DIPLOMA OF WHITENESS

D0841535

Jerry Dávila

DIPLOMA OF WHITENESS

Race and Social Policy in Brazil, 1917–1945

DUKE UNIVERSITY PRESS   DURHAM & LONDON 2003

2nd printing, 2006

© 2003 Duke University Press   All rights reserved

Printed in the United States of America on acid-free paper ∞

Designed by Rebecca M. Giménez   Typeset in Quadraat by

Keystone Typesetting, Inc.   Library of Congress Cataloging-in-

Publication Data appear on the last printed page of this book.

FOR LIV

CONTENTS

Acknowledgments, ix

Introduction, 1

1   Building the "Brazilian Man," 21

2   Educating Brazil, 52

3   What Happened to Rio's Teachers of Color?, 90

4   Elementary Education, 125

5   Escola Nova no Estado Novo: The New School in the New State, 155

6   Behaving White: Rio's Secondary Schools, 192

Epilogue: The Enduring Brazilian Fascination with Race, 233

List of Abbreviations, 244

Notes, 247

Bibliography, 271

Index, 287

ACKNOWLEDGMENTS

This project would not have been possible as either a personal or intellectual endeavor without the support, patience, and encouragement of many people in the United States and Brazil. Through their support, this project first became viable and then exciting. Above all, I must acknowledge my dissertation adviser, Thomas Skidmore, whose contagious passion for history and for things Brazilian, and his support and friendship in my years of study, are qualities I strive for but can never surpass. The other members of my dissertation committee, Doug Cope and Anani Dzidzienyo, have similarly been role models as scholars and advisers. Deans Bernard Bruce and Joan Lusk must also be acknowledged not only because their support made my research and writing possible but more importantly because their faith in me has kept me committed as an educator. I regret that Bernard Bruce did not live to see this book, but its completion is a testament to the unique spirit and energy he invested in his students. Dissertation research in Brazil was funded by a Dorothy Danforth Compton Fellowship as well as by grants from the Watson Institute for International Studies and a Foreign Language and Area Studies grant. Grants from Gustavus Adolphus College significantly aided my postdoctoral research and revisions, and my colleagues in the history department and the LALACS program offered ongoing support and encouragement.

I am also indebted to many in Brazil whose kindness and friendship made my research possible. Lucia Lippi de Oliveira, director of CPDOC at the Fundação Getúlio Vargas, invited me to work as a visiting scholar. Research at CPDOC was aided significantly by the support of Ignez Neidu; and formative discussions with Maria Helena Bomeny, José Murilo de Carvalho, Celso Castro, and Carlos Eduardo Sarmiento offered me much advice and assistance. Paulo Elian at the Arquivo Geral da Cidade gave me access to the as yet uncatalogued papers of Mayor Henrique Dodsworth. Marissa Werneck of the Rio Department of Education directed me to schools where I might find educational materials from the 1930s. Leonora Gama de Almeida, librarian of the Institute of Education, dug through the institute's records and collections for 1930s pedagogical material to identify unique and remarkable sources. José Silveiro Baía Horta at the Universidade Federal de Rio de Janeiro and Clarice Nunes at the Universidade Federal Fluminense helped to conceptualize the project and to track down dissertations on education during the Vargas era. Fúlvia Rosemberg of the Fundação Carlos Chagas provided assistance with the gender and statistical components of the project. Jamil Hermes of the Fundação Darcy Vargas was extremely generous with his time and with giving me access to the foundation and to the Darcy Vargas papers. The staff of the Arquivo Edgar Leuenroth in Campinas was especially understanding and helpful in the face of my tight research schedule.

A number of people connected to the Colégio Pedro II shared stories and experiences that have enlivened my narrative. I wish to thank Aloysio Barbosa, Wilson Choeri, Norma Fraga, Maria Yedda Linhares, Umbelina de Mattos, Fernando Segismundo, and Maria Cecilia Teixeira for the interviews they granted. I also owe a special debt of gratitude to Carolina Cortês-Brasilico, librarian of the Colégio Pedro II, and to the teachers and staff of the colégio, all of whom took me in as a friend and labored to help me find materials that helped recapture the day-to-day life at the school. Despite the school's funding problems, the faculty and staff of the colégio are engaged in a labor of love for their historic institution and for the students who find in the colégio a rare opportunity for a decent but free secondary education.

The form this book has taken owes much to the stimulating exchange of ideas with scholars at the Oswaldo Cruz Foundation and the Instituto de Filosofia e Ciências Sociais (IFCS) of the Federal University of Rio de Janeiro. These scholars have developed lively and innovative research on Brazilian race relations and public policy in the twentieth century. A great intellectual debt is owed Gilberto Hochman, Nisia Trinidade Lima, and Marcos Chor Maio at the Oswaldo Cruz Foundation, and to Marcos Luis Bretas, Peter Fry, Olivia Cunha Gomes, Flavio Gomes, and Yvonne Maggie of IFCS. In particular, I am indebted to Mônica Grin of IFCS for her ongoing support and friendship. Among the many others in Rio de Janeiro who deserve thanks for their help, encouragement, and friendship are José Neves Bittencourt of the Museu Histórico Nacional and Jürgen Heye of the Pontifícia Universidade Católica. Ana Maria de Almedia Lima, Andy Castonguay, Samantha Soifer Saenz, and Luis Valente have made me feel at home in Brazil over the years.

I have had the great pleasure during my years of research in Brazil of working in a field with a remarkably congenial, stimulating, and friendly group of international scholars. These include Desmond Arias, Amy Chazkel, Todd Diacon, James Green, Wiebke Ipsen, Mara Loveman, Zachary Morgan, Ben Penglase, Ori Preuss, Ken Serbin, Micol Seigel, Gail Triner, Daryle Williams, Erica Windler, and Joel Wolfe. Jeffrey Lesser, whose zeal for history is contagious, has given patient, demanding, and invaluable advice on my dissertation and manuscript. Peter Beattie, Dain Borges, Sueann Caulfield, Tamera Marko, and James Woodard have also generously read and thoughtfully commented on portions of this project.

Preparation of the book manuscript was aided by a Fulbright fellowship at the University of São Paulo in 2000. I am particularly grateful to the Fulbright Commission for the opportunities for research and writing that the fellowship afforded and to the faculty of the University of São Paulo who received me, especially Laura de Mello e Souza, Jorge Grespan, Ligia Prado, and Maria Helena Machado. Luis Filipe Silveiro Lima and Diana Gonçalves Vidal in particular offered welcome support and advice. The Latin American Studies Institute at Tel Aviv University has repeatedly sustained a forum for the presentation and exchange of ideas about Brazil, and two conferences (in 1999 and 2001) provided opportunities for debating and refining elements of this book. Thanks are due to Raanan Rein, Tzvi Tal, Rosalie Sitman, and the other organizers and participants of these symposia. Andre Luiz Joanilho and Lúcia Helena Oliveira Silva of the Universidade Estadual de Londrina provided stimulating advice and assistance as I completed manuscript revisions. My editors at Duke University Press, Valerie Millholland and Justin Faerber, have been great advocates and supporters, and the Press's two anonymous reviewers generously provided thorough, thoughtful, and incisive feedback. They have my deepest gratitude for challenging me into making this the book that it has become.

Finally, to my parents, Linda and Walter, my brothers Steven and Michael, and my grandmother, Marion, thank you.

INTRODUCTION

In 1944, at the height of the Estado Novo dictatorship and Brazil's participation in the war against fascism in Europe, a young girl of indigenous descent named Jacyra became the center of a public debate on the nature of racism in Brazil. Her adoptive parents had tried to enroll her in the school of the Sisters of Notre Dame. When the nuns running the school refused her admission because she was not white, her angry parents and their supporters took their indignation to the media. According to a letter to one of the main Rio de Janeiro dailies, the *Diario Carioca*, when the parents met with one of the (supposedly) German nuns who ran the school about matriculating their daughter, they asked whether she might face discrimination at the school. The nun asked to see the girl, and in the words of the letter writer, "said she could not accept the little Indian . . . because at the school there were only white students."[1]

The author of the letter, medical school professor Mauricio de Medeiros, attributed the act of racism to the fact that the nuns were of German descent— "countrywomen of Hitler." He argued that "in our country there has never been prejudice of this type. . . . Descendants of Indians have reached positions of distinction and respect in our country, including . . . [army Field Marshal Candido] Rondon." He added that when, among the mixture of races that characterizes Brazil, the indigenous traits are more visible, "it is with a certain pride that we call the person *caboclo*."[2]

A few days later, a Catholic supporter of the Sisters of Notre Dame, H. Sobral Pinto, replied to Medeiros's charges. Sobral Pinto explained that the nuns were not German but Polish, and that they had fled nazism and therefore abhorred racism. And, because they are not racists, he added, the nuns "are saddened by these values of Brazilian and North American parents." In his view the nuns did not discriminate against the girl but were afraid that the white children at the school would: "The religious women make no distinction by color or race. Still, as regards the students of the school, they cannot guarantee the same." They asked for the girl to appear before the Brazilian headmistress, who weighed her appearance against the "prejudices existent in many sectors of our society." To "protect" the girl, the school denied her admission and offered to enroll her in another school run by the nuns "where girls of all colors are received."[3]

Sobral Pinto inverted Medeiros's argument that the foreign nuns were introducing accusations of racism into a Brazilian society that many claimed was a racial democracy, free of intolerance and discrimination. Instead, he suggested that the nuns were trying to negotiate the racism already present in Brazilian society; racism that he equated with racial intolerance in the United States. Furthermore, Sobral Pinto suggested that Medeiros should be more sensitive to "exalted nationalism," because Medeiros himself had been a victim of intolerance when he was arrested during the anticommunist crackdown of 1936 by the regime still in power. Sobral Pinto reminded readers that Medeiros was singled out as a "direct agent of doctrines disrespectful of Brazil's historical personality," was jailed, and "unjustly" lost his professorship at the Rio de Janeiro School of Medicine.

The story became a press sensation. Coverage spread across the city newspapers, from the *Diario Carioca* to the *Diario de Noticias*, the *Folha Carioca*, the *Jornal de Comercio*, and *O Globo*.[4] What is more, these newspapers began reprinting the letters to the editor that appeared on their competitors' pages. At stake was not simply the question of whether Jacyra had been the victim of discrimination, but whether racism was a foreign or native entity—were Brazilians racists? Letter writers like Dr. Doraci de Souza added their opinions, criticizing the nuns for hiding behind the image of their racist students: "The function of a school, especially a Catholic school, is to educate their children with Christian principles . . . [what they have] admitted is that the school is unable to educate its students."[5]

This debate about the nature of racism alarmed the censors at the federal Department of Press and Propaganda (DIP), who on 18 March prohibited any further coverage of the Jacyra incident. Sobral Pinto was outraged that the censors had robbed him of the chance to defend the nuns against the latest series of attacks in the press. He asked the archbishop of Rio, Jaime de Barros Câmara, to use his influence to lift the silence imposed over the incident, because it would reflect poorly on the nuns and turn public opinion against the Church. He argued that the DIP's censorship "challenged the most legitimate rights of cultural thought of the Brazilian Nation."[6]

Archbishop Câmara took up the matter with Minister of Education and Health Gustavo Capanema, a longtime ally of the Catholic Church and of the conservative Catholic activists who had supported the regime.[7] Capanema declared discussion of the incident closed, stating only that "racial prejudice absolutely does not exist in this case" and that the facts point to "the hypothesis of a misunderstanding . . . between two well-meaning parties."[8]

While Jacyra's experience involved admission to a private school, this incident and debate reflect the paradoxical role of race in Brazilian schools. The leaders of public education in Brazil in the first half of the twentieth century did not block students of color from attending their schools. To the contrary, between 1917 and 1945 they engaged in a succession of school-system expansion and reform projects aimed at bringing public schools within the reach of poor and nonwhite Brazilians who at the turn of the century were largely excluded from school. These educators sought to "perfect the race"—to create a healthy, culturally European, physically fit and nationalistic "Brazilian race."[9] Between the world wars, Brazilians built school systems capable of extending near-universal elementary education.

Brazilian elites of the first half of the twentieth century tended to believe that the poor and the nonwhite were overwhelmingly degenerate.[10] By defining this state of degeneracy in medical, scientific, and social scientific terms, they claimed for themselves the power to remedy it and they assumed jurisdiction over public education. They treated schools as clinics wherein the national maladies they associated with Brazil's mix of races could be cured. Their beliefs provided a powerful motive for the construction of schools, and shaped both the ways these schools would work and the lessons they would provide. This volume analyzes ways in which an emerging white medical, social scientific, and intellectual elite turned their assumptions about race in Brazil into educational policies. These policies not only reflected elite views about degeneracy, they projected them into Brazilian society in ways that typically worked to the disadvantage of poor and nonwhite Brazilians, denying them equitable access to the programs, institutions, and social rewards that educational policies conferred. Because these policies were steeped in medical and social scientific logic, they did not on the surface seem to handicap any individual or group. Consequently, these policies not only placed new obstacles in the way of social and racial integration in Brazil but they left only scant evidence of their effects, limiting the ability of Afro-Brazilians to challenge their inherent inequity.

This study focuses on the work of education reformers in Rio de Janeiro between 1917 and 1945. Rio de Janeiro was then Brazil's largest city, and as the federal capital it drew the energies of education reformers from across the nation. The reformist period began with two events in 1917. First, a team of doctors involved in the country's public health and hygiene movement set off on an "expedition" to chart health conditions in the interior of the country. When they returned from the field, doctors Arthur Neiva and Belissário Penna published a report calling for the creation of a federal ministry of education and health.[11] Second, Afrânio Peixoto, a doctor who was the leading Brazilian exponent of legal medicine (he believed some individuals were hereditarily inclined toward crime) and a student of the relationships between race, climate, and degeneracy in the tropics, assumed the directorship of the city of Rio's Department of Education. He entered his post with a broad mandate to reform the city's schools to reflect the growing consensus that racial degeneracy could be reversed through scientific improvements in health and education.

When progressive white intellectuals and public officials began to establish universal public education in Brazil in the first half of the twentieth century, their motives and actions were influenced by racial ideology in three general ways. First, they built on centuries of domination by a caste of white European colonists and their descendants, who lorded over slaves, indigenous peoples, and individuals of mixed ancestry. For centuries, this white elite also turned to Europe to borrow culture, ideas, and self-definition. Second, although these intellectuals and policymakers became increasingly critical of that legacy (going so far as to celebrate racial mixture), they invariably came from the white elite and remained enmeshed in social values that, after centuries of colonialism and racial domination, continued to associate whiteness with strength, health, and virtue—values that were preserved and reinforced through the deprecation of other groups. Third, as they created educational policies in pursuit of a utopian dream of a modern, developed, and democratic Brazil, their vision was influenced by the meanings race held for them.

Brazil's self-styled educational pioneers turned the emerging public schools into spaces where centuries of white European supremacy was rescripted in the languages of science, merit, and modernity. The schools they created were designed to imprint their white, elite vision of an ideal Brazilian nation on those mostly poor and nonwhite children who were to be the substance of that ideal. The role of race within this process resembles Ann Stoler's description of race in European colonies, where

> the cultivation of a European self . . . was affirmed in the proliferating discourses around pedagogy, parenting, children's sexuality, servants, and tropical hygiene: micro-sites where "character," "good breeding," and proper rearing were implicitly raced. These discourses do more than prescribe suitable behavior; they locate how fundamentally bourgeois identity has been tied to notions of being "European" and being "white" and how sexual prescriptions served to secure and delineate the authentic, first-class citizens of the nation-state.[12]

In the societies analyzed by Stoler, whiteness was a threatened commodity and colonial officials preoccupied themselves with the task of shoring it up. For Brazilian elites, the problem was even more urgent—they believed their racially mixed nation already lacked the whiteness it needed to sustain its vitality. The task at hand, then, was to find new ways of creating whiteness. Thus, endowed with a commitment to forge a more European Brazil, and bound by a sense of modernity equated with whiteness, these educators built schools in which most every action and practice established racialized norms and meted out or withheld rewards based on them.

For Brazilian educators and their intellectual generation, race was not a biological fact. It was a metaphor that extended to describe the past, present, and future of the Brazilian nation. At one extreme, blackness signified the past. Blackness was cast in Freudian language as primitive, prelogical, and childlike. More broadly, white elites equated blackness with unhealthiness, laziness, and criminality. Racial mixture symbolized historical process, envisioned as a trajectory from blackness to whiteness and from the past to the future. In the 1930s, white Brazilians could safely celebrate race mixture because they saw it as an inevitable step in the nation's evolution. Whiteness embodied the desired virtues of health, culture, science, and modernity. Educators ranging from federal Minister of Education and Health Gustavo Capanema to child psychologist Manoel Lourenço Filho, composer Heitor Villa-Lobos, history textbook author Jonathas Serrano, and anthropologist Arthur Ramos all explicitly embraced this vision of race. Naturally, for them Brazil's future was white.

For these educators, race also worked as a social (rather than biological) category.[13] Because of the color of their skin or their ethnic origins, individuals might have been more likely to fit into a given racial category, but these categories were elastic. At the turn of the century, Brazilian elites, following the vogue of racial determinism in Europe, readily adopted the scientific racist belief that whites were superior and that those of black and mixed ancestry were degenerate. But by the second decade of the twentieth century these elites began to seek escape from the determinist trap that tied Brazil to perpetual backwardness because of its large nonwhite population. Instead, they embraced a notion that degeneracy was an acquired—and therefore remediable—condition. Blackness still held all of its pejorative connotations, but individuals could escape the social category of blackness through improvement of their health, level of education and culture, or their social class. Conversely, whites could degenerate through their exposure to poverty, vices, and disease. In other words, money, education, celebrity status, and other forms of social ascension increased whiteness.[14]

These elites, and Brazil's education reformers in particular, defined whiteness through both positive and negative affirmation. Whiteness was a way of affirming Europeanness, which in turn bore all the trappings of modernity—from urbanization to industrialization, rationalism, science, and civic virtue. In addition, whiteness conveyed a racial sense of healthiness, vigor, and Darwinian superiority. Whiteness was also, however, the absence of blackness, which was a negative affirmation of racial virtue similar to that developed in the United States and exemplified by Malcolm X's assertion that " 'white man' as commonly used, means complexion only secondarily; primarily it described attitudes and actions. In America 'white men' meant specific attitudes and actions toward the black man, and toward all other non-white men."[15]

Studies by David Roediger, George Lipsitz, and others have explored the ways blackness and whiteness in the United States have been exclusive in mutually reinforcing ways. Citing Ralph Ellison, Roediger argues that whiteness only acquired meaning because of the existence of blackness: "Southern whites cannot walk, talk, sing, conceive of laws or justice, think of sex, love, the family or freedom without responding to the presence of Negroes."[16] Yet, while Brazilian educators, scientists, and intellectuals affirmed the significance of whiteness through a discourse that associated degeneracy with blackness, there was a crucial difference between their vision and the vision developed in the United States. Using an elastic definition of degeneracy, white Brazilian elites did not see blackness and whiteness as mutually exclusive. Poor whites could be degenerate, and some Brazilians of color could escape degeneracy by whitening through social ascension. It is this crucial detail that infused Brazilian public education with its special significance.

The possibility of hastening Brazil's modernization by increasing the number of people of color who no longer fit into the social category of black drove intellectuals, scientists, doctors, anthropologists, psychologists, and sociologists into a sustained, concerted campaign to build state institutions attending to public health and education. The title of this volume, *Diploma of Whiteness*, is drawn from a December 2000 cover story in the Brazilian news magazine *Veja*, which explored the possibility of individuals being effectively white despite their skin color.[17] This phrase conveys what public education meant to the leaders of the school reform movement between the world wars: schools would provide the resources of basic health and culture that could earn children, regardless of their color, the social category of white. Educators, social scientists, and policymakers spared little energy or expense in building a state role in mediating Brazil's escape from the determinist trap of blackness and degeneracy.

The principles of public education established by these interwar elites remained in place throughout the twentieth century. As recently as 1996, the Brazilian congress continued to approve educational legislation based on interwar reforms. What has changed is not public education but rather popular perceptions of that education. Since the 1960s, the most visible division in public education has been based on social class: poor children would attend public school, those who could afford to do so would attend private school. Still, the patterns of racial inequality in Brazilian education have remained and have transcended social class barriers. Nelson do Valle Silva and Carlos Hasenbalg have demonstrated that patterns of educational attainment remain unequal even when social class is eliminated as a factor: whites of the same social class have higher literacy rates and remain more likely to attend school, to stay in school longer, to be advanced through school more rapidly, and to secure better-paying jobs given the same educational qualifications. Silva and Hasenbalg conclude that "white children's rates of school advancement are significantly more rapid than those of *pardo* [mixed] and *preto* [black] children. These differences result in profound educational inequalities that separate whites and nonwhites in Brazilian society."[18]

In part, these enduring racial inequalities have resulted from the fusion of educational reform movements and racial thought in the decades between the world wars. The rise of public education coincided with a wave of publications in Brazil that detailed scientific and social scientific studies to disprove the perceived inferiority of nonwhite Brazilians and to celebrate race mixture as a positive national characteristic. These texts included Gilberto Freyre's *The Masters and the Slaves* (1933), *The Mansions and the Shanties* (1936), and *The Northeast* (1937); Sérgio Buarque de Holanda's *The Roots of Brazil* (1938); and Arthur Ramos's *The Negro in Brazil* (1938) and *African Folklore in Brazil* (1942). These writers permanently transformed the mainstream understanding of race and the role of descendants of African slaves in Brazilian society. Their work reshaped popular thinking about race by taking the argument that blackness and race mixture were less significant than environment and culture as determinants of fitness and turning it into a mythology about Brazil's historic social evolution, which in turn served to comprehensively explain a Brazilian national experience.

Gilberto Freyre became the principal exponent of the idea that Brazil's racial diversity was a strength rather than a weakness by decentering that weakness from race and ascribing it to poor health and culture. In one clear example of this argument, Freyre prefaced *The Masters and the Slaves* by describing a scene he witnessed in New York. He watched Brazilian sailors—"mulattoes and cafusos"—descending from their battleship onto the soft snow of the Brooklyn naval yard. He reflected that, "I ought to have had some one tell me then what Roquette Pinto had told the *Aryanizers* of the Brazilian Eugenics Conference in 1929: that these individuals whom I looked upon as representative of Brazil were not simply mulattoes or cafusos but sickly ones."[19]

Edgar Roquette Pinto was, at the time, Brazil's leading anthropologist and director of the National Museum of Anthropology. Endorsing Roquette Pinto's ascription of black and mixed Brazilian's deficiencies to environment rather than race, Freyre then gave the nod to the science of eugenics as a way of managing racial conditions. He explained that "it is [Columbia University anthropologist] Franz Boas who, admitting the possibility that eugenics may be able to eliminate the undesirable elements of society, reminds us that eugenic selection should concern itself with suppressing the conditions responsible for the creation of poverty-stricken proletarians, sickly and ill-nourished."[20]

Eugenics was a scientific endeavor to "perfect" a human population through the improvement of hereditary traits—a notion that was popular throughout Europe and the Americas between the world wars. Scientists turned to eugenics as a catchall science that combined different theories about race, heredity, culture, and environmental influences into practices and prescriptions typically aimed at "improving" a national population. A "hard" eugenics based on removing individuals who possessed undesired traits from the reproductive pool through sterilization or genocide was practiced to varying degrees in countries such as Nazi Germany, Britain, and the United States. Much of Latin America and some parts of Europe adopted a "soft" eugenics that maintained that pre- and neonatal care, public health and hygiene, and an attention to psychology and to general culture and fitness would gradually improve the eugenic fitness of a population.[21]

This strain of eugenics fit well with the ideas about race held by Brazilian elites, who presumed the inferiority of both the poor and the nonwhite yet also sought the possibility of rescuing that population, and thus the nation. For the Brazilians who embraced it, eugenics was not a means for improving specific individuals or groups. It was a way of overcoming what they perceived to be the shortcomings of the nation by applying a range of scientific diagnoses and solutions. It was eugenic nationalism, and it brought together doctors, sociologists, psychologists, hygienists, and anthropologists. These scientific authorities sought avenues through public policies and institutions to apply their healing hands to a national population that they commonly regarded in gentle contempt. They banded together, across both scientific disciplines and geographic regions, to create public health and education programs that would be the sites where they could carry out their redemptive intervention.

The leading education reformers who built or expanded public school systems around Brazil between the world wars were not just pedagogues. Indeed, few had pedagogical training. They were doctors and social scientists drawn to public education as an arena for social action. These reformers established a vision of social value that privileged a white, middle-class appearance, demeanor, habits, and values. They made the school system into an engine that in ways both deliberate (furnishing poor and nonwhite Brazilians with the tools of whiteness) and unwitting (establishing barriers by reifying their narrow values) created a racial hierarchy in the school system that mirrored their own vision of social worth. Their hierarchy was particularly stable, effective, and longstanding because it relied on unimpeachable values of science and merit.

The schools these men built (although the overwhelming majority of teachers were women, all of the leading education policymakers were men) provided elementary education heavily infused with notions of nationalism, health, hygiene, physical fitness, and prevocational training. The leading reforms were conducted in city school systems in Rio de Janeiro and São Paulo, although they were echoed by reforms by the states of São Paulo, Rio de Janeiro, Minas Gerais, Pernambuco, Ceará, Amazonas, Pará, Bahia, Espírito Santo, Rio Grande do Norte, Paraíba, and Sergipe. Their reforms consisted of revised curricular content, renewed administrative procedures and professional standards, and an expanded reach for the school systems. Especially after the Revolution of 1930 created increased political and administrative openings for education reformers to carry out their goals, school systems expanded dramatically. This expansion brought public schools, along with their eugenic, whitening, and nationalist message, to poor and racially mixed neighborhoods.

Education reforms began to take root in the second decade of the twentieth century as nationalists began to adopt eugenic ideas about degeneracy and contemplated the possibilities for regenerating the vast racial and social underclass. By the 1920s, this movement had gained cohesion and national visibility. Education reformers began working with a common sense of purpose across their disciplines and across Brazil, although their energies were concentrated on the showcase school systems of the cities of Rio de Janeiro and São Paulo. The Revolution of 1930, which brought Getúlio Vargas to power, led to the almost immediate creation of a federal Ministry of Education and Public Health (later Ministry of Education and Health, or MES), as well as a changing of the political guard across the country that hastened the consolidation of reforms and drove the expansion of school systems.

The 1930s were a golden age for education reformers, who gained unprecedented opportunities to put their ideas into practice. Their reforms during this decade, both in Rio de Janeiro and in the states, were remarkable for the extent of school system expansion and depth of institutional reforms. Educators availed themselves not only of the sciences allied to eugenics, but they also embraced practices of systematic rationalization increasingly applied in Brazilian industry. The link between industry and education was more than casual and extended far beyond the sphere of vocational education. Many educators, such as Fernando de Azevedo and Manoel Lourenço Filho also participated in projects aimed at rationalizing the industrial workforce. Indeed, progressive educators and forward-thinking industrialists had much in common. Both shared a vision of a modern Brazil that would be created by applying rational and scientific paradigms to the organization of society. Both educators and industrialists believed this new society would be created through the reformed attitudes and behavior of the popular classes. Even more important, both educators and industrialists believed that these reformed attitudes would come not from the popular classes themselves but from technicians who would be capable of functioning as social engineers.

Barbara Weinstein's study of this social vision developed by São Paulo industrialists illustrates just how much educators and industrialists shared in a vision of a modern society rationalized by science. Although Weinstein focuses on the emergence and implementation of an industrialist discourse about the working class, she recognized a role for race within the industrialists' social project that is substantially similar to the role race played within educational policy. According to Weinstein, "most industrialist spokesmen eagerly adopted the view that Brazil was a 'racial democracy' and would not have regarded their unflattering construction of the Brazilian worker as related in any way to racial prejudice. In a narrow sense, it was probably not. But their very notion of the working class as morally and culturally inferior without ever resorting to explicit racial references . . . [and] the resemblance of this view to earlier stereotypes about immigrant versus 'national' (that is, nonwhite) workers cannot be dismissed as coincidental."[22]

Although there are substantial parallels between the social projects of industrialists described by Weinstein and the reforms of educators (while Weinstein describes engineers as educators, the pages that follow show educators acting as self-proclaimed engineers), the economic and political autonomy of industrialists resulted in a divergence of paths in the mid-1930s.[23] As the Getúlio Vargas presidency drifted toward the fascist-minded Estado Novo (the "New State," 1937–1945) dictatorship, many prominent educators were forced from their posts by conservative Catholics who opposed the reformers' resistance to religious education in the schools. Still, the struggle between progressive educators and the conservative Catholic activists who increasingly gained influence in the Vargas regime did little to change the course of public education.

While this study begins with the emergence of an elite consensus about race, medicine, and education, it ends with the Estado Novo, when the Rio de Janeiro school system came to be administered by military officers. Although the conflict between the progressive reformers and the Catholics was dramatic, the heyday of reactionary authoritarianism did little to alter the racially coded educational policies enacted in previous administrations. To the contrary, the Estado Novo's military educators continued and expanded the programs and practices that most directly dealt with race. The Estado Novo period illustrates that despite the political fractiousness that emerged in Brazilian national politics after 1930 and that continues to the present, an uncritical consensus about the meanings of race and degeneracy, along with the prescriptions for treating that degeneracy, remained intact.

Why study Brazilian race relations through education? The public school system was one of the principal areas of social action for those individuals most active in examining the significance of race in Brazilian society and most engaged in the pursuit of a socially and culturally white nation. Because education is an area of public policy, it reveals ways in which racial thinkers turned their ideas and assumptions into practice. What is more, during the period studied these practices were experienced by hundreds of thousands of people within the city of Rio de Janeiro, and millions across Brazil. Thus, not only does public education provide the historical resources for studying patterns of racial inequality in Brazil, it also provides the source for a different kind of reading that showcases some of the most significant and yet analytically elusive aspects of race relations in the nation: its ambivalence (the fact that race was meaningful yet that meaning was diffused into a broader medical and scientific discourse of degeneracy); its elasticity (that the meaning of race and of one's social race could change, and as a source of social prestige education mediated that elasticity); and especially its ambiguity (that school systems generally addressed race only indirectly, using coded medical and social scientific language).

Jacyra's story illustrates the analytical opportunities and methodological challenges this study confronts. There are a number of ways of interpreting the significance of Jacyra's exclusion. One way is to look at racist values among Brazilian elites or among immigrant communities like that of the nuns, as well as strategies of resistance to racism as shown in the outrage that erupted in the city's newspapers.[24] Jacyra's story could also be read as an example of the social inequalities faced by nonwhite Brazilians.[25] Perhaps more provocatively, the story could be read as one of frustration at not being able to "pass for white," in that the combination of white adopted parents, wealth, and supporters among the city's elite was not enough for Jacyra to overcome obstacles based on her color.[26]

The concern is to show how policymakers and educators formulated racial values and applied them as racialized practices. In other words, how did values of race and social place work when they did not erupt into the type of rare public debate that surrounded Jacyra's experience? In this analysis there is no dialectic between oppressors and resistors, and no dichotomy between specific discussions of racialized actions and more general discussions of the Rio de Janeiro educational system. This is not a study of social behavior nor of the clash of ideas. This text deals with the often ephemeral ways in which educators turned a discourse about race and nationhood into everyday practices wherein race was not commonly evident but always significant. A belief central to this analysis is that racial ideology is a metanarrative, meaning a complex of values and conceptual categories that guided the ways educators designed institutions and practices.[27]

The metanarrative of race in public education naturally influenced and was influenced by the metanarratives of gender, sexuality, social class, and nationhood. For example, as the hiring of teachers by the Rio school system became a gendered process, the favoring of female candidates over male ones placed teaching out of the reach of candidates of color who were male. Moreover, efforts by education reformers to define teaching as women's work were part of a broader process of professionalization that also made it harder for women who were of color or were poor to meet the criteria for becoming teachers. Similarly, efforts to teach children the meaning of being Brazilian, or of deciding to promote a child from the first to the second grade, were practices within which elite perceptions of the social roles of race, gender, and class all played an active role. This study analyzes the ways in which concepts of class, gender, sexuality, nation, and race influenced and reinforced each other, because these relationships generated many of the interactions through which race influenced social policy, and through which the metanarrative of race in Brazil can best be understood.

This volume returns to the years when the idea of a "racial democracy" took root and flourished, and it analyzes the ways in which educators' explicit views on race disappeared from view once they turned into policies. The idea of a "racial democracy" was embraced with great ease by individuals who had full faith that their public institutions were meritocratic, technical, and rational. Where could there be space for race within these modern institutions? By looking at the rare moments when discussions of race surfaced and, even more important, the more common experiences where no one spoke of race, this study reveals ways in which racial assumptions shaped the intentions and outcomes of public education. In other words, institutions and practices seemingly devoid of racial ideology were commonly those places where race played the greatest role. The reformers studied here wove the assumptions they held about race into the practices they created. Consequently, public policies tended to work to the disadvantage of the growing numbers of Brazilians of color who came into contact with them.

By its very nature, this is a difficult process to demonstrate. One way to conceive of the analytical framework employed here is to think of the waves of education reform and the rising tide of public education as forming a sea whose surface conceals the reefs of racial values and racialized practices. These reefs of racial values formed over a long period of time, and although invisible from the surface they remained firmly in place and shaped the currents of policy that surround them. This study adopts two strategies for mapping the often-hidden contours of race in public policy. First, by looking for those rare instances of turbulence on the surface of educational practices it identifies the racialized issues that lie sometimes quite close to the surface, as in Jacyra's case. Second, by following the rising tide of educational reform places can be seen where the seamlessness of educational policy has not yet washed over and concealed a question of race. By looking at moments in this rising tide of reform, such as the introduction of intelligence testing in schools, we see how new practices first confronted questions of race, revealing in remarkable clarity the ways in which white, elite responses to issues of race guided policies around these shoals.

The ways educators wove race into public policy meant that on the surface not much seemed to happen. Yet below the surface, and at the margins of educational policy, lay places where educators might be uncharacteristically open in their discussions about the meanings race held for them and the ways those meanings shaped their educational projects. At least as they were recorded these encounters were rare, but when they are analyzed within the broader context of institution building they become meaningful. In some ways very little happened here and yet everything happened: this is not a study of events but of the sets of meanings that events assumed for the privileged cadre of white men of science who forged the national model of education. Something as simple and as intimate as eating, brushing one's teeth, or washing one's hands—activities repeated over and again in the private space of homes—became the subject of public policies developed to stem the nation's racial degeneracy and save Brazil.

Each chapter of this volume is a vignette that illustrates the ways educators dealt with questions of race in different aspects of public education. While these snapshots build on each other, they are intended to stand as separate episodes. This is done in order to avoid giving the impression that this is a history of education reform, or of Brazilians of color in the school system. Just as the analytical lens of this text seeks to reveal a systematic vision of race within elements of public policy, the narrative structure of the text avoids replacing the vision of public policy as racially neutral with a new model defining a specific role for race within policies. Instead, each chapter shows a facet of the many ways in which race shaped public space.

This book begins with an episode in the creation of the foremost institution of public education, the federal Ministry of Education and Health. This episode, a debate over the appearance of the statue of the "Brazilian Man" that would be placed to greet visitors to the new ministry building, encompassed the debate over race and whitening through education. The chapter on the "Brazilian Man" traces the emergence of a discourse on degeneracy and the process by which an educational elite comprised of physicians, scientists, and social scientists coalesced around the belief that public education could resolve the nation's racial ills. "Educating Brazil," expands on the links between race, the emerging nationalism, science, and the state within the context of the new statistics-gathering and interpreting institutions created after 1930. Although the "statistical reality" produced by the Brazilian government provided a way of "seeing" Brazil that reflected the vision held by nationalists and social scientists, the data the new agencies generated also permit an analysis of the social, geographic, racial, and economic dimensions of the city of Rio de Janeiro during the period covered by this study.

"What Happened to Rio's Teachers of Color?" shows that the expansion of the role of the state in Brazilian society through the creation and expansion of social policies did not mean a proportionate degree of integration for afro-descendants within public institutions. To the contrary, a significant increase in the sophistication of the means of racial exclusion took place. Looking behind the processes of professionalization of the teacher corps, this chapter shows that policies for selecting and training teachers created subtle obstacles based on values of race, class, and gender. Education reformers sought a teacher corps that was modern, professional, scientific, and representative of a middle-class ideal. Their policies succeeded at producing the teacher corps that education reformers imagined, and this teacher corps was almost exclusively white.

"Elementary Education," examines the principal reform of the Rio de Janeiro school system, which was carried out by Anísio Teixeira between 1931 and 1935. Teixeira not only gave full expression to the reform currents underway over the past decades, his reform became the lasting blueprint for public education in Brazil. This reform combined the major scientific trends governing social policy: eugenic nationalism, systematic rationalization, and professionalization. "The New School in the New State," follows Anísio Teixeira's reform in the decade after he was purged from the school system by Catholic conservative opponents. In the years of increased authoritarianism culminating with the Estado Novo, public education in Rio de Janeiro was directed by military officers and fell under the influence of the Catholic Church. This chapter shows that despite the dramatic and at times violent politics surrounding public education during these authoritarian years, the technical side of public education remained untouched. Despite the breakdown of consensus over some aspects of educational policy, the ways in which elites of the Left and Right saw education and race and science and the nation continued to coincide.

"Behaving White: Rio's Secondary Schools," examines two facets of public secondary education in Rio de Janeiro. Despite the efforts of Teixeira and other reformers, public education scarcely surpassed the boundaries of the elementary school. Most children abandoned their schools after the third grade, and even those who completed their elementary studies had few city-funded opportunities to attend high school. Consequently, secondary education was a form of training for a narrow elite whose dreams of social mobility, and the process they underwent to realize them, were shaped by values of whiteness. A case study of the federal model high school, Colégio Pedro II, shows that students at the most prestigious public school in Brazil embraced the language of eugenic nationalism and behaved accordingly.

A NOTE ON THE LANGUAGE OF RACE

One of the consistent methodological challenges faced by scholarship on race in Brazil is developing a language for discussing racial categories. In this study the challenge is twofold because it analyzes racial discourse from the interwar period as well as the presence of Brazilians of color within educational institutions. Thus two methods are employed for describing racial categories: one that preserves the original language of race used by educators and the other to describe individuals within the school system.

When discussing school system policies or the rhetoric of educators, this study follows the original language as closely as possible. Educators and other agents of the state worked with a clearly delineated set of racial categories. Beginning in 1940, the Brazilian census employed four color categories: *branco, pardo, preto,* and *amarelo* (white, brown, black, and yellow).[28] *Pardo* was an especially elastic term because it was used to describe anyone of mixed African, indigenous, or European ancestry. While educators generally adhered to this set of categories, they at times substituted *pardo* with *mulatto*. Although educators believed that the link between degeneracy and race was contingent, they were clear in their belief that race existed and could be quantified. Moreover, while they seldom had reason to turn to scientific definitions of racial categories, when they did they commonly referred to the framework developed by anthropologist Edgar Roquette Pinto, who established a system of color gradations based on three main categories: *leucodermo, faiodermo,* and *melanodermo* (white skin, brown skin, and black skin).[29] Generally, these technical categories were employed to assess the progress of the physical whitening of the Brazilian population through the dilution of those racially mixed.

These categories were far removed from the ways in which individuals within the school system would have classified themselves. The self-classification of individuals and the ways in which they might have identified themselves or others varied considerably. This is especially true for teachers and other professionals within the school system because their level of education and social prestige could influence their sense of racial identity.[30] The sources employed in this study seldom provide sufficient information about individuals' self-identification to be able to make definitive statements about their identity. Consequently, this study cautiously employs the terms "white," "nonwhite," "of color," and "afrodescendant" to describe individuals. "White" and "of color" were two terms that individuals from the period would have been likely to use to describe themselves. "Of color" was an inclusive category that could be used to describe individuals of any degree of race mixture, as is "afrodescendant," a term increasingly used by contemporary racial activists. The greater ease with which these terms describe individuals who might vary considerably in color and appearance offers an advantage over the term Afro-Brazilian, also widely employed by activists.

The challenge of racial categorization is part of what makes social institutions such a rich source for historical study. Between the wars, millions of Brazilians with millions of identities shared a common set of educational experiences. These experiences were the product of carefully crafted policies created by a narrow administrative, technical, and intellectual elite that, as it turns out, had a focused and deliberate sense of the significance of race not only for schools but for Brazil. The process by which elites turned this consensus into the most far-reaching of social policies is the subject of the pages that follow.

1

BUILDING THE "BRAZILIAN MAN"

"How will the body of the Brazilian man, the *future* Brazilian man, be? Not the vulgar or inferior type, but the best example of the race? What shall be his height? His volume? His color? What will be the shape of his head? The form of his face? His physiognomy?"[1] In 1938 Minister of Education and Health Gustavo Capanema directed these questions to a group of anthropologists and nationalist intellectuals. He wanted to get to the bottom of a problem that was beginning to bother him: the statue of the "Brazilian Man" he had commissioned to grace the entrance of the new Ministry of Education and Health (MES) building looked racially degenerate rather than virile and Aryan, as he imagined Brazilians would evolve.

Capanema was troubled by the appearance of this sculpture because he envisioned the new MES headquarters as a statement on Brazil's future and on the role of the government in shaping it. The two themes that expressed Capanema's vision failed to meet in the sculpture. First, the "Brazilian Man" was to symbolize the outcome of the racial and social engineering that was Capanema's special responsibility. As he explained to Getúlio Vargas when he commissioned the piece, the sculpture would specifically be the "Brazilian Man" because the MES "is dedicated to preparing, to forming, to crafting the man of Brazil. It really is the 'ministry of man.'"[2] Second, the degenerate figure clashed with the modernist building.

In contrast to the sculpture, the building was a huge success. Capanema brought together French modernist architect Charles Le Corbusier and young

Brazilian architects Lúcio Costa and Oscar Niemeyer to design a modernist structure that earned international acclaim. Indeed, the design made such an impact, especially in the United States, that years later Nelson Rockefeller reassembled the team to design the United Nations building. The MES building design did its job: it cast the ministry as a portal to Brazil's white future, a future forged through public education. For Capanema, the MES building was proof that Brazil was finding its identity, defining itself as the nation of the future—no longer a weak nation that imitated stronger ones. To the contrary, it was now the foreigners who would imitate Brazil.

The statue of the "Brazilian Man" would complete the allegory by showing that public education would make Brazilians white and strong, worthy of their bright future. According to Capanema, "the building and the statue will complete each other in an exact and necessary manner."[3] Yet the figure of the "Brazilian Man" that sculptor Celso Antonio rendered from the stone represented everything Capanema hoped Brazil would leave behind. The figure was a *caboclo*, a racially mixed backwoodsman. To make matters worse, this *caboclo* was *barrigudo* (paunchy). The sculptor, Celso Antonio, justified his work by stating that as he looked about Brazil, that is what he saw. This figure was the average Brazilian man. Seemingly, he had neglected the allegorical significance of this monument to Brazil's future, a future that was white and strong.

The scientists were all in complete agreement. Edgar Roquette Pinto, director of the National Museum of Anthropology, advised against choosing any of the racial types that in his view would sooner or later disappear. Instead, the figure should be white and Mediterranean to represent the phenotype to which "the morphological evolution of the other racial types" is headed.[4] Jurist Francisco Oliveira Vianna agreed, replying that the sculpture should reflect "not only the whitened types which will result from the Aryanizing evolution of our mixed-bloods, but also the representatives of all the European races among us."[5] Juvenil Rocha Vaz, a professor at the Rio de Janeiro School of Medicine with extensive public health experience, reminded Capanema that this question "exuberantly" demonstrated the need for more federal research grants, and he agreed that although no final type had emerged from the "racial melting pot," the figure should nonetheless be white.[6]

The agreement between Roquette Pinto, Oliveira Vianna, and Rocha Vaz takes on added meaning in considering their diverging scientific philosophies. Roquette Pinto was the leading proponent in Brazil of Columbia University anthropologist Franz Boas's antiracialist thesis that there were no such things as superior or inferior races, and that people should be measured instead by their level of culture. By contrast, Oliveira Vianna, a reactionary social policy advisor to President Vargas, believed in outright Aryan biological superiority, a racialist position echoed by Rocha Vaz. Yet as they envisioned Brazil's future, the differences in their approaches ceded to a consensus about the nation's ills and their remedies. Oliveira Vianna, Roquette Pinto, and Rocha Vaz, like the mainstream scientific, social scientific, and medical community as a whole, held faith in Brazil's white future and the role of public education and health in creating it. Although there continued to be debate over the nature of blackness, degeneracy, and the possibility of racial improvement, there was consensus on the meaning and value of whiteness—consensus that expressed itself in masculine virtues of virility, strength, and courage, in Europeanness, and in the agreement that this was the race of Brazil's future.

Acting on the advice of his scientific advisors, Capanema spelled out for Celso Antonio the racial criteria the "Brazilian Man" must meet, requiring that the finished sculpture be reviewed by a special committee. According to Capanema, this committee "cannot be composed of international authorities, because the exam will mainly determine whether the figure matches the Brazilian type under development, and therefore only national specialists will be qualified to render judgment."[7] Celso Antonio refused, and he lost his commission for the sculpture. Capanema sounded out another artist, this time making his racial politics more explicit: the sculpture should be "a solid figure, strong, Brazilian. Not a pretty boy. A swarthy type of good quality, with an appearance bespeaking intelligence, elevation, courage and capacity to create and to accomplish."[8]

Soon, the disagreement between the minister and Celso Antonio spilled into the newspapers. A Nota agreed with Capanema, declaring that "the artist has committed a crass historical and ethnographic error in imposing a caboclo as our national type." Like Capanema's technical advisors, the writer concurred that although "there does not yet exist a definitively fixed Brazilian type," the sculpture should be white rather than the other groups being assimilated.[9] Another commentator, M. Paulo Filho, writing for O Correio da Manhã, saw the debate as a conflict between aesthetic ideals and contemporary reality, stressing that Celso Antonio simply created what he saw. Still, the commentator concluded, "the Brazilian man they both imagine does not yet exist."[10]

The fact that the minister, doctors, anthropologists, sociologists, and journalists all imagined the ideal Brazilian would be white is not surprising— Brazil's elite had projected idealized images of the nation's whiteness and Europeanness for generations. What is surprising is these scientists' unwavering determination to use the adverb "yet" in describing Brazil's racial makeup. Each one of the commentators awaited the moment when Brazil would finally be white (which might take as long as two hundred to three hundred years, according to Paulo Filho). Responsibility for achieving whiteness fell to Gustavo Capanema's Ministry of Education and Health. The statue of the "Brazilian Man," which was never completed, stood as testament and tribute to the work of educators and scientists in reaching Brazil's racial destiny.

BRAZILIAN EUGENICS

How were teachers and scientists supposed to create this future "Brazilian Man"? The answer, some felt, was through eugenics, the practice of "improving" the human race physically and mentally by manipulating genetic traits, primarily through controls on the act and context of procreation. Between the world wars, Brazil was a nation seduced by the idea that science could be the ultimate arbiter of social relations. This cause was championed by the growing caste of scientists and social scientists who claimed jurisdiction over social policies and promised capable and impartial application of foreign scientific theories to Brazil's national problems. Nearly every national problem had a racial subtext: Brazil's mixed-race and nonwhite underclasses were, by all accounts, culturally backward, and by some accounts racially degenerate. Eugenics could solve both of these problems.

As Nancy Stepan has argued, in the early decades of the century "soft" and "hard" camps of eugenicists debated whether a population could be genetically improved by strengthening health, hygiene, and education, or whether genetic improvement could be achieved by limiting the gene pool. This division loosely followed the division between the genetic theories of Lamarck and Mendel. Lamarck maintained that the behavior and environment of parents could shape the genes of offspring: tuberculosis or alcoholism, for example, would produce degenerate babies. By contrast, for Mendel genetic material could not be altered in the course of a lifetime. "Soft" eugenics allowed for racial improvement through attention to health, environmental influences, cultural values, and the circumstances of reproduction. "Hard" eugenics did not allow for the modification of traits, and focused instead on the elimination of undesirable traits through control of reproduction.[11]

In the interwar historical context, the difference between Mendelian and Lamarckian genetics had practical and moral implications for the practitioners of eugenics. Eugenicists who favored Mendelian genetics tended to focus on preventing reproduction, at times through forced sterilization.[12] Because the Mendelian approach implied the fixity of race, its use in whitening Brazil would have meant somehow preventing half of the country's population from ever reproducing. Instead, Brazilian eugenicists followed their intellectual compass and embraced a French Lamarckian genetics, which promised the most immediate and positive returns. This opened the path for modifying the traits of the existing population. If "Brazil is an immense hospital," as public health advocate Miguel Pereira declared in 1916, it can be cured.[13]

Who were the eugenicists? Brazilian eugenics was advocated by a confederation of doctors, scientists, and social scientists who were united by their nationalist desire to see Brazil brought back from the brink of degeneracy provoked by the mixture of races and cultures and by poverty and uncivilized and unhealthy customs. Beginning in the second decade of the twentieth century, these individuals began organizing associations to advance eugenics and address eugenic issues. The first, the São Paulo Eugenics Society, organized by Renato Kehl, included as its secretary the sociologist Fernando de Azevedo who later conducted reforms of the school systems of Rio de Janeiro (1926–1930) and São Paulo (1933–1934). Eugenics, Fernando de Azevedo observed, "called for the elimination of poisons, not people." Anthropologist Edgar Roquette Pinto, who participated in the Rio de Janeiro school system administration (1931–1935), was both a member of the Eugenics Society and the related Mental Hygiene League, for which he edited the journal Saúde (Health). Afrânio Peixoto, the doctor and legal medicine pioneer who directed the Rio school system from 1917–1922, was also a member of the Mental Hygiene League.[14]

Associations like the Eugenics Society, the Mental Hygiene League, the Biotypology Association, and the Pro-Sanitation League had overlapping memberships and worked as a lobby for an expanded state role in addressing the causes of degeneracy. The members of these associations were public intellectuals who came from Brazil's elite, and they found in eugenics a language that allowed them to converse across disciplines and to stake a claim for their disciplines as the bases for social policy. As they sought to consolidate their respective fields, they succeeded in making them the basis of a range of federal, state, and municipal programs of not only education and health but also areas of public action such as government hiring, criminological practices, military recruitment, and treatment of the insane. Through their creation of these programs and of the educational instruments that trained their technicians (by the 1930s formal teacher training throughout Brazil included varying degrees of the eugenic disciplines of sociology, psychology, hygiene, physical education, and puericulture, the science of pre- and postnatal care), these eugenic pioneers assured that the core sciences of eugenics would be widely taught and practiced.[15]

Brazilian eugenicists differed from those in other countries in the degree to which they drew eugenics out of the laboratory and into public policies aimed at improving the physical and medical state of the population and reshaping their cultural values. There were two reasons for the unique public role of eugenics in Brazil. First, it provided the emerging scientific, medical, and social scientific authorities with a shorthand for explaining ideas of racial inferiority and defining strategies for managing or ameliorating that inferiority. Second, eugenics armed this group with a scientific solution to what was basically a social problem. Contemporaries believed science transcended politics, thus policies framed in eugenic language depoliticized debate over racial norms. Moreover, the prestige of science meant that eugenic programs competed effectively for resources.

Beginning with the public health and hygiene movement of the second decade of the twentieth century, policies meant to whiten the composition of the population through European immigration began to share space with new policies meant to whiten behavior and social conditions. The consensus among policymakers was that schools were the front lines in the battle against "degeneracy." Educators turned schools into eugenic laboratories—places where ideas about race and nation were tested on and applied to children. Eugenics became the rationale for expanding and allocating educational resources. Curricular and extracurricular practices were wed to eugenics in ways that continue to resonate today. To give one example, physical education and fitness became so fundamental to "perfecting the race" that a generation later sports announcers would declare that scoring four goals in one game made the soccer star Pelé "racially perfect."[16]

The eugenicists enshrined their goals in the ideal of a *raça brasileira*, or "Brazilian race." The *raça* was a work in progress—a common ethnicity that all Brazilians would belong to once they shed inferior cultural and hygienic conditions. Teachers taught students that being a part of the *raça* was the key to citizenship and success. In practice, this meant behavioral whitening: that is, discarding African and indigenous cultural practices. Even Brazilians not of European descent could be members of the *raça*. Elite concern over the "eugenic perfection of the race" meant the allocation of resources to mitigate some of the effects of poverty on children. The promise of balanced lunches and health care were major reasons parents sent their children to school, as shown in the records of parents' correspondence with public officials. While the idea of a *raça brasileira* may not necessarily have meant much to the public, the programs that the *raça* inspired linked elites and the poor in a common enterprise that had lasting repercussions on the definition of race in Brazil.

The educational projects of eugenicists, which took root in the 1920s and gained their fullest expression during the Vargas era, shed light on one of the most paradoxical questions about modern Brazil: How did the idea that Brazil was a racial democracy become the nation's guiding myth for the better part of the twentieth century, especially in face of such visible racial inequalities? The trick that allowed both Brazilians and foreigners to have accepted this idea lies in the way the practice of eugenics submerged the management of racial hierarchy within social scientific language that deracialized and depoliticized the image of Brazilian society.

EDUCATION AND HEALTH

The eugenic projects of educators emerged between the 1920s and 1940s from the public health and hygiene campaigns of the first decades of the century. In turn, advocates for public health and hygiene were innovators whose projects countered a widely held belief in the racial degeneracy of black and mixed-blood individuals. This idea of degeneracy combined European scientific racism with white Brazilian fears of the African slave population. Could a black wetnurse (a figure indelibly imprinted on the Brazilian national mythology as the *mãe preta*, literally "black mother") convey her diseases (perhaps syphilis or tuberculosis) or general degeneracy to white infants, thereby sapping their vitality? Were mulattoes psychologically unstable and given to criminal behavior? These were the types of beliefs that stood at the root of white fears and that served as the basis of the research of scientists who imbibed racial theories crafted by European white supremacists who sought to impose scientific barriers along the racial frontiers of European empires.[17]

The Brazilian most closely associated with this position, Bahian anthropologist Raimundo Nina Rodrigues, was a turn-of-the-century proponent of the idea that nonwhite Brazilians constituted a group so inferior to whites that they should not even be held to the same legal standards in criminal proceedings. But while Brazil arrived at the twentieth century laden with the burden of scientific racism and the stigma it applied to the racially mixed nation, this current soon gave way to the environmental and cultural approach to degeneracy. Concern about endemic diseases in the first decade of the century expanded into Miguel Pereira's condemnation of Brazil as a "vast hospital" in 1916, reflecting the development of political consciousness about the relationships between state and society and between health, race, and degeneracy. By 1917, Arthur Neiva and Belissário Penna, two doctors and public health advocates sent by the National Academy of Medicine to study conditions in the interior of Brazil, published a report calling not for a Ministry of Health, but for a Ministry of *Education* and Health.

This intellectual trajectory has been traced by Thomas Skidmore, Mariza Corrêa, Nisia Trinidade Lima, and Gilberto Hochman. These scholars credit the emergence of countercurrents to scientific racism in Europe and the United States (especially the influence of anthropologist Franz Boas), as well as the pragmatism of Brazilian elites, who found the vision of degeneracy as a medical, cultural, and psychological problem to be a more serviceable idea than the older racial theories. This new view of degeneracy was a boon to pioneers of the social sciences in Brazil, whose practices now spoke to the most serious problem in national identity, offering not only a diagnostic language but an unprecedented array of purported treatments.[18]

The transformation of a recurring character in the essays of the writer J. B. Monteiro Lobato illustrates this shift in consciousness. A leading intellectual figure in the early decades of the century and a popular author of nationalist children's literature, he was the most visible convert to the environmental camp of racial ideology. In a 1914 essay, Monteiro Lobato introduced the character Jeca Tatú ("hillbilly"). Jeca was *sertanejo* (from the interior) and epitomized all that was wrong with Brazil's racially mixed underclasses: "[He] exists merely to hunker; he is incapable of evolution and is immune to progress."[19] The openly racist essay depicted the backwoodsman as the cause of the nation's economic and political weaknesses. Monteiro Lobato's Jeca was the equivalent of the original, degenerate, "Brazilian Man" statue that caused such conflict twenty-five years later.

But in 1918, in the midst of a growing debate over whether the nation's poor and rural populations were inferior because of their racial background or because of their conditioning, Monteiro Lobato revised his interpretation of Jeca Tatú. His collection of essays, *The Vital Problem*, included a parable called "The Resurrection of Jeca Tatú" in which the backwoodsman was cured of degeneracy by a traveling doctor, whereupon he was able to transform his farm through hard work and become happy and wealthy and travel the world. The moral of this story, which was distributed widely in the interior as a children's fable, was that "Jeca wasn't born that way, he became so." *The Vital Problem* (and along with it, Jeca's redemption) was jointly published by the Eugenics Society of São Paulo and the Pro-Sanitation League, as these groups began to assert their ideas of cultural and environmental degeneracy in the debate over race in Brazil. As "The Vulture of Our Progress," a 1935 pamphlet declared, "Jeca is illiterate because he lives in misery! He lives in misery because he is sick! He is sick because he is illiterate!"[20]

The public education movement grew out of this new consensus that degeneracy was acquired and could be mitigated. Beginning with the call by doctors for a Ministry of Education and Health, doctors and educators (who were mostly trained in the social sciences) worked together to apply eugenic theories to the complex of problems they called degeneracy. Numerous doctors and public health specialists, like Afrânio Peixoto, occupied educational administration posts. Meanwhile, educators joined the professional organizations of doctors and public health advocates, such as the São Paulo Eugenics Society, the Mental Hygiene League, and the Pro-Sanitation League.

Concern for "redeeming" Brazil joined education and health in a common endeavor. It blurred the distinctions between different professions and scientific disciplines. It also created a national network of professionals working on local problems. Political scientist and historian of medicine Gilberto Hochman provides an analysis of the public health and sanitation movement's pressure to rethink the constitutional relationship between federal and state power: because epidemic disease did not respect state boundaries, *sanitaristas* (as advocates of public health and sanitation were known) succeeded in pushing for a looser reading of the constitutional balance of powers and forged federal responsibility for public health. Nationalization of education evolved differently. Education remained local, but it was administered by a national elite. For instance, it was Monteiro Lobato who would secure the appointment of Anísio Teixeira to reform and direct the Rio school system in 1931.

Similarly, in 1922, the state of Ceará recruited a twenty-five-year-old professor of educational psychology at the São Paulo Normal School, Manoel Lourenço Filho, to reform its school system. In the decades after his appointment in Ceará, Lourenço Filho emerged as a pioneer child psychologist, setting nationally embraced standards and practices. In the 1930s, he directed the Institute of Education in Rio and later organized and headed the federal department of educational research, the National Institute for Pedagogical Studies (INEP). Manoel Lourenço Filho's experience in Ceará not only reflects the nationalization of local education, but also illustrates the way such educational reformers saw Jeca Tatú, the backwoodsman, and sought his redemption.

As Lourenço Filho set out to expand the reach of the school system within the interior of Ceará, he sent surveyors to towns across the state to count the number of children. His team experienced difficulties with the town of Juazeiro, which repeatedly expelled the surveyors. Juazeiro had been the site of an uprising in 1913 in which demagogic priest Father Cícero led its inhabitants in arms against the state government. Father Cícero's rebellion succeeded, and he remained a regionally powerful figure because the federal government saw the rebellion as a convenient way to rid itself of Ceará's opposition faction of the national ruling Republican Party. The state government fell, Father Cícero remained, and Juazeiro retained relative autonomy, which it reasserted in the face of state school system officials sent by Lourenço Filho.[21]

The young educational psychologist resolved to take upon himself the task of bringing Juazeiro into the system. He assembled a motorcade and mounted an automotive expedition into the interior, where such a thing must have been a rare sight. Lourenço Filho found Father Cícero ailing and on his sickbed. The young secular social scientist who was building the state came to an agreement with the aging religious patriarch. Later, Lourenço Filho wrote of this experience in prose resembling Joseph Conrad's *Heart of Darkness*. His book *The Juazeiro of Father Cícero* (1928) reframed Monteiro Lobato's model of cultural and environmental degeneracy in the context of education. In *Juazeiro*, Lourenço Filho explored the mentality of the people of Juazeiro and offered a disparaging psychological profile of the demagogic priest and his sickly and uneducated followers.

Lourenço Filho drew a contrast between backwardness and modernity that could be measured in terms of both race and culture. He saw the rural Catholic clergyman as largely responsible for the state of ignorance of the inhabitants of Juazeiro. Conversely, the public schools he sought to install would provide the secular, technical, and cultural resources through which the people could overcome centuries of accumulated backwardness. The dichotomy between secular school and religious power drawn by Lourenço Filho foreshadowed the battles in which he and his cohort of educational reformers would engage against a resurgent Catholic Church in the next decade.

In *Juazeiro*, Lourenço Filho related his journey to the "horrid jungle" as travel backward through time, measured in the darkening skin of the people he encountered: "Our own ethnographic evolution could be studied in such a journey to the interior. On the coast whites dominate, demonstrating the Aryan preponderance of our people of today; shortly we see results of the most violent mixing of the three primitive races, with the rare presence of the pure black." At the end of this regression through the path of human evolution, Lourenço Filho reached Juazeiro, where "the backwardness of the backlands is concentrated, creating the worst regression and causing formidable maladjustments within which lurk mentalities behind by centuries."[22] As Capanema did with his imagined "Brazilian Man," Lourenço Filho again related race and time, equating the coastal whites with progress and civilization, and looking back through the ages where primitivism and backwardness were written in the darkening pigments of the skins of those people he encountered.

For Lourenço Filho the people of the backlands, and especially of Juazeiro, were "miserable, without hygiene or work . . . sick and crazy." Lourenço Filho described a scene of almost total "degeneracy," where the population was unlearned, sick (84 percent of its children had trachomas), jobless, and crazy. The solution was education: "The mental situation of the population can be summarized like this: twenty percent know how to read, the rest don't."[23] The essence of Lourenço Filho's argument in Juazeiro can be summarized by three points. First, the misery that Brazilians of the interior endured was responsible for their "degeneracy": their ignorance, ill health, psychological maladjustment, and perpetual agitation. Second, rather than alleviate this condition, the federal government actually encouraged degeneracy by waging short-term political games between local factions. Third, the redemption of these Brazilians would come from building schools and reorienting the priorities of elites.

CITY, RACE, AND NATION

That the Ministry of Education and Health only built its first permanent headquarters in 1938 illustrates how late the federal government became actively involved in Brazil's decentralized and limited educational system. Created in the immediate aftermath of the Revolution of 1930, the MES replaced the previous regime's second-tier Ministry of Telegraphs, Mails, and Public Instruction. The new ministry did not centralize public education. To the contrary, while the national educational movement's leaders participated in MES endeavors, the true center of education reform in the 1930s and 1940s continued to lie with the educators, doctors, and social scientists active in different areas of the eugenics movement and in public education, who rotated through posts in Rio de Janeiro, São Paulo, Recife, Belo Horizonte, Fortaleza, and Salvador. During the Vargas era, the MES helped coordinate their endeavors, and soon states that had been outside of the circle of education reform—such as Amazonas, Sergipe, Espírito Santo, and Paraíba—enacted legislation restructuring and expanding their educational systems to reflect the evolution of education in regions like Rio and São Paulo, often receiving federal resources to implement reforms.[24]

While Lourenço Filho was one example of the educational pioneers who moved across Brazil conducting reforms and expansions of the school system, he was far from alone. Rio de Janeiro school system director Fernando de Azevedo (1926–1930) came from São Paulo, while Afrânio Peixoto (1917–1922) and Anísio Teixeira (1931–1935) came from Bahia. Antônio Carneiro Leão, a native of Recife who directed the Rio school system from 1922 to 1926, returned to Pernambuco in 1928 to reform the state's public schools. His return and his reform help illustrate the flow not only of people but of ideas among state and municipal school systems.

Carneiro Leão was a committed eugenicist whose reform of the Rio school system introduced to daily practice such institutions as the *pelotão de saúde*, or student health brigade, in which designated students in each classroom oversaw the health and hygiene of their classmates. He also pioneered the practice of physical education in elementary schools, believing it would "combat vices and illnesses, making it decisive in elevating the race." In 1924, his Department of Education produced a documentary, *For the Grandeur of the Race*, that showcased twelve thousand students performing calisthenics in order to promote physical education in other parts of the country. Consistent with his scientific vision of education, Carneiro Leão expanded professional teacher training.[25]

When Carneiro Leão returned to Recife to direct the state of Pernambuco's Department of Public Education, he brought with him the eugenic, rationalizing, and professionalizing norms he had put to work in Rio de Janeiro. He turned the state's normal school into the first Brazilian institution to offer regular courses in sociology, and selected fellow Pernambucan Gilberto Freyre to serve as Brazil's first professor of sociology. Freyre's curriculum taught sociology as "a healer of the social ills, alerting the youth to the ills that came from marriage between sick individuals by encouraging prenuptial exams and abstinence from alcohol, promoting eugenics and the fight against sloth, thus avoiding the proliferation of hospitals and prisons." Borrowing lessons of scientific rationalization from industry, Carneiro Leão created a Technical Educational Administration to manage the school system. The Technical Administration offices were charged with making the schools more scientific and with instituting practices aimed at "the perfection of the race, eugenics, vitality, and productive capacity" among students.[26]

The Carneiro Leão reforms of both the city of Rio de Janeiro and the state of Pernambuco show how the main principles of reform (eugenics, professionalism, and rationalization) ultimately rested in the hands of individual educational leaders. Even after the creation of a Ministry of Education and Health, education reformers continued to work at the local level. Indeed, the Rio de Janeiro school system was more of a magnet for leading education reformers than was the MES. Rio de Janeiro was the target of the reformers' zeal since Afrânio Peixoto's tenure in 1917. It was the largest school system in Brazil, and reformers developed it as a showcase of public education projects that could be developed by other school systems across the nation. Carneiro Leão made this clear in his 1922 inaugural address when he stressed that the city school system must be seen as "a model for the entire Republic and a reference point of our national pedagogical and cultural progress."[27] Not only did they treat the Rio school system as a model, they used it as a space where they could develop and refine the eugenic sciences and social sciences that underwrote the educational mission of building the "Brazilian race."

By the time Anísio Teixeira gained appointment as director of the Rio school system in 1931, the coalition of scientists, doctors, and social scientists was fully devoted to eugenic nationalism. They agreed that degeneracy was acquired through a lack of culture, health, and environment and that public education and health could reverse it. Nonetheless, the challenge of mapping out specifically how cultural and environmental factors created degeneracy, and of developing the precise measures that would overcome degeneracy, still had to be faced. Teixeira assumed this challenge and turned the Rio school system into a laboratory that attracted the nation's leading eugenicists. Individuals like Roquette Pinto, Arthur Ramos, Lourenço Filho, and Afrânio Peixoto were all drawn again to the Rio school system in order to research degeneracy, develop health and education programs for addressing it, and apply these programs within the city's schools.

The Rio de Janeiro school system presented eugenicists with a perfect environment: nearly one hundred thousand schoolchildren of all races and social conditions, along with a Department of Education that gave the eugenicists an almost free hand to study the children and treat their perceived inadequacies. At the outset of his administration, Anísio Teixeira created the Institute for Educational Research (IPE), which was based on the Institute for Education Research at the Columbia University Teachers College in New York, where Teixeira studied under John Dewey and other leading U.S. progressives. The IPE would conduct some of the most advanced educational, sociological, eugenic, and psychological research of its time in its four sections: Tests and Measures, Educational Radio and Cinema, Orthophrenology and Mental Hygiene, and Anthropometry.

Testing and Tracking dealt with psychological and intelligence testing and tracking of students, and was originally headed by Isaias Alves, an educator who like Teixeira had studied at the Columbia University Teachers College. In the Testing and Tracking section, Alves was responsible for applying intelligence tests developed in the United States in order to separate students into different classrooms based on their aptitudes. The main measure he used, the Terman Group Test, was developed with the specific belief that the eugenic fitness of some children was inherently better than others. As test developer Lewis Terman asserted in 1916:

> The common opinion that the child from a cultured home does better in tests solely by reason of his superior home advantages is an entirely gratuitous assumption. Practically all of the investigations which have been made of the influence of nature and nurture on mental performance agree in attributing far more to original endowment than to environment. Common observation would itself suggest that the social class to which the family belongs depends less on chance than on the parents' native qualities of intellect and character. . . . The children of successful and cultured parents test higher than children from wretched and ignorant homes for the simple reason that their heredity is better.[28]

Although Lewis Terman believed in the inherent hereditary superiority of some intellects, his test was easily adapted to the Brazilian vision of degeneracy because Alves and others read the test results as indicative of the poor cultural and social conditions of the Brazilian subjects. Still, the tests had the effect of separating white students from students of color and wealthy students from poor students.

The IPE's Department of Educational Radio and Cinema, headed by Edgar Roquette Pinto, explored means of delivering education to remote regions of the interior. The division operated a radio station, PRD-5, which was entirely dedicated to educational issues. It supported a number of educational programs such as weekly lectures on mental hygiene, broadcasts of instructions for administering psychological tests, and an *Hour of the Teacher* that addressed curricular and professional issues. The principle behind the radio and cinema program was that through such media the school system might reach the illiterate and unfit individuals of the interior, where degeneracy was believed to be the most severe. Radio and cinema could bring messages about health and lessons of basic education to these people before they moved to the cities, bringing with them their profound maladjustments.

Orthophrenology and Mental Hygiene, headed by Arthur Ramos, studied child psychology and psychological/sociological adaptation to modern society. The service conducted research, developed educational programs for schools and the community, and managed the education of "problem children." This section combined influences that ranged from Freudian psychology to Italian criminology and cultural anthropology. In Ramos's view, Afro-Brazilians and children fit into a similar category of primitive and prelogical development. Finally, Anthropometry, headed by Bastos D'Avila, explicitly dealt with the physical aspects of degeneracy and eugenics, again borrowing from the Italian school of criminology, which studied the links between physical and phenotypic characteristics and criminality. One of this movement's leading advocates, Nicola Pende, "believed that by means of an inventory of human biotypes in a population the biological resources of a nation could be harnessed efficiently to the goals of the state. Such an endeavor, said Pende, was of vital concern to the fascists and the work of Mussolini."[29]

Each section of the IPE managed a different element of the eugenics program. They maximized the potential of the school in perfecting the race by dealing with the psychological adaptation and physical development of children. Unlike other aspects of education in Rio, which were battered by the political turbulence of the era, the IPE's programs reflected consensus among elites over racial ideology and were uncharacteristically stable. Although the director of the IPE resigned in protest over Anísio Teixeira's dismissal in

1935, all of the section chiefs remained, departing only years later with timing and reasons that seemed disengaged from national politics.[30]

The resource base used by the I P E's researchers were the records, or *fichas*, that were gathered concerning the city's schoolchildren. In some cases, these records were confidential and were collected without the knowledge of the student or their parents. A *ficha antropométrica* kept a record of the student's phenotypic and physical development, while a *ficha de higiene mental* tracked them psychologically. These records followed students throughout their studies and were used by school system officials to classify children into different classrooms or programs. The *fichas* also provided the basis of further psychological and anthropometric research. Researchers used this data both to fine-tune the school system's eugenic programs and to further a national science of eugenics that applied foreign theories to Brazil's particular mix of races and conditions.

The school system's head biometrician, Bastos D'Avila, used the *ficha antropométrica* to gather data for such projects as refining a measure called the Lapicque Index, which he hoped to use in order to detect the existence of latent African characteristics among individuals who appeared to be white.[31] D'Avila's report on the introduction of the *fichas* noted that the index "lets us compare the physical development of the child to define his particular environmental situation."[32] In a letter to Lourenço Filho he expressed the need for the school system to purchase some cephalometers (instruments used to measure skull size) in order to test the reliability of the Dubois Cephalization Index, which "might lend itself to categorizing the students as normal, supernormal, or sub-normal, which is extremely interesting."[33]

D'Avila's "Essay on Brazilian Raciology: Populations of the Federal District" reflects the aims of his research. It was published in the quarterly journal *Revista de Educação Pública*, which the Rio de Janeiro Department of Education circulated to teachers in the city and to school systems throughout the country. The article briefed teachers about theories of whitening or forming a homogenous race, echoing the "Brazilian Man" debate by explaining that "it's too soon to speak of a 'Brazilian race,' a race that technically speaking does not yet exist. . . . There is no reliable forecast that can be made of the type that will result from the effervescence of the *melting pot* within which the

Brazilian people brew."[34] Because the future was unwritten, schools should redouble their efforts to shape the race.

In the same essay, D'Avila also tried to explain away the disappointing results of eugenic research on the patterns of growth among Rio's school-children. Although D'Avila tried to measure race-linked differences, his study was muddled by class issues: contrary to his expectations, the study showed that black children gained weight and height faster than white children. D'Avila strained to reconcile his data with the accepted notion that whites had superior conditioning. He reasoned that the wealthiest children did not attend public schools, and if their growth had been sampled the ranking of white children would have surpassed that of nonwhite children. According to D'Avila, "studies by the Anthropometry section support this theory by demonstrating that the white children in our schools are, for the most part, of the physically deficient type."[35]

Although the white children in public schools were generally poor, and therefore "deficient," the opposite held true for the black children. D'Avila explained that "they are from the better-organized families—those which seek out the public schools—since the less-cared for children, be it through parental negligence or ignorance, are never even matriculated."[36] Whiteness was the control for D'Avila's research: it was a value that signified vitality. Nonwhite children could achieve that standard, and only particularly unfit whites could depart from it, but when this was the case researchers felt compelled to carefully explain the failure of white students to meet eugenic expectations.

In his publications, D'Avila displayed a consistent assumption that environmental considerations influenced physical development. By 1945, he lamented that the *fichas*, which had been modeled on the records maintained by the National Museum, dealt with absolute racial types to the neglect of other environmental factors that bore on the development of the individual. He explained that "the children are measured without considering their state of hygiene," and he sought ways to develop an "index of somatic architecture" that would reveal a child's "state of hygiene."[37] D'Avila tested indices on twenty-nine hundred candidates for admission to the Institute of Education during their eliminatory health exam. Because all these candidates were women, follow-up tests were done on another ten thousand students to gain data on males. And although by 1945 D'Avila had still not perfected a workable measure, research continued.

That the school was a place where children of all races could be observed as they developed over months or years was not apparent to D'Avila alone. Noted anthropologist Arthur Ramos used the Rio school system for his case studies on the cultural aspects of improving the race. Ramos combined psychological and anthropological studies of race, reflecting the elasticity of disciplinary boundaries in the context of eugenics. From 1933 to 1938, Ramos headed the Orthophrenology and Mental Hygiene section of the IPE. Previously Ramos had studied Afro-Brazilian culture in Bahia, identifying elements of cultural "inferiority." Seeking to foster adaptation of Afro-Brazilian culture to modern society, he turned his attentions to child psychology and preventive mental hygiene. In his 1945 curriculum vitae, he expressed his "preference for the study of human behavior, especially in certain conditions of deficiency: children, primitives, ethnic minorities, the insane, and neurotics."[38] The combination of his interests in problem children and in Afro-Brazilian cultural deficiencies drew Ramos to the Rio de Janeiro school system, where he was provided with the resources and research base to carry out his studies.

A 1934 pamphlet written by Ramos and published by the school system for distribution among parents shows how he integrated child psychology with what was perceived as the cultural improvement of the Afro-Brazilian population. As Ramos explained: "The racial inferiority complex has blocked our progress. . . . There are no superior or inferior races. But there are social groups that are culturally advanced or retarded." Ramos saw himself as a disciple of Raimundo Nina Rodrigues, one of the principal turn-of-the-century scholars of race. Although Nina Rodrigues had been one of the principal exponents of scientific racism, Arthur Ramos (along with Afrânio Peixoto) considered himself a member of a Nina Rodrigues school of thought. Ramos was intent on bringing Nina Rodrigues's empirical methods for the study of race to his analyses of Afro-Brazilians as a cultural community.[39] For Ramos, racial mixture did not result in inferior hybrids as Nina Rodrigues had believed. Instead, he stated, "give him good physical and mental hygiene and the alleged inferiority will disappear."[40]

While negating racial inferiority, Ramos measured differences in cultural development. He singled out aspects of Afro-Brazilian culture that he considered pathological, and he labored to eliminate them. As he said, "we must not neglect the ways retarded cultures and prelogical thought make our work in the schools difficult." Ramos defined Afro-Brazilian culture as prelogical, and he believed schools should help children "escape the insidious influence of hoax and superstition[,] combat the slow and invisible effect of *macumba* [a syncretic Afro-Brazilian religious practice] and fetishism that infiltrates our lives [and] focus on proper spiritual growth, guided toward the currents of true scientific values."[41]

Ramos situated his views within a broader discourse on eugenics, linking both mental faculties and culture to prenatal care: "Attention to mental hygiene must begin at even the prenatal and preconception periods. At this point, mental hygiene gives way to racial hygiene, through the proper methods of this new science." He lauded the work of eugenicists, who "engineer the mental and physical transformation of peoples."[42] Ramos believed in the primacy of culture over race in conditioning human potential. The Orthophrenology and Mental Hygiene Service provided him with the resources—literally thousands of *fichas de higiene mental*—with which to disprove biological determinism, which he called "racial hygiene," demonstrating instead the "immense and complex . . . influence of the cultural environment."[43] Ramos relied on the behavioral and psychological records of Rio's students to develop his *The Problem Child: Mental Hygiene in the Elementary School*, which explored reasons for the maladjustment of children.

Ramos argued that behavioral, adaptive, and psychological problems emerged from culturally or environmentally unfit social conditions, attributing children's maladjustments to bad influences in their homes. Blaming parents for the physical and psychological maladjustments of their children meant blaming their culture and skin color. Ramos described a culture of poverty in which the domestic influences on children living in inferior conditions translated into pathological behavior. As he explained, poor performance in school was caused by "the powerful influence of maladjusted environments, domestic conflicts, emotional neglect, terrible role models, and fatigue from malnutrition and work."[44] Ramos argued that alcoholism and addiction were not causes of maladjustment but were symptoms of broader social problems. Documenting the existence of a culture of poverty buried explanations of racial degeneracy as well as larger structural causes of poverty. Poor children were case studies of inferior culture being passed on generationally.

For Ramos and other Department of Education researchers, schools were at once a medium for diagnosing the maladjustments in the society and the instrument for breaking the cycle of poverty. These schools intended to reach whole families through schoolchildren. As one school nutritionist argued, "if a child acquires certain healthy and well-oriented 'alimentary habits' in school, she will very naturally try to follow them outside of school; and can even transmit them in the home to parents and siblings."[45] This was a common aim of school programs: nutritionists, hygienists, psychologists, and teachers tied to the school system knew that the nation's problems were not rooted in its children, and that to remedy these social ills meant using the children to teach the society.

The formula applied by educators—defining a cultural or behavioral deficiency as linked to a population defined by class or color, and addressing it through public policy—was also applied in other areas of governance. As head of the INEP, for example, Lourenço Filho lamented to Minister Capanema that the federal biometric laboratory never had the opportunity to conduct research because it spent all its time screening candidates for government jobs. During the war, when Brazil fought alongside the Allies, the IPE tested the intelligence of soldiers. As was so often the case with comparisons between students of different colors, the author of the IPE report on the wartime testing of soldier intelligence dedicated himself to explaining away the awkward detail that white candidates performed less well than others—perhaps many of the whites were immigrants who, although literate, did not understand the test as well as did native Brazilians.[46]

Rio Department of Public Works Director Pedro Monteiro Machado developed a survey of his department's workers' culture and behavior to determine the "causes of job instability." Believing that it was the civic-minded thing to do, as well as necessary to safeguard the "economic interests of the country," Machado wanted to survey the cultural situation of the city's public works staff in order to take measures to make them more efficient workers. His primary concerns were alcoholism, poor food preparation, and recourse to inappropriate medical care. Among the first questions, Machado's survey inquired about the race of the employee, reasoning that this would determine the "cultural level" of the worker. To illustrate this point, Machado affirmed that a white Brazilian descended from Portuguese or Italian parents prepared meals that were more nutritious and rational than those of other Brazilians. He pointed to the "serious and constant shortcomings" in food culture, a symptom of the way that Brazilian races "adapt easily to civilization and technology" but retained "primitive cultures."

Nowhere was this more evident than in worker health and hygiene. Machado explained that any doctor knew that lower-class Brazilians, especially nonwhites, only sought sound medical care "after a painful pilgrimage to *macumbeiros* [Afro-Brazilian spiritual leaders] . . . sessions of low spiritism or, worse, the counters of fraudulent pharmacists, where ignorance is compounded by exploitation."[47] The survey of worker health practices was all the more salient because the city's mayor, Pedro Ernesto, who was a close Vargas ally and a doctor, established public health clinics throughout the city. Together with the public education reform program, the mayor's extensive public health program made the capital into a model for Brazil's emerging social welfare state.[48]

HEALTHY CHILDREN FOR A HEALTHY SOCIETY

The Department of Education's research institute, the IPE, developed analytical models for understanding the national social problems that appeared in schools and prescribed remedies for them. A child going to school stepped into a laboratory and unwittingly became a scientific subject. Children regularly underwent a battery of tests of their psychological, physical, and eugenic development, intelligence, and maturity. These tests were used to determine the norms against which children would later be measured and classified. These tests also further completed the analytical framework of eugenics by providing evidence that supported new classificatory schemes that substantiated interpretations of race and society.

These inroads by eugenicists into Rio's schools were only the most visible elements of the eugenic orientation of public education. School health, nutrition, and hygiene program directors endeavored to substitute deficient cultures with practices that built the race. Researchers divulged their findings and procedures through the school system journal, in national conferences, and in other publications, all with the aim of reaching a national audience. Still, the research end of the eugenics program was overshadowed by daily eugenic practices and programs in the schools. The health and nutrition programs of the school system were a key element of what administrators and politicians boasted was a model for the nation.

By the 1940s, the Department of Education divided the city into medical space: fifteen sanitary districts, all administered by the Department of School Health. School system officials proclaimed that the basis for administering the schools within these zones was "medical-pedagogical." In other words, decisions to place students in a certain classroom, and to pass them or hold them back, were based not only on maturity and intelligence testing and or classroom performance but also on assessments of health. The sanitary districts became the administrative units along which educational health, hygiene, and nutrition programs were implemented.[49]

The most visible example of the health and hygiene program in the city's schools was the "health brigade," or *pelotão de saúde*. This was a group of students—one per classroom—who were charged with inspecting the hygiene of their classmates. *Pelotão* members wore armbands with a red cross and inspected the students in their classrooms daily, recording the state of their hygiene on a chart on the door of the room. The health brigade checked dental hygiene, general cleanliness and neatness, hands and nails for proper washing and trimming, and hair for lice. Students got a yellow cross for good hygiene, green for fair, and red for poor hygiene. Those with poor hygiene were sent to the principal's office for a lecture on hygiene or even an intervention with their parents. This hygiene chart illustrates the daily ways in which eugenics and nationalism were woven together in the daily school practice of building the race: good and fair hygiene were represented by the colors of the Brazilian flag, bad hygiene was red.[50]

Educators saw a lack of hygiene among more affluent children as a lack of discipline subject to reprimand. Among poorer children, a lack of hygiene was considered a result of environment, so punishment was substituted with instruction on proper cleaning of the teeth, ears, and hair. One inspector recalled watching the principal of the Escola Estados Unidos show a student how to brush her teeth. The student did not have money for a toothbrush, so the principal explained how to put some charcoal in a rag, fold it over, tie it, and then rub her teeth with the rag.[51]

The resources that schools devoted to the development of hygienic habits varied. Each school had a fund of public money and private donations that provided shoes and uniforms for the poor or strengthened the school lunch. The Escola Vicente Licínio went a step further than the Estados Unidos in making hygienic practices possible. The principal believed that "it is inefficient if not ridiculous that the school promote the advantages of good habits and attitudes without providing the means to put them into practice."[52] The school solicited donations with which it bought toothbrushes, hair brushes, soap, and towels. Students acquired habits like brushing teeth, washing hands, combing hair, and shining shoes by performing them daily in the school.

In addition to the *pelotão* in place in all schools, each third-grade student at the Escola Vicente Licínio was responsible for the cleanliness of a group of first graders. The principal reported that "it was truly endearing to see them take care of the little ones, trimming their nails, washing their hands, etc. with the responsibility and care of little mothers."[53] At the local level, these ritual steps toward "perfecting the race" took on a different aspect—one of adults caring for children and children learning to look after each other. The teachers who administered these practices found them endearing, but they had also been drilled about the importance of hygiene in eugenics through their normal schooling, by radio, and in teacher journals.

The journal *Revista de Educação Pública* repeatedly stressed to teachers the importance of health and hygiene in addressing the nation's deficiencies. Furthermore, the journal emphasized the importance of these women as the technical professionals who would redeem the race. According to one school doctor: "Today doctors and teachers are carrying out a common task, which is the psycho-somatic perfection of the human being, so that he can realize his greater destinies."[54] Not only were teachers like doctors, the school was like a hospital: "School hygiene . . . has eliminated the boundary between the school and the hospital," one school-system doctor observed.[55] At a time where few women entered the prestigious ranks of medicine and the liberal professions, making the case that the women who taught in the city's elementary schools were performing work of such professional caliber and national importance was flattering. By fulfilling the task of improving the race, teachers became respected and valuable agents of the nation's progress.

The metaphor that "Brazil is an immense hospital" lent itself easily to describing the teacher's work in the classroom, healing Brazilians of their bad habits and unhealthy cultures. The comparison of schools to hospitals, however, was more than allegorical. As students enrolled, they underwent "detailed clinical, radiological, and laboratory exams in which the state of sanitation of the student is determined."[56] From this exam a permanent medical record was formed and periodically updated. Regular health and hygiene was dealt with at the school and in the classroom. Serious medical problems were ideally treated at the school system's medical and dental clinics, located in each of the fifteen sanitary districts or at the Educational Medicine Center.

In practice, the medical needs of all students exceeded the capacity of these facilities, and many went without the care the city purported to provide. The principal of the Escola Vicente Licínio reported that of the students referred to the dental clinics located at the Escola Colombia and in the Department of Education's Pediatric Dental Clinic, "unfortunately, few could be attended to, relative to the number who needed treatment."[57] Publicly, the school system promised comprehensive medical and dental care, but privately it recorded the inadequacy of its measures.

Parents made similar complaints. Medical care and free school lunches were two of the tangible benefits of the school that attracted students and drew the support of their parents. Parents knew when the promises made by the city or by the school system were not met. Although medical and dental care was supposed to be systematic and available to all students, letters from parents either to the school system or to Getúlio Vargas—who received thousands of petitions from "simple" or "humble" Brazilians for a pension, space in a school, or access to a clinic—show that the system did not have the reach boasted by the administrators.

In November 1943, retired "simple second lieutenant" Waldemar Pinto Victorio of Rio's working-class suburb Realengo wrote Vargas explaining the difficulty of raising his children and educating them in the absence of the promised medical care. Of his twenty children, eight had died "for lack of financial means." Of the nine still under his care, two had to be taken out of school in order to work "to buy what aren't even modest clothes, and I too work at a factory so that we may live honestly." Victorio cautioned that from his experience it was not advisable to have so many children, because "the growth in the number of children is exactly why my family is so destitute."[58]

Victorio asked for help in getting his children medical and dental care. He explained that like other working-class parents, he had never been given the opportunity of dental care as a boy. He asked if his children could have access to a free dental clinic through the school. Savvy to the pattern of unkept promises, he added that "the school dentistry office should not be 'for the English to see' like most are." This expression referred to actions taken to impress sophisticated foreigners, like the Parisian boulevards that had been carved into the center of the city at the beginning of the century; essentially Victorio suggested that the dentistry clinics were merely window dressing. Finally, Victorio stressed that: "Your Excellency has excellent ideas, but they do not reach those who need them."[59]

Getúlio Vargas was the "chief of the nation" and cultivated an image of father of a national family.[60] In pursuit of this role, letters and petitions by thousands of ordinary Brazilians were taken seriously by administrators. Each letter opened a file and was relayed to the appropriate federal or local government administrator for action. The files sent to Henrique Dodsworth, mayor of Rio de Janeiro during the Estado Novo, were kept among his papers. They reveal the inquiries and actions taken on dozens of requests. In this case, the school system did not waver from its official line: Dodsworth replied to Vargas that "his children can find medical and dental care in any sanitary district, or in any city school where they matriculate."[61]

Just as the school system had difficulty accommodating all of the demands for education, it had even greater trouble meeting its publicly stated goals regarding health and hygiene. Programs that involved classroom education or that could be carried out without specialized equipment or staff were widespread. In 1935, for instance, as public school enrollment in Rio surpassed one hundred thousand students, the Department of Education employed fourteen doctors and twenty-four dentists, and subcontracted another forty-four.

One dentist was a woman, reflecting both the entrance of women into the medical profession and the importance of expanding school systems in creating employment opportunities for women.[62] More intensive or specialized treatment was available only occasionally, reflecting school system objectives rather than regularly meeting needs.

It appears that only one school set up as a prototype, the Escola Barbara Otoni, enjoyed the full effects of the vaunted child and infant health care system. But the prototype proved the point that educators had emphasized for years: good health was the foundation for learning. Each year, 98 percent of students moved on to the next grade (well above the city average of roughly 50 percent). Colonel Pio Borges, secretary of education during the early years of the Estado Novo, explained that the students at the Escola Barbara Otoni proved "that the hands of the children became applied and diligent once they were placed under the care they needed to reach a normal state of health and hygiene."[63]

Educators saw nutrition as the most important part of the physical, intellectual, and cultural development of the child. As the head nutritionist of the school system wrote in 1942: "Adequate nutrition is necessary for the eugenic perfection of the race," and "good eating habits are the seeds of other habits of hygiene, discipline and work."[64] Because of the importance of nutrition to eugenics, free lunches were provided by the school. For many of Rio's children, these lunches were the only balanced meal of the day. One parent described a situation common to many poor children: "His only meal is the school lunch. When he gets home I give him a little soup, some coffee, and bread."[65]

The lunch program was one of the eugenically influenced practices that was most widely and consistently carried out. School lunches were available to all needy students. In some suburban schools, nearly all children qualified. Lunch consisted of milk, a plate of greens, rice, and meat or eggs. It did not take eugenics to realize that growing children needed nutritious meals. Still, that "the physical, mental and moral health of the future citizen, and consequently, the strength of the race" depended on nutrition gave the free lunch program added support.[66] If the school system was unable to meet all its established goals in health and hygiene, it was nonetheless capable of fulfilling certain basic objectives. Nutrition and basic hygiene were among these.

Physical education was another fundamentally eugenic program. Although school system administrators intended physical education to reach all children in all schools, it did not have the scope that the regulations and programs described on paper suggested. Many urban schools lacked space for physical education activities. Although some schools used nearby plots of land or made arrangements to share facilities with nearby schools, the idea that physical education classes should be a daily or weekly activity was far from the reality of many children. By 1944, there were just over a thousand physical education teachers in Brazil, and the education legislation had made it a mandatory part of the curriculum. Still, many urban schools, including the Colégio Pedro II federal model high school, had difficulty in finding suitable space for physical education activities.[67]

The concern for physical education began in the aftermath of the First World War when leaders in the military and nationalists worried about the physical fitness of potential army recruits. Indeed, the first public school physical education teacher training was provided by the army, which set up the army Physical Education School. By the 1920s, normal schools began to include this training in their curricula. The physical education techniques developed by the army and extended to the normal schools were introduced by the French military mission and were attuned to the French Lamarckian school of genetics. This technique emphasized mental and physical discipline. Biometrician Peregrino Júnior, director of the National Physical Education School that was established in the 1930s at the Universidade do Brasil, characterized physical education as part of Vargas's "politics of the Man." He explained that "the politics of physical education inaugurated by the National Government is one of the fundamental chapters of the plan to renew and build Brazil. . . . [It is how] the healthy Man, the strong Man, the happy Man of tomorrow is prepared."[68]

In Rio de Janeiro, physical education was introduced with the 1923 Carneiro Leão reform. Almost a decade later, the federal Francisco Campos secondary education law made it mandatory for all high schools. Rio de Janeiro's practices were more extensive: the city made physical education part of the curriculum for all elementary school students. These programs played the dual roles of disciplining students and promoting their sound physical development. To this end, physical education teachers worked in tandem with biometricians to record the progress made in the courses.

Physical education was one of the few aspects of the eugenic movement that caused conflict with the Catholic Church. In 1940, a letter to Vargas by the bishops of São Paulo condemned physical education for ignoring "all moral or religious concerns, with the complete absence of guidelines about sports decency, contemplating gymnastics from a strictly muscular standpoint, compounded by the emphasis of the sensual aspects" of bodily movement. Physical education worked to "corrupt our youth and make way for the establishment of anarchy in Brazilian society." The bishops even suggested that the programs had "materialist orientation, perhaps unconsciously communist."[69]

The bishops objected to coed physical education, to the "indecent" clothing students wore, to public physical education demonstrations involving girls, and to the physical examination of girls by male biometricians. Regarding the *fichas* recording indiscreet measurements of women's bodies, they stated "[the records are] contrary to the most basic notions of decency, abusively indiscreet and excessively detailed." The bishops insisted that they were not against the physical development of the body, and that there was no contradiction between moral duty and true physical need. Instead, apparent contradictions arose in this, the materialist century, from flawed notions of hygiene. Hygiene "with the pretext of physical culture, opens to lawlessness the doors that decency and tradition closed." Physical education as practiced was against the Sixth and Ninth Commandments (relating to adultery and covetry).[70]

Capanema replied to the bishops with one of the rare acts of federal defiance of the Church on matters of education. He stated simply that there was no conflict in coed physical education because both sexes wore clothing that was modest yet provided freedom of motion. Second, male biometricians did not measure girls, this was always done by female nurses. Third, all of the information on the records was both decent and necessary: "These measurements are justified by the use we get from them [in coordinating physical education], not to mention the scientific studies in anthropology, sociology, medicine, and eugenics that are nourished from this data, collected technically and without violating the natural modesty of the girls."[71]

That the federal government chose to defy the Church on this issue underscores the importance of eugenics. On other occasions, the government accommodated the Church's growing political and educational activism, taking seriously accusations by the Church hierarchy or lay Catholic nationalists that certain educators or educational programs were communist or unconsciously communist. Yet in this case, Minister Capanema dismissed the Church's concerns. Eugenics was the science used to address longstanding notions of Brazilian biological or cultural inferiority. These issues saturated public policy more deeply than did the Church's preoccupation with immorality, even when the Church suggested that physical education was causing the imminent collapse of the moral order.

Eugenics resonated throughout the education community. Policymakers focused on Brazil's "racial situation" and were versed in the scientific aspects of addressing it. Eugenic solutions were apparent throughout educational policy and practice. School administrators and teachers in Rio de Janeiro received a continuous education in the cultural and behavioral theories that explained racial deficiencies, and they were trained in the techniques that reversed them. Some projects did not reach all of the city's schools but others did. Expensive or complicated solutions seldom made it far from paper; approaches to eugenics and to hygiene that could be carried out by teachers or schools without much equipment or external resources were regularly and systematically applied.

In Rio during the Vargas era, eugenics was not relegated to professional conferences and remote laboratories, but rather was a collective, participatory endeavor. Teachers, parents, and children were taught to work together to realize the ideal of the future "Brazilian Man" that was to stand outside the MES building. Within the school system, eugenicists put their ideas to work for the first time, learning and practicing the programs for perfecting the race. Their research showed what they wanted it to believe: that white, wealthy students were more qualified in some quantifiable way. In the cases where a test revealed the opposite, the researcher went to great lengths to explain why the tests or the subjects somehow skewed the actual results from the conditions known to be true. In other words, poorer or darker children were deficient because the tests showed it. Consequently, the underclass remained deficient even if the tests did not show it. Research inductively quantified and qualified impressions about race and class instead of recording observations about social conditions revealed in the schools.

The results of these programs benefitted children in some ways. They were provided with free meals, some degree of medical and dental care, and a large dose of hygienic and nutritional education. On the other hand, they were reduced to objects of science, subjects of experiments whose conclusions were used as scientific proofs to sustain a system of assumptions about class and race that discriminated against the majority of public schoolchildren. The science of eugenics provided a bridge between racial ideology and popular culture, defining a culture of poverty. By the waning years of the Vargas era, this connection had become so strong that it could endure beyond the administrative endorsement of the science that guided it. Although eugenics lost legitimacy in the aftermath of the Second World War, the institutions, practices, and assumptions it gave rise to endured.

2

EDUCATING BRAZIL

In 1946, Mário Augusto Teixeira de Freitas, director of the Brazilian Institute for Geography and Statistics (IBGE) (the powerful agency created by Getúlio Vargas to survey the national landscape; charged not only with running the census but with collecting and interpreting all sorts of statistical data about Brazil) prepared a report on the level of education of the generation born in 1922. Because this year marked the centennial of Brazilian independence, Freitas employed the generation of 1922 as a symbol of the nation's progress. Seen from the perspective of educational attainment, the view was bleak:

> Of a whole generation that had begun to assume its social responsibilities, only 133,361, or 17 percent of its survivors, can be considered educated (having completed the third grade)—even if poorly educated. And of them, no more than a quarter (4 percent of the total), received an intermediate education. . . .
>
> In 1946, if the generation had its components distributed in squads, each one headed by two of the 7,319 leaders that have received higher education (be it military, civil, technical, or religious);—if we so organized that generation, which is, without a doubt, the "best" the "most rich in value" that the Nation has yet produced in all its history, we would see each of these teams comprised of the following: 2 leaders, 7 subleaders, and 201 followers.
>
> This last category would include the following:

- 27 "qualified" workers (not because they have any intermediate education, but because they passed the third grade).
- 24 barely "subqualified" workers that are reasonably literate, having made it through second grade.
- 42 workers that are "nonqualified" by any educational process beyond the most rudimentary first grade education.
- 100 "disqualified" workers; that is, workers who live in a subsocial quality of life, without any culture, any education, without notions or habits of hygiene or of preserving themselves or their families, without a basic civic or even human consciousness, even though a fifth of them had at some point attended a school that simply did not know how to educate them.

From this we conclude: each squad of 210 individuals has only two leaders (one per hundred citizens), a total of 7 subleaders (or one for twenty followers), and of these followers, only a fifth can be considered to be social values conscious of their professional and civic duties, those that education has pulled out of the condition of being a simple "human cattle."[1]

Freitas's declaration illustrates both how much and how little had changed in the twenty-four years since the centenary. Much had happened in the political arena in the lives of these twenty-four year olds, including the Revolution of 1930, the provisional government of Getúlio Vargas, the promulgation of a progressive constitution in 1934, the national state of emergency that gave Vargas broad powers beginning in 1935, the imposition of the Estado Novo dictatorship in 1937, Brazil's participation in the Second World War, and the deposition of Vargas in 1945. These political moments brought with them a sea change in the ways the federal government functioned.

One outcome of this transformation was the creation of the IBGE and other agencies charged with gathering and interpreting a raft of statistical data about Brazil. By 1946, it was possible to look at the generation of 1922 in ways that would have been impossible when its members were born. This statistical x-ray by Freitas supported the work of politicians, bureaucrats, educators, and nationalists, and it highlighted the importance of the educational reforms underway in Brazil. How could a growing, urbanizing, and industrializing country ever get ahead if it possessed one educated leader for every two hundred people? How could the country progress if half of this best-educated generation was "human cattle"? More important, how could this national problem be solved?

Freitas's "human cattle" category fit solidly within the discourse about race and degeneracy. The degeneracy he cited came from a lack of education. If these people had been educated, they would possess the virtues of hygiene and civic consciousness, they would know how to preserve the institution of the family, and they would be able workers. His vision echoed that of Monteiro Lobato, Roquette Pinto, Capanema, and the other leading intellectuals confronting questions of race and education. Freitas's unique—and consequential—contribution to this discourse was the ability to measure and quantify the degree of the problem faced by the perfectors of the race.

The work of Freitas at the IBGE combined ideology, method, and purpose. The ideology was a strain of nationalism that emerged in the first decades of the century. The intellectual leader of this nationalist movement, turn-of-the-century jurist Alberto Tôrres, expressed a desire for state-driven national integration and development. Tôrres's writings served as a rallying point for mid-century intellectuals who condemned the disregard for social policy and the uncritical Europhilia so widespread among Brazilian elites. Freitas's method consisted of employing statistical sciences to "know" the nation. His purpose was to find a way out of economic, social, and cultural backwardness that the combined degeneracy of the masses and the Europhilia of the elites had wrought. By the 1940s, after two decades of developing institutions aimed at "perfecting the race," educators and statisticians like Freitas were at ease discussing with clinical precision social problems at a national level. The new statistical lens permitted a new discourse on social change and a new level of focus for shaping national policy.

The Revolution of 1930 created the openings through which many of the policies analyzed in this study could be put into practice. Through the events following the installation of Getúlio Vargas, new transcripts of race, nationhood, and science (in its most general sense of producing knowledge) gained robust institutional expression. From here we will look at the vision and the methods of Freitas to see the bridge between nationalism, institution building, and the creation of an analytical apparatus. Freitas's studies offer a profile of public education throughout Brazil that helps bring perspective to the scope of education reform. Then, we take a look at the city of Rio de Janeiro with the help of the fruits of Freitas's apparatus, along with a reading of the work of others who employed Freitas's methods, most notably French urbanist Alfred Agache, who completed a survey of Rio de Janeiro in 1928, and sociologist L. A. Costa Pinto, who studied race in the city of Rio. The previous chapter showed how cultural and environmental definitions of racial degeneracy contributed to the drive for federal social policies after 1930. This chapter shows how that stake in social policy was analyzed and interpreted through statistics, and it borrows that interpretive model to build an understanding of the city where this history took place.

What roles did race play in the rise of a statistical worldview? First, it shaped the new nationalism, which confronted a perceived vacuum of social organization left by the abolition of slavery and provided the perception of social degeneracy that the nationalists reacted against. Second, within Freitas's project, the study of race through statistics emerged as an analytical endeavor in its own right. The 1940 and 1950 censuses devoted an almost unique degree of attention to race and racial difference in Brazil, providing much of the basis for mid-century studies of Brazilian race relations.[2] Finally, these statistical analyses show how racial difference shaped the city of Rio, and how Rio (especially because of its unique geography) shaped race relations.

Freitas was one of the master architects of the Vargas era, and the institutions and processes he created have left a lasting mark on Brazil. While education reformers in Rio de Janeiro had a national vision, they acted locally. By contrast, Freitas's analytical vantage point had such breadth that his analyses demonstrate the extent and depth of the sophisticated social policymaking put into effect during the Vargas era. Freitas's statistical analyses developed a sense of the social and racial dynamics of the city of Rio, shaped a profile of national education, and reflected the nationalist ideology that served almost as a moral compass for the political and intellectual mainstream.

THE REVOLUTION OF 1930

The Revolution of 1930 ushered in a new political era for Brazil by bringing together Getúlio Vargas and his alliance of regional political bosses, nationalist intellectuals, and the emerging industrial, professional, and managerial middle classes. This new political coalition replaced a forty-year-old decentralized political system that concentrated political power in the hands of regional oligarchies, most notably the powerful coffee barons of São Paulo. The Vargas era of 1930 to 1945 at first widened the space for political dialogue and policy experimentation, but a growing reliance by Vargas on the military and on authoritarian tactics gradually narrowed the space for dissent and innovation. Still, the Revolution of 1930 ignited expectations that a new regime would narrow the social gap and pave the road to a modern industrial and urban nation. The new regime also engaged in extensive institution building and adopted the new nationalism as its official ideology.

Tangible—if limited—innovations were made during this time, including the creation of a Ministry of Labor that administered an emerging system of labor relations, and the creation of a Ministry of Education and Public Health, which endeavored in earnest to expand public educational opportunities (although with more success in the cities than in the countryside). Both of these new ministries were part of a broader campaign to expand the role of government in preserving social welfare, as well as expand the terms of political, social, and cultural integration. Other areas of federal policy also reflected the drive to increase social inclusion. These included the extension of political autonomy to the government of the Federal District of Rio de Janeiro, the enfranchisement of women, the introduction of meritocratic government hiring practices, and the creation of limited social security benefits.

Although these innovations were part of a broader cycle of political change made possible by the Revolution of 1930, they alone offer an incomplete vision of the revolution and its aftermath. What *was* the Revolution of 1930? Was it actually a revolution? Did it mark the victory of the industrial bourgeoise over the coffee barons and other traditional elites? Did it usher in a revolution in government from the liberal and decentralized Republic to a nationalist, modernist, and centralizing regime? Did it usher in the industrialization of Brazil? The integration of the working class? Was this even something new? Although historians will always debate the significance of the Revolution of 1930, one outcome is clear: the political events that brought Vargas to power unleashed a revolution of expectations that touched both traditional and emerging elites, as well as radicals on both the Left and the Right, the emerging urban working and middle classes (and a small segment of the rural poor), nationalists, progressives, artists, and intellectuals. The expectations that these groups held for a "postrevolutionary" Brazil, whether met or frustrated, were symbolically borne by Vargas.

In assessing whether the Revolution of 1930 represented the triumph of new groups such as the industrial bourgeoise and the working class over the traditional planter oligarchy, historian Boris Fausto finds broad evidence for the political participation and reformist attitudes of the emerging groups. Yet he does not believe the industrial bourgeoise or the middle class displayed a clear opposition political program.[3] Instead, Fausto suggests that the clear existence of an emerging consciousness among these groups did not translate into political action toppling the prevailing order. The Revolution of 1930 was not a class conflict simply because social classes were involved.

Instead, Fausto suggests that 1930 marked a watershed in which both international and domestic political changes weakened the hegemonic potential of the planter oligarchy. This group could no longer monopolize power. Yet the revolution did not mean the defeat of the oligarchy nor the triumph of emerging sectors. Instead, Fausto proposes that a compromise state emerged from 1930. Without a clear social, political, or economic victor, the state was forced to mediate between competing groups and popular pressures. This was not a "social tie" but a delicate balancing act that took Brazil through decades of short-lived populist and authoritarian governments.[4] Although a long-term structural transition from an agrarian society to an industrial one was related to the Revolution of 1930, it did not cause the revolution nor did the revolution resolve it. Instead, it was a symptom of a widening sociopolitical gap.

Historian Edgar de Decca has challenged the concept of a "compromise state," arguing instead that by 1930 the São Paulo industrial and economic elite had already established a new model of state-society relations and a new political philosophy, both of which were gradually absorbed by the federal government after 1930.[5] Barbara Weinstein echoes this analysis in her examination of São Paulo industrialists' adaptation of the principles of scientific rationalism from a system of industrial management into a social philosophy that placed the state in the role of mediator between workers and industry and laid the foundations for a limited system of social welfare.[6] Certainly, this vision of the state as cultural mediator and social manager was echoed within the realm of public education. Although the principles of education reform were visible as early as the second decade of the twentieth century, only after 1930 did the political opportunity and institutional momentum make it possible for the most substantial of these reforms to take root at the federal level.

THE RISE OF THE STATISTICAL WORLDVIEW

Many of the political and social reforms after 1930 were inspired by the nationalism that had surged in preceding decades. While this nationalism was tangibly adopted by most leading politicians, administrators, intellectuals, and educators of the era, there was no clearer interlocutor of this ideology than Mario Augusto Teixeira de Freitas. His activism within the Vargas regime demonstrates the extent to which leading nationalists gained not only authority but also broad powers of authorship over the post-1930 federal government. For Freitas, this nationalism took on the power of morality. It called for the federal government to invest itself in two parallel projects: developing a system for understanding Brazil politically, socially, and economically, and using that knowledge to coordinate national energies and resolve national problems. Freitas assumed responsibility for the first project and aided those involved in the second.

Freitas coordinated statistics gathering and analysis for various ministries, from Education and Health to Agriculture, gradually consolidating them into a central organization, the IBGE. His creation of a statistical vision of Brazil was one of the most far-reaching institutional changes of the Vargas era. Indeed, almost all of the numbers through which it is possible to gauge the expansion of public education beginning in the 1930s were the fruit of Freitas's labors. Statistics as a way of knowing provided Freitas with the means to turn the nation's eye inward—elites had always looked toward Europe for guidance. Contemporaries believed that this eye would see Brazil for what it actually was, because statistical data could be rigorously technical and objective.

The census and other forms of statistical analysis could, for Freitas, define Brazil in a new, more accurate, and more honest manner. Statisticians working for the IBGE, the Ministry of Education, and other government agencies forged a technical and scientific vision of Brazil shaped by the questions that were of greatest concern to contemporary nationalists. The ability, for example, to compare Brazilian regions illustrated the great economic and demographic diversity of Brazil. Yet by facilitating a detailed regional comparison, these analyses made it possible to integrate these regions into both discourses and policies about Brazil as a single entity. Statisticians included race as a leading analytical category, along with detailed studies of immigration and birth rates in order to understand the rate at which Brazil was whitening through intermarriage with Europeans.[7] While statisticians held faith in the unimpeachable scientific rigor of their studies, the decisions they made about what and how to study were determined by the ways they wanted to imagine Brazil. In Brazil, as in the postcolonial Asian societies studied by Benedict Anderson, "the census tried carefully to count the objects of its feverish imagining."[8]

By 1946, when Freitas wrote the passage at the opening of this chapter, he could say things about Brazil that had not been said before, and he could do so with greater scientific precision and objective credibility than anyone else. By 1940, it was possible to compare educational, economic, and agricultural data across regions. A decade earlier, such a feat was unthinkable. But thanks to agreements between the Health and Education Statistics Service (SEES), the IBGE, and state and local governments, all manner of data became not only available but standardized and comparable. The numbers of schools, teachers, and students—as well as educational spending, patterns of attendance and attrition, participation by gender and race, and rates of literacy across Brazil—could and would be carefully scrutinized.

For Freitas, this social knowledge filled a conspicuous gap in the nation's self-understanding. Especially frustrated with the failure of public authorities to contend with the miserable realities of Brazil's interior, he wrote in the *Jornal do Comercio*, "the state of abandon of rural men surpasses the energies of this admirable race . . . afflicted by a dantesque array of physical miseries ranging from the most horrible and devastating diseases to the ramshackle homes, half-nakedness and malnutrition, that gives these millions—tens of millions—of unhappy Brazilians the most beast-like of lives."[9] Freitas's career and the institutions that he helped build were dedicated to drawing attention to the country's social conditions, not only by writing about them but by demonstrating them in the ostensibly apolitical and scientific language of statistics.

As Freitas saw it, he drew his authority from the strength of his numbers, giving the data a voice of its own. He often invoked technical authority for defining Brazil and its condition through statistics rhetorically, giving speeches with titles such as "What the Numbers Say about Primary Education in Brazil." He explained that "obeying the mandate that was conferred on me in the name of Alberto Tôrres, whose memory I revere as a disciple and as a Brazilian, I come with these words, to bring you a 'message' that the numbers from Brazilian statistics want to send to the nation."[10] For Freitas, the numbers spoke for themselves.

At the time of this 1936 address, Freitas was simultaneously head of the Education Statistics Service; the Ministry of Agriculture's Department of Information, Statistics, and Dissemination; the National Institute of Statistics, (precursor to the IBGE); the Brazilian Association of Educators (ABE); and a leader of the Society of Friends of Alberto Tôrres, a loose association of nationalist intellectuals. Freitas's direction of the principal statistics-gathering agencies and presidency of the ABE show his prominent role in developing the statistical grounding of national education and served as the basis for his role as the mediator between progressive educators and the increasingly authoritarian central government. His membership in the Society of Friends of Alberto Tôrres reveals the nationalist underpinnings of Freitas's agenda.

By declaring himself a disciple of Alberto Tôrres, Freitas aligned himself with a spirit of statist, developmentalist nationalism that had grown in Brazil in the first decades of the century. Tôrres had been a jurist who participated in the formation of the Republican regime, serving as minister of justice and justice of the Supreme Court. Toward the end of his life he became a bitter critic of the political order he helped establish, denouncing it as a "flowery game of theories set on a field of miserable realities."[11] Tôrres's writings were a bridge in the trajectory between the proclamation of the liberal Republic in 1889 and the nationalist Revolution of 1930. His criticism of the political generation with which he had come to power served as the rallying cry for the political groups that took the reigns with Getúlio Vargas. The nationalist language Tôrres coined became the lingua franca of politicians, ministers, and administrators in the years after 1930. In the words of one of the leading ideologues of the Vargas era, Alceu Amoroso Lima, "no Brazilian sociologist holds greater prestige today."[12]

In the eight years between Tôrres's retirement from the Supreme Court until his death in 1917, he built his critique of Brazil's political culture and published a series of articles in the *Jornal do Comercio* offering nationalist cures for the nation's ills. Several of these articles were reprinted in 1914 in separate volumes as *National Organization* and *The Brazilian National Problem*.[13] In these essays, Tôrres concluded that "we have a country which lacks economic organization and education, capital, credit, an organized work force, politics adapted to the means and ways of the population: in sum, ours is a disgoverned country." Although an abolitionist and antiracist, Tôrres was so disturbed by the corruption and disorganization of Republican Brazil that he reflected that "slavery was one of the few elements of organization that this country has ever possessed. . . . Socially and economically, slavery gave us all of the labor and all of the order that we possessed, and is the basis of all the resources that we still have."[14] Still, Tôrres was one of the earliest elite adherents to the environmentalist view, arguing that Brazil was a "museum of races" that disproved the theories of racial supremacy that Europeans used to justify their imperial claims.[15]

But Tôrres saved his harshest criticism for Brazil's elites, whom he considered alienated from their national reality: "[They live] in the big cities, dress in the clothes fashion brings them from Paris, receive current ideas from foreign papers, and transform their malaise into disbelief in the race and the fatherland, adopting as their creed the negative type of patriotism that consists of exaggerating our shortcomings, our vices, our corruption and our ignorance." For Tôrres, Brazil lacked elites that both knew the country and were capable of guiding it. In the end, Brazil was "a land still completely in need of being studied."[16]

Mario Augusto Teixeira de Freitas saw his mandate as fulfilling Tôrres's call to know the country and to educate it. As a member of the Society of Friends of Alberto Tôrres, created in 1932, Freitas joined with some of the other leading political and intellectual figures of the era to apply Tôrres's vision. The society's members included Oliveira Vianna; hygienists Belissário Penna and Saturnino de Brito; Roquette Pinto; Minister of Agriculture and eventual presidential candidate General Juárez Távora; and Plínio Salgado, leader of the fascist Integralist movement. The society, created to advance Tôrres's ideas and shape debate over the 1934 Constitution, was especially active in opposing immigration and promoting eugenics through health, hygiene, and education.[17] Alongside the society, many of the junior officers, or *tenentes*, who had been active in the nationalist dissident movements that culminated in the Revolution of 1930 were guided by Tôrres.[18]

The society, like Freitas, reflected the marriage between liberal progressive ideals and reactionary, even fascist, authoritarianism. Freitas himself believed in a strong central government role in shaping education—even calling for the army to take charge of rural education and establish "educational missions" in the interior—and he seemed at ease with the authoritarian drift of the Vargas regime. But he was also the individual principally responsible for keeping progressive educators involved with the regime and in drawing local educators to posts in the national ministry. He attracted Manoel Lourenço Filho, director of Rio's Institute of Education, to become the founding director of the National Institute for Pedagogical Studies (INEP). He also commissioned sociologist Fernando de Azevedo, who had been at odds with the Estado Novo, to write *Brazilian Culture*, the sweeping introduction to the 1940 census. He also labored, without success, to draw Anísio Teixeira to the MES shortly before Teixeira was purged as director of the Rio de Janeiro school system in 1935.

THE MINISTRY, AND THE REACH OF PUBLIC EDUCATION IN BRAZIL

The statistical programs of the Vargas era had their origins within the Ministry of Education and Public Health (MES) and the Ministry of Agriculture, which jointly hired Freitas to administer their statistics departments. Freitas's work with educational data reflects the intentionally limited role of the MES in a country in which education remained the constitutional responsibility of state and municipal governments. Despite the nationalistic and centralizing politics of the Vargas era, and especially of the Estado Novo, the MES never followed the lead of Latin America's next-largest countries, Mexico and Argentina, in establishing federal control over public education.[19] At most, the federal government established norms for states and municipalities to follow. But it attempted neither to directly administer the nation's schools nor to establish mechanisms to enforce its educational mandates, with the exception of the school inspection system imposed on the country's few, mostly private, secondary schools.

Beyond gathering data and supervising secondary education, the MES created an educational research agency (INEP) and "Brazilianized" the immigrant colony schools in the south of the country by banning the use of foreign languages and requiring teachers to present Brazilian birth certificates. The MES created the University of Brazil and managed the model high school Colégio Pedro II. It invented itself as the manager of the nation's artistic, cultural, and historic patrimony and absorbed the public health functions of the old National Department of Public Health.[20] The MES's role in elementary education was indirect (except in 1939 when it nationalized the colony schools), and primary education spending normally accounted for 0.5 percent of the MES's budget.[21]

On 3 November 1930, in his first address as provisional president of Brazil, Getúlio Vargas promised to immediately contend with the "moral and physical *saneamento*"[22] of the people by inaugurating a Ministry of Education and Public Health.[23] This new organization (which soon changed to the MES) was headed by Francisco Campos, a nationalist intellectual enamored of Mediterranean fascism, who as state secretary of justice and the interior for Minas Gerais had directed the state's public educational system and had recently reformed the state normal school. During his tenure at the MES from 1931 to 1932, Campos directed little attention to elementary education, focusing instead primarily on the development of legislation governing secondary and higher education.

Campos established Brazil's first modern university, the University of Brazil, in Rio de Janeiro, and issued a reform of secondary education that bears his name. The Campos reform emphasized the sciences over classical studies, instituted physical education, and gave the MES jurisdiction over the national secondary educational curriculum (previously, high schools were simply required to follow the curricula of the federal model high school, the Colégio Pedro II).[24] In addition, Campos created a network of school inspectors that accredited secondary schools to permit their graduates access to higher education. By focusing exclusively on secondary education (largely private and available almost exclusively to the higher social classes), and by reinforcing its links to higher education, Campos reinforced a class division that was already well defined: the poor were concentrated in public elementary schools, and while the wealthy might enroll their children in a public elementary school they would pass from there to the private secondary school system, which would prepare them for higher education.

While Francisco Campos organized the MES, the ministry's mission was defined by Gustavo Capanema, a Catholic nationalist also from Minas Gerais who served as minister from 1934 until the end of the Estado Novo in 1945. More in touch with the modernist artistic and cultural currents that swept Minas Gerais as in other parts of the southeast, Capanema developed the MES's presence in the artistic, cultural, and historical life of Brazil by hiring the poet Carlos Drummond de Andrade as his chief of staff and supporting the poet Mário de Andrade with several MES appointments. In 1937, he created the National Service for Historic and Artistic Patrimony (SPHAN), which appropriated historical spaces from Brazil's diverse regions and used them to celebrate a national history. Similarly, the MES subsidized and supported figures like Gilberto Freyre as cultural ambassadors, sponsored book publishing, hosted international congresses on education and culture, and assumed jurisdiction over several historical museums and historic sites.[25]

By 1945, the MES held a sweeping presence over Brazilian intellectual, cultural, educational, and medical life, possessing or interacting with subsidiary or local institutions throughout the country. In the area of public health, aside from a national network of leper colonies and tuberculosis sanatoriums, the MES administered the Oswaldo Cruz Foundation, which worked with health education and tropical diseases. The MES also administered a growing network of historical museums that glorified episodes in Brazil's colonial and imperial past. Attending to the teaching demands of the eugenically oriented physical education programs instituted across the country, the MES established a National School of Physical Education to train teachers. A National Vocational School was also established to meet the same need in vocational teaching. The MES also administered the Colégio Pedro II and several vocational schools, and it maintained both the University of Brazil and the National College of Philosophy.[26]

Although under Capanema's guidance the MES continued to have a limited influence over elementary education, the ministry was nonetheless active in reshaping Brazilian education. The Capanema reform of 1942 attached to the Campos law a national curriculum for vocational and commercial secondary education and in 1946 established national curricula for normal, agricultural, and elementary education. The MES also established the National Service for Industrial Training (SENAI) and the National Service for Commercial Training (SENAC), partnerships between businesses and the federal government that provided on-the-job industrial and commercial apprenticeships. Although these programs were created in 1942, their real impact would not come until the industrial surge of the 1950s and 1960s, when they would emerge as the primary means of industrial training in the country.[27]

In 1938 the Vargas government determined that the immigrant colonies concentrated in the south of Brazil did not assimilate and thus threatened the nation's integrity, especially as the mother countries of these colonies (most notably Germany) prepared for war. Thus in another major federal education initiative, the MES moved to "Brazilianize" these colonies' education by shutting down foreign language schools and replacing them with state-run public schools with Brazil-born teachers who lectured in Portuguese. Because the affected states lamented that they did not have the resources to replace the closed schools, the MES provided subsidies to make the change.[28] Similarly, in the 1940s the MES proposed a national elementary education endowment that the states and federal government would pay into. This endowment would primarily be directed toward funding state-run rural education and was intended to overcome the economic disparities between the impoverished northeast and south regions of the country. This idea died with the end of the Estado Novo.

Finally, the MES created the Health and Education Statistics Service (SEES) headed by Freitas, and the National Institute for Pedagogical Studies, headed by Manoel Lourenço Filho. Even if the MES were not regularly active in the nation's elementary education, by the late 1930s the SEES and INEP were able to monitor the work of Brazil's state and municipal school systems and the effects these programs had—or failed to have—on Brazil's population. These agencies tracked the considerable educational reformism underway across Brazil. Although this movement was most evident in the southeast (especially Rio de Janeiro and São Paulo), it also reached such northern and northeastern states as Amazonas, Paraiba, Sergipe, Pará, and Ceará.[29] The local educational reform movements that began in the 1920s expanded student enrollments, fortified teacher training and professionalized teaching, and drank from international currents of educational thought, giving special attention to ideas coming from the United States.

The zeal for public education netted impressive results according to a confidential internal report prepared by the Ministry of Education in 1941. Ministry of Education and IBGE statistics showed that by 1939 the number of active students per 1,000 Brazilians had climbed to 89, more than doubling the figure of 41 in 1920 and tripling that of 29 in 1907. Between 1932 and 1939 alone, 13,000 new schools were added to the 27,000 already in existence; the number of teachers climbed from 56,000 to 78,000; and the national student body expanded from 2 million to 2.5 million. Involved in elementary education were 90 percent of these students and 75 percent of the teachers. By 1940, the school system had become a major source of employment dominated by women, and although the public school by no means reached every family, it had irrevocably emerged as a principal point of contact between the public and the state.[30]

This change in the number of Brazilians involved in public education, both as teachers and as students, did not happen on its own. On a national scope, government resources were allocated to education, reflecting a country-wide pedagogical optimism that education would transform the country. Table 1 illustrates the increase in public spending on education as a portion of overall government expenditure between 1932 and 1941. The greatest change was in the area of municipal education (broadly meaning urban school systems).

Another major change in education between the wars affected the role of women in Brazilian society. By the beginning of the century, teaching had become a female-gendered profession. Although some men continued in administration, vocational education, and secondary schools, women dominated the ranks of elementary teaching and administration. As more women sought entrance to the liberal professions, demand for limited space in public normal schools spurred stiff competition that pushed nonwhite men and women who had once held many of these jobs to the side. In the first half of the century, public school systems concentrated on elementary education and on training the teachers to staff their schools. Thus they neglected general secondary education with the exception of the high schools linked to the teachers colleges. School systems offered a disproportionate educational opportunity to young women.[31]

But the benefits of the expanding educational systems did not only accrue to professional women and those few female students taking advantage of

Table 1. Education and Culture as a Percentage of Public Spending

	1932	1941
Federal	2.1	3.1
State	13.8	13.0
Municipal	9.3	11.9
Total	6.3	7.7

Source: "Custo do ensino público, primário geral, no decênio de 1932/1941," Freitas Collection, AN, AP 48, Box 55, Folder 116.

targeted secondary educational opportunities. By 1940, there were slightly more literate girls than boys in the five to fourteen age group, a tendency that strengthened by 1950. That beginning in the 1930s literacy rates were higher among girls is all the more striking because among adult women (age twenty and higher), literacy rates lagged 10 to 25 percent behind men. Women's gains in literacy were nationwide—measureable across all regions of the country, among the major racial categories, and among both urban and rural women.[32] Lower-class women, whose literacy rates and educational attainment lagged relative to men, formed the group to benefit the most from the expansion of education in Brazil, closing the historic gap in levels of education.

DECENTRALIZED EDUCATION

At a national level, the reach of public education expanded considerably, and all regions of the country benefited to an extent. Still, because public education remained in the unchallenged custody of state and municipal governments, education was characterized by considerable variation in investments and outcomes. Given the centralizing tendencies of the Vargas regime and the nationalism of the leading educators, as well as the gradual centralization of public health and hygiene programs, the decentralized nature of public education remains surprising. Political scientist Gilberto Hochman, in his innovative analysis of the centralization of public health, suggests that endemic and epidemic diseases themselves pushed health policy out of the decentralization established by the 1891 Constitution. As he argues, disease did not obey state borders or respect the decentralization of power, and epidemic diseases contributed mightily to the campaign for a greater federal role.[33] Thus by 1921 the

National Department of Public Health held almost exclusive jurisdiction for public health across Brazil.

Advocates of nationalized education could not fall back on contagion as an argument for centralization. Illiteracy was localized and spread by migration rather than by mosquitoes. Like disease, though, illiteracy and a lack of education affected some parts of the country, some social classes, and some racial groups more than others. Yet public education of the lower classes did not benefit the upper classes as directly as did public health, and it remained locally administered. However varied the motivations for expanding public education (motives that ranged from projecting a more civilized image of Brazil and the eugenic perfection of the race to the development of a skilled labor force or the mitigation of the extremes of poverty), between the wars Brazilians dedicated an extraordinary array of resources and energies into education. Hochman stresses that 1910 through 1920 was a unique time for the intensity of official concern for public health. The same holds true for education in the 1920s and 1930s.

Strikingly, this zeal for educational reform and expansion was not directed by a single national institution. Instead, the movement was sustained locally and was evident throughout Brazil. A national educational elite did emerge, was moved from state to state, and eventually gravitated to the MES, but this elite had its roots at the state and municipal level. Manoel Lourenço Filho is a good example. In 1922, at the age of twenty-five, he left his position as professor of psychology at the normal school in São Paulo to reform and direct the school system of the northeastern state of Ceará. He traveled from a state with one of the best organized and most innovative school systems in the country, and one where a majority of children attended school, to a state in which by 1935 fewer than a quarter of children attended school and per capita spending on education was among the lowest in the country.[34] In 1927 Lourenço Filho returned to São Paulo to resume his research on psychological testing, and in 1932 he was appointed director of the Institute of Education in Rio de Janeiro. In 1936, he was commissioned to establish and direct INEP, the research institute that initiated comparative analyses of education in Brazil across different regions.

Indeed, that comparison showed regional variation mattered more than any other factor in defining Brazilian education. These differences applied not only to enrollment patterns and rates of literacy but also to curricula, pedagogy, teacher training, and public investment. As Everardo Beckeuser, president of the National Commission on Primary Education (an advisory board to the MES), lamented, Brazilian children moving from one state to another encountered "immense if not insuperable difficulties. The subjects were ordered differently, making it hard to place students in the same grade. Teaching approaches differed. Books differed, and were generally narrow regional descriptions exalting the accomplishments of Brazilians born in that region."[35] Indeed, going to school in a different state, he added, was like going to school in another country.

But more important than the difference in curricula and educational techniques was the gap in public spending, school attendance, and educational attainment between the north and south of the country. In 1940, in the southern state of Paraná, literacy reached 45 percent, while in the Federal District it peaked at 77 percent. Meanwhile, typical of the north, literacy in Bahia was only 21 percent, and in Rio Grande do Norte it was only slightly higher at 27 percent.[36] The low literacy rate was symptomatic of the broader limitations to public education in the north and northeast of Brazil. By 1944, states in the south spent annually nearly Cr$23 (US$1.50) per inhabitant on education (above the national average of Cr$15). Meanwhile, states in the northeast spent on average under Cr$6. The two school systems that spent the most per capita on education were São Paulo, at Cr$33, and the Federal District, at Cr$67.[37]

Table 2 shows the link between the northeast's high rate of illiteracy and those states' low financial commitments to public education. In some states—Bahia, for example—school attendance rates did not even reach half the national average, which in turn was only one in every three students. Similarly, all of the states that in 1935 had attendance rates higher than 50 percent were concentrated in the south and southeast of Brazil. The disparity between the north and south in literacy and school attendance reveals another educational disparity: the difference between urban and rural education. The Federal District's school system stood out in the national context not only because of the zeal of its educators but also because it was a largely urban school system; and while it did reach rural enclaves in the capital area these were nonetheless proximate to the city. The MES's annual report on national education in 1939

Table 2. Percentage of Children Age 7–12 Attending School in 1935

State	Total Population	Population Age 7–12	Age 7–12 in School	Percentage of Children Age 7–12 in School
Distrito Federal	1,707,354	285,283	184,973	64.8
Santa Catarina	983,203	164,439	103,730	63.1
Rio G. do Sul	3,007,864	502,740	269,102	53.5
São Paulo	6,585,104	1,100,466	588,756	53.5
Amazonas	419,675	70,124	33,783	48.2
Mato Grosso	363,096	60,670	25,760	42.5
Espírito Santo	692,811	115,763	48,812	42.2
Paraná	1,011,865	169,073	68,877	40.7
Rio de Janeiro	1,982,098	331,191	127,222	38.4
Minas Gerais	7,349,408	1,228,020	402,200	32.8
Pará	1,505,580	251,569	71,526	28.4
Rio G. do Norte	756,000	126,321	34,350	27.2
Ceará	1,590,665	265,786	62,084	23.4
Sergipe	522,581	87,473	19,615	22.4
Pernambuco	2,894,865	483,706	106,724	22.1
Alagoas	1,157,385	193,389	40,372	20.9
Goiás	732,462	122,388	25,465	20.8
Territorio do Acre	110,279	18,581	3,654	19.7
Paraíba	1,352,748	226,032	44,415	19.7
Piauí	815,904	136,330	23,916	17.5
Bahia	4,055,338	677,610	101,583	15.0
Maranhão	1,140,685	190,598	26,675	14.0
Brazil Total	40,736,970	6,807,552	2,413,594	35.5

Sources: "População geral e em idade escolar, em 1935," Secção de Documentação e Intercâmbio, INEP, 1939, Gustavo Capanema Collection, CPDOC, 35.12.14g., INEP. "Ensino Primário Geral, Organização Escolar e Movimento nas Unidades Federativas em 1944," Freitas Collection, AN, AP 48, Box 19, Folder 36.

drew attention to the disparity between urban school systems like that of the Federal District and rural education. According to the report, the state capitals held only 14 percent of the population but had 37 percent of the teachers and 27 percent of the students. Students in the state capitals accounted for 37 percent of school children completing elementary studies and 63 percent of those beginning secondary education.[38]

The gap between education in the state capitals and in rural areas and secondary cities was even more dramatic. Although only a third of the population lived in urban and suburban areas, these areas held 70 percent of the teachers and 64 percent of the students. By 1946, the educational system reached 91 percent of the country's 2.5 million urban school-age children, but only 40 percent of the 7.5 million school children nationwide. One result of this disparity was the gap between urban and rural literacy: although 73 percent of the urban population was literate by 1950, the same percentage of the rural population was illiterate.[39] As Freitas explained, "putting aside the metropolitan centers and perhaps a few of the tributary centers along the coast, we can call Brazil a vast rural reserve," unserved by education.[40] Even by the end of the Second World War, to speak of public education in Brazil was to speak of urban education.

A report by Raimundo Pinheiro, a schools inspector for the northern state of Pará, captures some of the difficulties faced by the precarious rural school systems. One of the principal problems he cited was that trained teachers preferred the comfort of the city and would not accept posts in the countryside. Consequently, teachers were hired directly in communities and lacked the professional, intellectual, or physical means for the task. He asked, "What can be expected of an untrained, undernourished or sick teacher who finds herself forced to stop class just as soon as it has started, swooning with fever . . . ? And the children? Aside from [being] malnourished and sick they have to wander roads and trails for two to three hours to get to school!"[41]

Dismal as the situation in Pará sounds, it was one of the northern states with the highest rates of school attendance and a rate of educational spending nearly on par with the national average. Pinheiro's was one of the few voices calling for federal intervention in local education, arguing that the problems of rural schools outweighed the capacity of the states to solve them. Freitas was another such voice, calling for the federal army to establish rural "educational missions" in order to bring "knowledge of Brazil's social reality, revitalizing the administrative apparatus . . . and aiding the rural masses . . . integrating them into the greater national life, today almost totally restricted to our ill-formed cities."[42] Despite these isolated calls for federal action and the unsuccessful attempts to fix percentages of government spending to education, no plans to centralize rural or public education were realized.

Much as Brazil's public educational networks failed to reach the mostly poor rural population, school systems failed to reach the mostly poor non-white population. The states with the highest concentrations of people of African, indigenous, or mixed ancestry also had the lowest rates of educational spending. Bahia, a state in which less than a third of the population identified itself as white in the 1940 census, had a school system that reached fewer than one in every six children.[43] But even in those states where governments were more active in promoting public education, *preto* (black) and *pardo* (brown, or mixed) children lagged considerably behind white children in literacy rates, school attendance, and course completion.

Table 3 illustrates the striking gap in literacy rates along racial lines in 1940. The gap was greatest in the northeast, where in Rio Grande do Norte and Bahia whites were three times as likely as *pretos* to be literate. The gender division of literacy is no less poignant. A woman of color in Bahia stood just better than a 10 percent chance of being literate. By contrast, in the Federal District the more extensive educational system had reached a greater number of people of color, and over half were considered literate. Indeed, a *preto* man in the federal capital was more likely than a white man in Paraná or Bahia to be literate. Still, a *preto* woman in the capital was barely half as likely to be literate as her white counterpart. Here, as will be shown, the higher rate of illiteracy among *preto* women was potentially caused by the heavy migration of women of color from the interior of Rio de Janeiro and Minas Gerais to the Federal District.

Nationally, the tendency in these states is confirmed. In 1950, 53 percent of whites were literate, more than twice the rate of those who declared themselves nonwhite. Among nonwhites, the difference between *pretos* and *pardos* was not large: 24 percent and 27 percent respectively. The most literate group in the country were Brazilians of Asian descent and origin (well ahead of the other group averages at 78 percent).[44] Among Brazilians of African descent, between the wars there were no disproportionate gains in literacy made relative to whites as there were for women relative to men, although by 1940 among afrodescendants as with other groups girls outpaced boys in developing literacy.

What is most striking about afrodescendant literacy rates is that, with the exception of the Federal District, across Brazil their rates of literacy remained

Table 3. Percentage of Literate Population over Age 5 in 1940,
for Selected States

	White		Preto		Pardo		Total	
	M	F	M	F	M	F	M	F
Bahia	42	34	16	11	24	16	25	17
Federal District	86	81	59	44	76	64	81	73
Mato Grosso	54	46	29	16	—	—	46	42
Paraná	51	39	29	16	36	21	49	37
Rio Grande do Norte	48	39	13	12	22	21	28	27

Note: Mato Grosso data include age 6 and up; category *pardo* is folded into *preto*.
Source: "Alfabetização em relação à côr, nos estados," Gustavo Capanema Collection, CPDOC, 35.12.14g (569).

roughly half that of whites. Literacy rates varied considerably by region, and yet the relative social position of afrodescendants remained consistently subordinate to that of whites. As other scholars have shown, *pardos* did outpace *pretos* in literacy rates, but not significantly. Nor did *pardos* approximate whites or really comprise any sort of middle category. Still, the substantially higher literacy race for afrodescendants in the Federal District—a literacy rate well above the national average for all groups—raises questions about the nature of urban education in closing these gaps. More study is needed about the education of afrodescendants in other cities, especially São Paulo. As this study shows, the higher literacy rate in the Federal District is indicative of the nearly universal reach of the school system, although it does not reflect other barriers afrodescendants in the capital faced as they sought to advance their education.

EDUCATION IN RIO DE JANEIRO

Between the world wars, Brazil remained regionally divided and sustained a growing gulf between urban and rural worlds. Public education—decentralized and mostly urban—reflected and reinforced these divisions. As Brazil's southern cities, led by the Federal District and São Paulo, industrialized, the gaps widened between north and south and between rural and urban. Still, these regions remained linked by many factors common to all of Brazil.

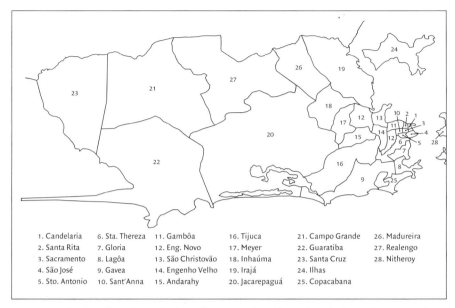

1. Candelaria	6. Sta. Thereza	11. Gambôa	16. Tijuca	21. Campo Grande	26. Madureira
2. Santa Rita	7. Gloria	12. Eng. Novo	17. Meyer	22. Guaratiba	27. Realengo
3. Sacramento	8. Lagôa	13. São Christovão	18. Inhaúma	23. Santa Cruz	28. Nitheroy
4. São José	9. Gavea	14. Engenho Velho	19. Irajá	24. Ilhas	
5. Sto. Antonio	10. Sant'Anna	15. Andarahy	20. Jacarepaguá	25. Copacabana	

MAP 1. Districts of Rio de Janeiro in 1928. Source: *Planta do Distrito Federal (Na Administração do Prefeito Antonio Prado Júnior, 1928)* (Rio de Janeiro: Diretoria Geral de Obras e Viação, 1928).

Between the wars, public education expanded considerably, drawing a growing share of resources and reaching a growing number of people. Within education, gender differences in literacy and educational attainment diminished while racial differences persisted. Illiteracy and low rates of school attendance continued across Brazil. Throughout the country, public education became a common part of life and a major part of the way in which the government and the public interacted. Although this education changed some aspects of Brazilian society, it did not change others.

The Federal District presented the best case for the accomplishments of public education in Brazil. The city of Rio de Janeiro school system attracted the principal reforms, had the highest rate of spending, the most extensive network of schools, the highest rates of enrollment and course completion, and the greatest national visibility in terms of leadership, research, and publications. Two-thirds of the city's children age seven to twelve attended school in 1935. Per capita spending on public education was more than double that of São Paulo and nearly four times the national average. By 1944 the city had 1,475 public and private schools, over 9,000 teachers, and nearly 250,000 elementary school students. Indeed, the city had more teachers than any entire state in the country except São Paulo, Minas Gerais, and Rio Grande do Sul.[45]

The Rio school system was as close as Brazil came to universal public education, a remarkable feat given the explosive growth of the city over the course of the century. Already the largest city in the country, Rio's population doubled from 1890 to 1920, making it the first city in Brazil with over 1,000,000 inhabitants. The population doubled again by 1950. In 1940, Rio had a larger population than the cities of Recife, Salvador, Belo Horizonte, Porto Alegre, Fortaleza, and Belém combined. Nearly half of the city's 1,157,873 inhabitants in 1920 were from somewhere else: 20 percent were foreign-born immigrants and 25 percent were born elsewhere in Brazil and migrated to Rio.[46] This growing population transformed Rio de Janeiro from a commercial port city that also served as the federal capital into one of the engines of social and economic change in Brazil.

Public education kept pace with these changes. As immigrants and migrants disconnected from the traditional networks of patron-client relations that had previously managed social relations, the school became a virtual patron by allocating social services, projecting criteria for citizenship, and integrating the growing population into the social fabric. As the city industrialized, public education provided vocational training. And, as women's roles changed, schools became a major source of employment, provided education that closed the literacy gap, and sought to anchor such traditional roles as motherhood. As both the city's school system and its nonwhite population grew, many afrodescendants gained access to public education for the first time. Still, the level of integration and mobility they enjoyed was less than that of whites.

Although Rio de Janeiro was different in some regards from the rest of the country—it was largely urban and under the nose of the federal government—it remained connected to national events. It was subject to many of the same currents, and its history is especially suggestive of the urban experience in Brazil as shaped by migration, expanding industrial and commercial opportunities, and persistent inequalities based on race and class. Moreover, public schools between the wars were primarily urban institutions, and the city of Rio's school system was the most extensive in the country. The Rio de Janeiro school system illustrates the reformist tendencies in education and the ways reforms contended with race, class, and gender. Rio's schools also provide a way to see how the educational system related to its city and responded to the particular circumstances created by rapid growth and industrialization.

This analysis is made possible by the same statistical eye that was applied to national education. Nationalist statisticians like Freitas were not satisfied with demographically charting the country. They were aware of the dynamics of change in Brazil and they developed detailed statistical analyses of the currents of internal migration, patterns of racial stratification, the changes in social roles of women, and the urbanizing industrialization of the south. Three studies in particular stand out for the analysis of a changing Rio de Janeiro: French urbanist Alfred Agache's 1928 urban reform survey; the 1940 census; and Brazilian sociologist L. A. Costa Pinto's 1953 study of race in Rio, which comprised part of the 1950 UNESCO study of Brazilian race relations. The 1928 Agache survey and the 1940 census did not primarily target racial difference, but the UNESCO study did. The study was comprised of research projects by a cohort of Brazilian, North American, and European scholars who sought to analyze and quantify claims that Brazil was a racial democracy. Interest in this project stemmed from the international reaction to the Holocaust, Brazilian efforts to project a positive national image, and the research concerns of Brazilian scholars of race relations such as anthropologist Arthur Ramos, one of the architects of the project.

These studies show the transformation of Rio de Janeiro from an administrative and commercial center to an industrial metropolis, and they frame the social setting of the nation's leading public school system. What these studies reveal is a city that burst out of its nineteenth-century shell and expanded to the north, west, and south. In the process, Rio became a segregated city. The wealthy moved to the "tourist map" portion of the city—the south end along the coast—settling affluent neighborhoods such as Copacabana and Ipanema. The city's poor and its recent migrants were concentrated in the industrial suburbs to the north and the west, principally along the rail lines. Patterns of race and class division were mirrored in the urban geography, blurred only by the favelas (shanty towns) that hugged hillsides across the city and by the almost invisible population employed in the service sector of the affluent addresses.

The shattering of Rio de Janeiro into a city of far-flung neighborhoods was an unanticipated consequence of the urban reforms led by Mayor Pereira Passos at the beginning of the century. Intended to give Rio a more European appearance by creating wide boulevards and lavish public buildings, the reform had a policy of eliminating visible poverty that began decades of slum clearance.[47] Moreover, although the reform updated the downtown, it deferred responsibility for extending utilities and public services to the urban poor by casting them out of the improved areas. The poor resettled in communities along the Central do Brasil and Leopoldina rail lines, which connected the port with the centers of production in the interior. Some of these new neighborhoods were in the expanding industrial areas to the north, while others settled in the semirural west end. In either case, the poor were cut adrift from the currents of urban reform and social policy.

Meanwhile, the wealthy left the city center for neighborhoods to the south, stretching from the presidential palace in Catete down the coast of the bay and along the ocean to Ipanema. By collecting and mapping the addresses, where available, of the politicians, administrators, educators, doctors and hygienists, feminists, and other prominent figures in this study (table 4), we see the self-segregation of the wealthy and powerful in a small section of the city (see map 2). Anísio Teixeira lived on Avenida Atlántica; Fernando de Azevedo lived in Botafogo; Afrânio Peixoto lived in Flamengo; Francisco Campos lived on Avenida Pasteur, between Botafogo and Urca; and General Goes Monteiro, army chief of staff during the Estado Novo, lived in Copacabana. None of these prominent figures lived in the suburbs and few lived in the city center. The turn-of-the-century neighborhoods of Tijuca and São Cristovão generally lost their appeal to the upper classes and to the emerging professional and bureaucratic elite. Only Manoel Lourenço Filho lived in one of these formerly fashionable neighborhoods, São Cristovão, presumably because of its proximity to the Institute of Education, which he directed. By and large, both the most progressive and the most reactionary political figures all identified with the modern neighborhoods of the Zona Sul.

Rio de Janeiro became two cities, both growing along their own social and

Table 4. Names and addresses of Vargas-Era Educational and Political Elites

Francisco Campos	Av. Pasteur, 184, Urca
A. Carneiro Leão	Prudente de Morais, 218, Ipanema
Milton da Silva Rogrigues (SGEC director, 1938)	Djalma Ulrich, 201, Copacabana
Manoel Lourenço Filho	R. Maracanã, 81, São Cristovão
Euzebio de Oliveira (ABE treasurer, 1935–36)	Cons. Lafayette, 53, Copacabana
Marieta Medeiros e Albuquerque (ABE V.P., 1935–36)	Joana Angelica, 116, Ipanema
Maria do Carmo Neves (ABE V.P., 1935–36)	Visconde de Pirajá, 239, Ipanema
Conceição de B. Barreto (ABE V.P., 1935–36)	Figueiredo de Magalhães, Copacabana
F. Venancio Filho	Toneleros, 195, Copacabana
Afrânio Peixoto	R. Paissandu, Flamengo
Alceu Amoroso Lima	D. Mariana, 149, Botafogo
Celso Kelly	Fonte de Saude, 128, J. Botanico
Jonathas Serrano	Pires de Almeida, 15, Larangeiras
Juarez Távora	Marques de Abrantes, Botafogo
General Góes Monteiro	Julio Castilhos, Copacabana
Ana Amelia C. de Mendonça, (LBPPF V.P.)	Marques de Abrantes, 189, Botafogo
Jeronyma Mesquita (LBPPF V.P.)	Senador Vergueiro, 238, Flamengo
Diva de Miranda Moura (LBPPF treas.)	Visonde de Pirajá, 238, Ipanema
Gerogina Barbosa Vianna (LBPPF sec.)	Sta. Clara, 38, Copacabana
Lina Hisch (LBPPF sec.)	Passeio, 70, Centro
Paulina Waisman (LBPPF sec.)	Catete 92, casa 9, Catete
Commandante Mário Gama e Silva (Escola Naval)	Vieira Souto, Ipanema

economic logic. The south end and the few well-to-do enclaves around the city center possessed the city's economic and political power and rewarded itself with the amenities of modern urban life. This is where the city's limited public school system of the first decades of the century was concentrated, along with utilities and sanitation services, public transportation, and other benefits of urban planning. In the north and west ends—together the suburbs—transportation, basic health and hygiene, and other public infrastructure and social services were precarious or altogether lacking.

In 1927, Mayor Antonio Prado Júnior commissioned a study of the city by French urbanist Alfred Agache to lay out a blueprint for a new reform of the city, parts of which would be undertaken during the Vargas years. But while Prado continued the tradition of relying on outside help, especially French, in imagining the city, and while the survey still gravitated toward the creation of

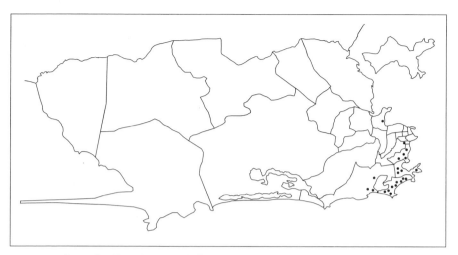

MAP 2. Places of residence in Zona Sul of Rio's educational and political elites.

monumental spaces, the similarities between the Pereira Passos and Agache plans ended there. Stating that "urbanism is a science," Agache grounded his plan in statistical analysis of the 1920 census and data gathered by his team of urban planners, mapping the city as an entity rather than an idea.

The Agache plan was a point of reference for future reforms of the city. Anísio Teixeira's education reform that began five years later relied on the demographic projections for population growth and distribution that Agache had assembled. The construction of new buildings for the Ministries of Education and Health, Labor, Finance, and War also followed the plan. The plan also inspired the major urban reform undertaken by the Estado Novo: the construction of President Vargas Avenue. The monumental avenue was two full city blocks wide and a mile long. In the process of paving those two blocks (and clearing another block on each side for redevelopment) Brazil's widest street gutted the heart of the Jewish and Arab neighborhoods and erased Praça Onze, home of the city's Carnival.[48]

As a showcase of the city's new official architecture, such as the art-deco Central do Brasil rail station and the Ministry of War, the avenue was a stage for the rituals of power. From the steps of the imposing Ministry of War building, Vargas watched military and youth parades and addressed the nation on the civic and nationalistic holidays that cluttered the calendar of the

Estado Novo. The avenue was the symbol of Vargas's power to erase the past and build the future. But more than a manifestation of the state's jurisdiction over modernization, the new avenue also linked the north and south ends of the city. The avenue cemented the recognition that the downtown had been transformed into a buffer between the two halves of the city, and it connected the expression of state power with the integration of hundreds of thousands of north end residents into the life of the city. Avenida Presidente Vargas reflected the imperative of connecting the sprawling suburbs with the formal city.

Although the Pereira Passos reform helped set the direction along which the city would grow, the growth itself was caused by industrial expansion, immigration, and internal migration. By 1920 Rio already lagged behind São Paulo, which concentrated a third of the nation's industrial production, but still Rio was responsible for almost a quarter of Brazil's industry. According to Agache, industrial production had tripled between 1907 and 1920. Although almost half of the city's factories produced textiles, others produced foodstuffs, pharmaceuticals, and consumer goods.[49] In 1920, 150,000 workers held industrial jobs, and nearly a third (40,000) of these industrial workers were women, predominantly employed in the production of textiles. In 1940 the total number of industrial workers remained unchanged, although a decline in the textile industry cut womens' industrial employment in half.

The 1940 census shows that another area of huge occupational growth between the wars was employment in the rapidly expanding government sector. Between 1920 and 1940 the number of people employed by either the federal or municipal government in Rio, excluding teachers, doubled from 50,000 to 94,000. The number of women employed by the government increased fivefold, reaching 14 percent of nonmilitary employees. Similarly, the combined number of public and private schoolteachers in the city climbed from 7,300 to 12,300, of which 70 percent were women. Still, the largest source of income for women in Rio remained domestic service, which employed 59,000 women in 1920 and 65,000 in 1940. Among men, the largest sources of employment outside industry were commerce and transportation services, together accounting for 162,000 jobs in 1940.[50]

As the physical dimensions of the city changed and its economic opportunities expanded, the immigrants and migrants that inundated Rio de Janeiro during the first half of the century divided themselves by race, class, and occupation. Despite its attraction to recent immigrants involved in commerce, the city center declined in population between 1920 and 1940. Immigrants were drawn to the city center by pre-established ethnic communities. Also, according to the 1920 census a full 20 percent of immigrants worked as merchants, and the center remained Rio's commercial hub. Agache noted that one of the center neighborhoods had remained demographically stable "by consequence of the Syrian colony (more than 20,000 in 1920) that lives above their own stores."[51] Middle Eastern immigrants were concentrated in a downtown commercial neighborhood along Rua da Alfândega, in an area they called the SAARA (a play on the word Sahara).[52]

Added to the city's 240,000 immigrants in 1920 were nearly 300,000 migrants from other parts of Brazil. By 1940, while the number of foreign-born inhabitants remained the same, the number of internal migrants in the city would soar to 673,000 (close to the size of the city's entire population at the beginning of the century).[53] These internal migrants were concentrated in the suburbs and in the favelas. Although the majority of immigrants were men and most were literate, most of the internal migrants were women and were illiterate, and many were of African descent. A contemporary journalist characterized the migrants as people pushed out of the economically pressed countryside, who "arrived in total financial ruin, with no preestablished employment possibilities, and without skills that would assure them immediate placement in industrial jobs."[54]

So many of the migrants arriving in Rio were women that by 1940 there were 4 percent more women than men in the city. Furthermore, such a large portion of the migrants were women of color that there were 10 percent more *preto* women than men in the city, a gender imbalance of 22,600 people. Costa Pinto explains that because afrodescendant women who migrated to Rio typically lived at the bottom of hierarchies of race, class, and gender in the countryside, they were more likely to seek the greater social and economic fluidity of the city. The large number of women migrants in Rio was part of a

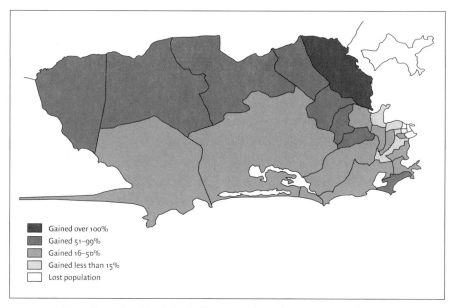

Gained over 100%
Gained 51–99%
Gained 16–50%
Gained less than 15%
Lost population

MAP 3. Rate of growth of the Federal District population between 1906 and 1920. (Note: to compensate for the changes in districting in the Federal District during this period, the district of Realengo is counted in Campo Grande. The districts of Anchieta, Pavuna, and Penha are included in Irajá. Piedade and Madureira are included in Inhaumá.) Source: Alfredo Agache, *Cidade do Rio de Janeiro: Extensão, remodelação e embellezameto* (Paris: Foyer Bresilien, 1930), 99.

broader national trend. Although the beginning of the 1950s saw a mostly male migratory current from the north of the country, from the 1920s to the 1940s a large regional migration took place. Women left the countryside for regional cities. In these two decades, over 600,000 women alone migrated from the states of Rio de Janeiro and Minas Gerais to the city of Rio de Janeiro and to São Paulo, accounting for 18 percent of the total migratory population in Brazil counted by the 1940 census.[55]

As these migrants settled, the suburbs grew exponentially in size. According to a census of buildings in the city, the suburban zone doubled in density of development between 1920 and 1930 alone.[56] Some suburban neighborhoods, such as Inhaumá, Irajá, and Madureira, increased fourfold in size between the 1906 and 1940 census surveys. Observers unanimously condemned living conditions in the vast suburbs. Agache noted that the suburbs had grown spontaneously, without any urban planning, and therefore their

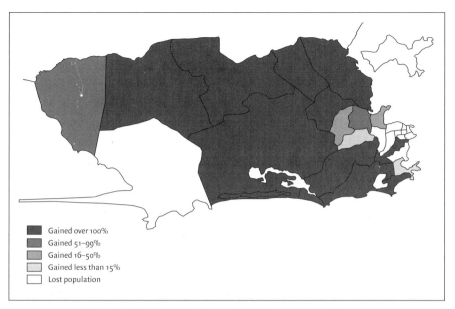

MAP 4. Rate of growth of the Federal District population between 1920 and 1940. Sources: IBGE, *Censo Demográfico—População e Habitação: Série Regional, parte XVI: Distrito Federal* (Rio de Janeiro: Serviço Gráfico do IBGE, 1940), 54; Alfredo Agache, *Cidade do Rio de Janeiro: Extensão, remodelação e embellezameto* (Paris: Foyer Bresilien, 1930), 99.

road systems did not connect neighborhoods easily to each other or to places of work, and the majority of the roads that did exist were unpaved, turning to mud in the rain. The neighborhoods lacked gardens or parks, the water supply was inadequate, and sewers were nonexistent.[57]

A city official responsible for mapping the creation of new schools in the early 1930s went further in his criticism, declaring that "the neighborhoods that are along the Leopoldina rail line present a miserable spectacle that is today an embarrassment to the Municipality's urban planning."[58] City planners began to realize that the Pereira Passos reform not only deferred the responsibility for bringing public services to the poor to a later generation, but also increased exponentially the eventual cost of doing so by scattering the poor over such a vast area. Another school system official condemned the "dispersion of the population into remote neighborhoods beyond the reach of the means of communication and the basic elements of hygiene . . . [thereby] rendering public services incalculably costly and complicated." He concluded:

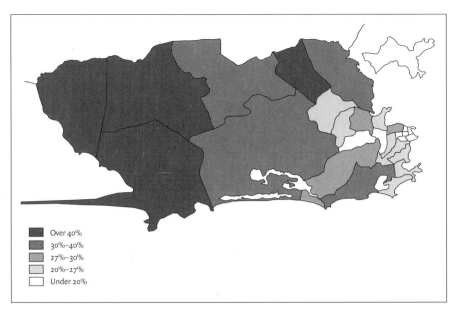

MAP 5. Percentage of nonwhite district populations in 1940 (Federal District average is 27 percent). Source: IBGE, *Estudos sôbre a composição da população do Brasil segundo a côr* (Rio de Janeiro: Serviço Gráfico do IBGE, 1950), 117.

"Such demographic dispersion of the population has brought nothing but onerous administrative responsibilities."[59]

These crowded neighborhoods, bereft of effective roads and sanitation and far from schools and workplaces, grew at such a rapid rate that by 1940 the suburbs, stretching twenty kilometers and an hour's train ride west of the city center, were home to the majority of Rio's residents. These neighborhoods were overwhelmingly poor and housed the bulk of the afrodescendant inhabitants of the city. In the 1940 census, while 27 percent of the city's inhabitants declared themselves nonwhite, 35 percent of the suburbanites declared themselves nonwhite. The nonwhite proportion of the population increased according to distance from the city center. The heaviest concentration was in the western regions of Santa Cruz, Realengo, Guaratiba, and Jacarepaguá—areas that had previously produced food for the urban market but were increasingly becoming residential.

Much of Rio's afrodescendant community lived in favelas, which were often located near the city center or south end, closer to sources of employment. According to Costa Pinto, 70 percent of the inhabitants of the favelas were people of color, and according to the 1950 census two-thirds of the favelas were populated by migrants.[60] The favela was identified with blackness and accumulated all of the attendant racial stereotypes. Journalist José Alípio Goulart defined the word favela as meaning "an area of social disintegration, maladjustment, and fragmentation." Agache called them "infected neighborhoods" that created serious obstacles to the social order and public safety, adding that "without precepts of hygiene, fresh water or sewers, sanitation, order . . . they create a permanent risk of epidemic infection and a fire hazard for all the neighborhoods they infiltrate. Their leprosy soils the surroundings of beaches and beautiful neighborhoods."[61]

Goulart and Agache echoed popular perceptions that the favelas were dens of disease and criminality, although Agache recognized that their greater proximity to places of employment and their fresher hillside airs made them desirable relative to the crowded suburbs. Despite the pejorative perceptions of the favelas, they housed much of the city's productive labor force, mostly in the areas of service, transportation, and commerce. Nonetheless, public officials tended to see the favelas as a menace and sought to eliminate them, sometimes tearing down the very hills they were settled on, as was done with the Morro de Castelo and the Morro Santo Antonio in the city center, settlements that an Estado Novo propaganda brochure declared "have caused much trouble for public administration and the justice system."[62]

Although the favelas and suburbs housed the overwhelming majority of Rio's afrodescendant population, there was also a large population of people of color that resided in the south end, who were employed in the service of the area's wealthy inhabitants. Most of these people of color were women working as domestic servants. In 1940, 86 percent of domestic servants were women, and three-fourths of them were of color. Indeed, one out of every three *preto* women in Rio over the age of twelve was a domestic servant.[63] The prevalence of women of color as domestic servants in the south end meant that in these neighborhoods 24 percent of the population was nonwhite. Yet across the south end, two-thirds of the people of color were women. In the trendiest neighborhood, Copacabana, three-quarters of the nonwhite population were women.[64]

Although living among the homes of the wealthiest cariocas, afrodescendants in the south end were in some ways more marginalized than their counterparts in the favelas and suburbs. Copacabana, whose mostly wealthy inhabitants typically sent their children to private school, had the smallest public elementary school capacity of any neighborhood in the city. In 1932, the Department of Education estimated that the school age population of the neighborhood was 8,500, but its two schools had capacity for only 640 students (which was increased to accommodate 850 students by running in triple sessions). To the director of school construction, Nereu de Sampaio, "this example shows the difficult situation of the First Educational District, located in one of the best neighborhoods of our city and where the poor population is hidden in collective dwellings at the center of city blocks, in old lots and other spaces rather than in shanties."[65]

Sociologist Costa Pinto was perhaps the first scholar to look specifically at the afrodescendant community of Rio de Janeiro. His The Black in Rio de Janeiro, published in 1953 as part of the UNESCO study on race in Brazil, is a landmark of statistical and demographic analysis. Costa Pinto depicted a city that was economically and geographically segregated by race. Residents of color were concentrated in the suburbs, the service quarters of the wealthy neighborhoods, and in the favelas, which Costa Pinto characterized as "segregated population centers for poor and colored people, concentrated precisely in the neighborhoods where whites constitute the greatest majority."[66]

The UNESCO project was proposed by anthropologist Arthur Ramos to study Brazil's perceived racial democracy as a counterexample of the racial intolerance unleashed by the holocaust. Research by Brazilian, European, and North American social scientists was supported by UNESCO and framed generations of scholarship on race relations. The researchers supported by UNESCO concluded that widespread inequalities based on race did exist, yet they reasoned that these inequalities were rooted in class difference. The main analytical vein to emerge from these studies, led by sociologist Florestan Fernandes and termed the "São Paulo School," argued that racial inequality would tend to disappear as afrodescendants gradually integrated into the labor market and became fuller participants within class society. Fernandes argued that contemporary inequality was rooted in the cultural, social, and economic disadvantages that accumulated on afrodescendants during slavery.

Although Costa Pinto also adhered to an economic analysis of class-based inequality, he did not blame perceived problems in afrodescendant cultural anomie as Fernandes did. Instead, he argued for redistribution of wealth, and he based his analysis on an extensive statistical survey of the patterns of racial inequality that transcended social class.

Costa Pinto's study noted that "in Rio, physical distance reflects social distance."[67] Between the south end and the suburbs, the distance could be measured in kilometers, while between the wealthy neighborhoods and the favelas "distance is measured vertically, from street level up the hillside, where the poorest population lives," thereby inverting the class pyramid. The distance could also be measured by the infant mortality rate: 123 per 1,000 among whites compared to 227 per 1,000 among nonwhites. Similarly, the distance was evident in employment patterns: afrodescendants were concentrated in the manual trades and service economy, and while 7 percent of whites were listed as employers in the 1940 census, only 1 percent of *pretos* and *pardos* were. For Costa Pinto, a wide physical, social, and economic gulf divided white from nonwhite in Rio.[68]

Educational attainment followed these patterns of inequality. As Costa Pinto explained, "education plays an important role in this process of differentiation, especially because it has traditionally been monopolized by whites in our society, as well as being . . . enormously significant in differentiating a *preto* from the mass of *pretos* and promoting him to a social position closer to whites." Costa Pinto suggested that evidence of the potential social mobility of afrodescendants through education could be measured in the indices of afrodescendant male literacy: the closer they were to the center of the city the more likely they were to be literate. He proposed that as some afrodescendants ascended socially, they "dispersed ecologically" by moving to more affluent neighborhoods, while the areas of greater afrodescendant density concentrated the less literate and more socioeconomically marginal members of the community. In the overwhelmingly nonwhite favelas, for example, 62 percent of the population was illiterate in 1940.[69]

Still, in the city of Rio, unlike the rest of Brazil, the majority of the afrodescendant population was literate by 1940. Given the large size of the city and its rapid rate of growth, the success of public officials in expanding public education between the world wars is remarkable. The growth of the school system outpaced the growth of the city, and it made Rio one of the first places in Brazil to break the "traditional white monopoly on education" described by Costa Pinto. The information about the growth of the suburbs, the surveys of the Agache urban reform plan, and the study that showcased the shortage of public schools for the service-sector families of Copacabana were all used by officials to plan the expansion of the school system into these communities. By the early 1930s, the school system even began opening schools in the favelas.

Metropolitan Rio de Janeiro in the 1920s and 1930s was socially and economically diverse and geographically complex, as urban planners well knew. It was also cosmopolitan and seductive. Half of its inhabitants came from somewhere else. Tens of thousands spoke foreign languages, while hundreds of thousands had come from other parts of Brazil, lured by the social, cultural, and economic fluidity of urban life. Still, the lines that divided the city were the same that divided the rest of Brazil. A small, geographically concentrated, predominantly white population monopolized power and access to social and urban resources. A much larger population, mostly nonwhite, lived in various kinds of fringes of this elite world. Either they lived in the suburbs, the favelas, or the service corridors.

Most of the afrodescendant inhabitants of the city were poor and most lived in insalubrious conditions, densely confined in neighborhoods that lacked the fundamentals of public sanitation and hygiene. Residents of the favelas were visible, so they were perceived as a social menace. Residents of the suburbs were invisible and their needs were ignored. Servants in the wealthy neighborhoods were even more invisible, except insofar as they were "necessary and useful to the wealthy population of the neighborhood."[70] Following the pattern set by the Pereira Passos reform, afrodescendants lived physically, socially, and economically at the margins of life in Rio de Janeiro. Whether in the suburbs or the favelas, the majority of the afrodescendant population lived in environments perceived by public officials as degenerate.

Yet Rio de Janeiro was also a place where the relationship between afrodescendants and public life changed. The city government broke the "monopoly" on education, and beginning in the 1920s it drew students of color into schools in such numbers that their rates of literacy climbed past the averages for many white Brazilian communities. This change raises questions. Why did the historic pattern of exclusion change? Did it mean full integration? What were the terms of inclusion? By creating Brazil's first universal public school system, Rio de Janeiro was the first to confront these questions and set lasting terms for the selective inclusion of afrodescendants into the nation's social, economic, and public life.

3

WHAT HAPPENED TO RIO'S TEACHERS OF COLOR?

Two photographs taken thirty-five years apart illustrate a dramatic change in the type of person who could become a teacher in Rio de Janeiro, as well as how that person became a teacher. Figure 1 shows a group of afrodescendant teachers among the staff of the Orsina da Fonseca vocational school. Figure 2 shows white teachers and their professors at the 1946 graduation ball of the former normal school, which in 1932 became the Institute of Education. These photographs, like scores of others contained in the Augusto Malta archive in Rio, in Institute of Education yearbooks, and in other sources point to a strong presence of afrodescendant teachers and administrators in Rio de Janeiro schools. More dramatically, these photographs show the gradual reduction in the number of afrodescendants until, by the late 1930s and 1940s, practically none were visible. This chapter explores the historical processes that led to the gradual whitening of the Rio de Janeiro teacher corps.

Although the photographs raise many questions, the focus here is on the dynamic of whitening, especially through the processes of the professionalization of teaching and teacher training. While education reformers saw professionalization as a meritocratic and technical process, it was an inherently political action that produced winners and losers. In the case of the professionalization of teaching, the politics involved combined values of race, class, and gender. The imagined teacher corps—indeed, the modern teacher corps that education reformers had created—was white, female, and middle class. Broader social changes contributed to the creation of this teacher corps, including a gradual decrease in the number of men seeking work as teachers, as well as the growing labor-market participation of middle-class white women. But these processes accompanied a deliberate project by reformers to forge an identity of the city's teachers. Their policies all but precluded men from gaining teacher training and created norms that made it increasingly difficult for poor or afrodescendant candidates to begin teacher training.

Combining the Malta archive photographs with an analysis of the professionalization of teaching underscores the complexity of writing about the pervasive role of race in shaping public policy. The policies that reformers put into practice were not specifically intended to bar any particular group from access to the teaching profession. The historical problem lies, instead, in what reformers imagined the modern professional teacher to be, and how they sought to achieve their goals. An analysis of teacher training reform—specifically of the teacher selection and training processes at the Rio de Janeiro Institute of Education—shows the implementation of practices that made it difficult for candidates who fell short of the vision of a modern teacher to gain access to the profession. The photographs, interviews, and other sources pointing to the experiences of individuals, and of afrodescendants in particular, are no substitute for a history of teachers of color in Brazil, but the sources offer a more concrete image of the broader historical process, as well as highlight the stakes involved in the politics of teacher training. The combination of this reading of iconographic sources and analysis of institutional processes highlights the tension between the ambiguity, elasticity, and ambivalence of race in Brazil on one hand, and the pervasiveness of race as a force shaping Brazilian public life on the other.

BACK WHEN THERE WERE TEACHERS OF COLOR

The Augusto Malta photo archive offers a glimpse into one of the most striking changes in the patterns of race and education in Brazil. At the turn of the century, the Rio de Janeiro school system had numerous teachers, administrators, and school directors of color. The story these images tell contrasts sharply with the collection's photographs from the 1930s, and with the photos of the teachers graduating from the Institute of Education in the 1930s and 1940s.

FIGURE 1. Teachers from the Escola Orsina da Fonseca, 1911. Augusto Malta Collection, MIS, Secretaria de Estado de Cultura e de Esporte do Rio de Janeiro, 127n/f009325.

FIGURE 2. Professors and graduates of the Institute of Education, 1946. Zilá Simas Enéas, *Era uma vez no Instituto de Educação* (Rio de Janeiro: Zilá Simas Enéas, 1998). Special thanks to Zilá Simas Enéas for permission to reproduce this photograph.

Malta was the city's photo chronicler, and his work spanned the Republic. Although his job was to record the pace of progress, his style was less that of a twentieth-century publicist than it was that of a nineteenth-century landscapist: he captured spaces. Because public schools were government projects, Malta photographed hundreds of buildings, classrooms, facilities, teachers, and students. He took most of the photos at the beginning of the century, although the collection reaches to 1935. Malta's more than four hundred photographs of schools and classrooms revealed a pattern: although many teachers during the first two decades of the century were visibly afrodescendant, this was no longer true by the 1930s. Roughly 15 percent of the teachers Malta captured before 1920 were of color, some of whom were quite dark, like the teacher shown in figure 3. By the 1930s, this number dropped to around 2 percent, and individuals in this group were mostly light-skinned mulattoes. Two other patterns are evident: first, the teachers of color early in the century tended to be younger, while the few present later tended to be older. Second, while most of the white teachers were women, a number of the teachers of color at the beginning of the century were men.

Men of color participated primarily in vocational instruction and in school administration. Malta reveals the city's vocational schools as a resource for poor and destitute boys, mostly of color, and often barefoot or in tattered shoes. One photograph (figure 4) depicts the inauguration of a type press at the Escola Profissional Souza Aguiar. Afrodescendant youths hold a lead engraving plate, and before them sits their afrodescendant instructor. The children are flanked by journalists of color attending the inauguration. Although poor, these boys had access to adult male role models in their teacher and the assembled journalists. The photograph also suggests linkages through education between a small professional middle class and large working class of color in Rio. Other photos show school directors of color, which includes the director of the city's normal school (later the Institute of Education) (figures 5–7).

By the twentieth century, most public school teachers were women. Researcher Dain Borges shows that in Bahia by the 1890s more than half of the schoolteachers were women, a number that would grow to 90 percent by 1924. Borges also suggests that "it may be that opportunities for women increased at the expense of opportunities for black and mulatto men. Through

FIGURE 3. Teacher of color at the Escola Pedro Varela, 1923. Augusto Malta Collection, MIS, Secretaria de Estado de Cultura e de Esporte do Rio de Janeiro, 127r/foo9529.

FIGURE 4. Inauguration of the type press at Escola Profissional Souza Aguiar, 1920. Augusto Malta Collection, MIS, Secretaria de Estado de Cultura e de Esporte do Rio de Janeiro, 127a/foo8680.

FIGURE 5. Directors of the Escola Visconde de Cayrú, 1908. Augusto Malta Collection, MIS, Secretaria de Estado de Cultura e de Esporte do Rio de Janeiro, 127a/foo8677.

FIGURE 6. Staff of the normal school in Rio de Janeiro, 1906. Augusto Malta Collection, MIS, Secretaria de Estado de Cultura e de Esporte do Rio de Janeiro, 127f/foo8970.

FIGURE 7. Teachers at the 2nd Mixed School, 1908. Augusto Malta Collection, MIS, Secretaria de Estado de Cultura e de Esporte do Rio de Janeiro, 127s/f009554.

the late 1870s in Salvador, and later in the interior of the state, educated black men constituted a notable part of the ranks of schoolmasters."[1] The same held true for Rio de Janeiro and seemingly for other parts of Brazil, where photographs, newspaper articles, and other anecdotal sources suggest that by the beginning of the century the number of men of color involved in public education dwindled, followed by a decrease in the number of women of color, until by the 1930s and 1940s the overwhelming majority of teachers were white women. By 1920 over 80 percent of (both public and private) schoolteachers in Rio were women.[2]

Schools photographed by Malta in the first decades of the century commonly included several teachers of color. While in most cases these teachers were a minority of the people in Malta's compositions, the extent of racial integration is nonetheless striking. In many photos, teachers of color posed standing together, which suggests that they—like the journalists of color at the Escola Souza Aguiar—may have shared a racial identity, if identity is defined as a performance of solidarity.[3] The elegance with which these teachers dressed suggest that they were individuals of social standing. They held authority over mostly white children and worked in a respected profession. Their presence as teachers, along with the afrodescendant men who appear as teachers, administrators, and journalists in other photos, suggests the existence of a professional and middle-class afrodescendant community in Rio de Janeiro.

Malta's photographs point to a set of historical problems. The existence or absence of different social groups within the teaching profession at the beginning of the century is difficult to corroborate. Census data, for example, offer little guidance. Although the 1920 census did not differentiate by race, the 1940 census combined the categories of public schoolteacher and government employee. By 1940, only 7 percent of Rio de Janeiro women working in the public sector identified themselves as "black" or "brown," although women of color constituted nearly a third of the female population of the city. In 1940, 11,747 women were listed as working in public school teaching and public service in Rio de Janeiro, but only 178 of these women identified themselves as being "black" and 697 as "brown."[4] Census data do not offer a sense of change over time, or even a number of active public schoolteachers. Although the census data are all the more complicated by the fact that individuals self-identified, it is nonetheless notable that so few women employed in teaching and public service identified themselves as being of color.[5]

The lack of systematization of educational institutions in Rio de Janeiro before the Fernando de Azevedo reform of 1927 resulted in a paucity of school-system documentation that might speak to the issue. There are some isolated complaints registered in Afro-Brazilian newspapers and by members of the Frente Negra Brasileira (Black Brazilian Front), a social and political organization based in São Paulo and present in some other Brazilian cities. There is also a quickly eroding oral memory. But perhaps the most extensive source on the subject is composed of the scores of photographs showing phenotypically diverse teachers in the first decades of the century. These teachers seemed proportionately divided between vocational schools, elementary schools, and the more prestigious normal school.

The Augusto Malta photographs are an incomplete lead. The images point to a palpable presence of teachers of color, reaching—depending on the type of definition used—up to 15 percent of the subjects Malta photographed. This number decreased over the course of the first three decades of the century, so that after 1930 it becomes as difficult to find teachers of color in Malta's photographs as it is to spot them in other sources, such as the Institute of Education yearbooks. But although the photographs signal the presence, and the near disappearance, of the teachers of color, they offer little additional information. They are mute on the key questions. Who were these teachers? Their names do not appear with the photographs. Did they come from middle-class families? How did they become teachers? What training did they have? How did they identify themselves socially, ethnically, and racially? Why did their numbers seem to decrease? Is there anything the photographer Malta neglected to reveal? For instance, did he have a preference for photographing one type of teacher over another? The photographs offer no answers for these questions, and the documentary evidence that touches on them is scant.

How did these teachers identify themselves? It is impossible to say that the teachers had a uniform sense of their color, race, or ethnicity. As state-employed professionals they may have assumed a whitened identity. Or they may have seen themselves as persons of color. The concern here is not to classify them but instead to analyze the patterns of the individuals present in the photographs, the trend of change over time, and the links that can be made between the photographs and other sources. The ways these teachers may have identified themselves notwithstanding, the photographs reveal a striking phenomenon: over time, a sizable number of teachers and administrators who bore tangible afrodescendant phenotypes decreased. Using consistent analytical criteria, a palpable change took place over the thirty-year period the photographs cover.

The photographs offer a clue to the sense of color and ethnicity held by at least some of the teachers. In several photographs, the individuals with darker phenotypes appear congregated together. Other types of sources also show that at least some teachers saw themselves as afrodescendants. One of the first issues of Getulino, a weekly newspaper from Campinas, São Paulo, which described itself as "an organ for the defense of men of color," printed a letter from a public schoolteacher who declared that "reading GETULINO, I understood what a newspaper that works for the emancipation of our color can accomplish."[6] Along the same lines, the memoirs of members of the Frente

Negra state that several of the organization's leaders in the 1930s were teachers.[7] Whether they embraced an afrodescendant identity, or considered themselves white because of their professional social status, the teachers unavoidably adopted some sort of racial identity.

A similarly limited set of sources speak to the social origins of these teachers, or to the path they took to their careers. Norma Fraga, a retired teacher of color who studied in the Rio public school system and at the Colégio Pedro II during the Estado Novo, suggests that these teachers of color came from mostly poor backgrounds and had been educated by religious charities. They used their basic education to teach "first letters" in the public schools.[8] Indeed, in the first half of the twentieth century fewer than half of practicing schoolteachers had earned a specialized teaching degree, which became a major source of criticism by education reformers. Although in the late nineteenth century state governments began to organize normal schools that provided teacher education, by 1950 only 60 percent of teachers held normal school degrees.[9]

Instead of receiving professional training, elementary schoolteachers commonly held a secondary degree, or at times less. Frequently, they also possessed a powerful patron who could intervene with the school system and help them gain their appointment. Maria Yedda Linhares, who studied in private schools in Rio in the 1930s and served as state secretary of education for Rio de Janeiro during the Leonel Brizola administration (1988–1992), recalled that school systems hired teachers who "had a pistolão, a protector."[10] Aristides Barbosa, who had been a member of the Frente Negra in São Paulo, recalled several colleagues who as teachers fit this profile: "Arnaldo Ovídio was an amateur professor, he didn't even have a [high school] degree. There was a shortage of teachers in São Paulo, and he applied." Another Frente Negra member was not so lucky: "Back then it was very common to complete high school and start teaching, and he wanted to find work. His aunt, who knew several politicians, . . . arranged to get letters for him to go I don't remember where, but the letters failed."[11]

The Malta collection photos and other evidence show that there was an afrodescendant teacher corps that in the early decades of the century taught in urban public schools. These teachers gained their employment through a combination of their comparatively high level of education (according to

IBGE statistics, in 1946 only 4 percent of twenty-four year olds in Brazil had completed secondary education), and the potential influence of a patron.[12] The photographs suggest the possibility that the teachers of color assumed an afrodescendant identity, and other sources show that some teachers assumed an Afro-Brazilian social and political consciousness. The photographs also show that the number of these teachers declined visibly over time: most appeared in photographs taken between 1900 and 1920, while very few were present in photographs taken after 1930.

The gradual dilution of teachers of color in Rio de Janeiro again is not the direct subject of much historical documentation. By far the most direct source was a speech given at the 1934 Afro-Brazilian Congress in Recife. The congress was organized by Gilberto Freyre in his home city directly after the publication and overwhelming public reception of *The Masters and the Slaves.* The meeting brought together an eclectic mix of anthropologists, eugenicists, and other social scientists, on one hand, and members of Afro-Brazilian religious and social organizations, on the other. The volume of published papers included a brief declaration made by a member of the Frente Negra from Pelotas, a city in the southern state of Rio Grande do Sul: "Many young Ethiopians who gain their diploma as teachers struggle to be able to teach and have to settle for giving private lessons, given the impossibility of working for the State. The majority just give up in the face of painful examples, and become seamstresses, which is the most that a women who possesses characteristics of African descent can hope for."[13]

In 1934, the Frente Negra spokesman saw a tendency against hiring teachers of color even though they had their teachers' diploma, and although he spoke of this problem from his experience in Pelotas he described it in general terms to a national audience. A decade earlier, the Afro-Brazilian newspaper *Getulino* ran a profile of Norberto de Souza Pinto, a schoolteacher in Campinas who also seemingly had his teachers' degree. The profile presented Souza as a young, virtuous, and applied gentleman. But "in another environment where modesty is not an obstacle to general learning, Professor Norberto de Souza Pinto, through his general training, would have reached a position of distinction in public school teaching, without those injustices that he has experienced."[14] While *Getulino* did not specify what these injustices were, the word its editors chose to describe them, *preterições*, refers to actions that are taken in disguise: while publicly affirming one thing the opposite action is taken, thus describing the form of discrimination in which the racial motives are denied behind an ostensible racial democracy.

These descriptions of the obstacles faced by teachers of color came from different parts of Brazil. Within the experience of the city of Rio de Janeiro, however, it is possible to witness the creation and the implementation of policies for selecting and training prospective teachers that created conditions hostile to afrodescendants and lower-class Brazilians seeking to become teachers. Beginning in the second decade of the twentieth century, the succession of reformers—Afrânio Peixoto, Antônio Carneiro Leão, Fernando de Azevedo, and Anísio Teixeira—expanded and reformed the city's teacher training programs, putting into practice values that defined teaching as a white, female, middle-class profession. While the Malta photographs leave many questions for which there are few answers in the documents, the reformers' transformation of the public school system into a rational and scientific network of institutions left a documentary trail that permits an analysis of the ways values of professionalization systematically marginalized teachers of color.

IMPORTING A VISION OF THE NEW TEACHER

The leading education reformers all saw the training of the teacher corps as the key to education reform. Each commonly expressed their disdain for the teachers previously hired by the city school system and those continuing to be hired in other parts of the country. These reformers felt that the teachers lacked professionalism, technical capacity, and moral force. They envisioned instead a teacher corps that was comprised of a properly selected and trained, exclusive and gifted professional elite. Fernando de Azevedo, secretary of education from 1926 to 1930, believed that the social order depended on a well-trained elite, because "without the creation of elites capable of guiding them, the education of the popular masses would result in a mass movement toward the worst demagoguery." Consequently, Azevedo lent his weight to a process of professionalization underway for a decade by building a lavish new normal school building, expanding the scope of teacher training, and "banishing political favoritism in hiring and promotion."[15]

In his preamble to the city decree that turned the normal school into the Institute of Education, Azevedo's successor Anísio Teixeira sounded an even more urgent note on the need for professional reform, because "the school must give our people their certificate of health, intelligence, and character, which is indispensable for modern life. Such a task . . . cannot be entrusted to anyone, much less a corps of men and women who are insufficiently prepared, who lack intellectual or social vision, and who could do no more than bastardize the educational process down to the demoralizing level of technical inefficiency and spiritual indigence that it finds itself in many cases." Writing five years after the Fernando de Azevedo reform, Teixeira expressed relief that the situation in Rio de Janeiro was better than in other parts of the country because "a certain degree of social selection has been carried out in the public teacher corps, which . . . has given us a teacher force with enviable moral qualities."[16]

Manoel Lourenço Filho directed the normal school in Rio from 1932, the time it became the Institute of Education, until 1938, when he left to organize and direct the federal National Institute for Pedagogical Studies (INEP). In his report on the transformation of the normal school into the Institute of Education, he decried "the shamelessness with which any person in Brazil assumes the title *professor* . . . [and the fact that] that popular sentiment does not differentiate between those who have or have not passed through a teacher training institute. Thus, anyone who knows or presumes to know how to read can call themselves a teacher, not only those *who know or should know how to teach*."[17]

These reformers struggled with what they perceived as the backwardness of Brazil, and because they sought to create a new society they modeled their vision increasingly on the United States. Education was their means of achieving this transformation, and the reform of teacher training and the professionalization of teaching were a microcosm of their ideas. As the preamble to the state law regulating normal schooling in Minas Gerais stressed, "[reform] can only be achieved . . . in the domain of normal schooling, which guides elementary education, that only by renovating and readjusting the former can the spirit of the latter be reformed."[18]

For reformers, the existing teachers symbolized this backwardness with their clientelism, lack of professional training or even general education, and the unmerited assuming of elite airs. These were the teachers who taught in schools that "still slept their colonial *siestas*," Azevedo reflected.[19] In the place of these backward teachers, reformers sought a modern corps that better fit their image of a modern elite as scientifically trained; highly educated; reflecting the most rigorous norms of health, temperament, and intelligence; and possessing a corporate sense of identity and social class that paralleled that of military officers. Mário de Brito, director of the Institute of Education secondary school (which was responsible for the screening and selection criteria for aspiring teachers), captured the spirit of the transformation when he declared, "for new methods, it is indispensable that we have new personnel."[20]

When these reformers set out to modernize Brazil by reinventing education, none of the ingredients of their formula could be found at home. As Brazilian elites had done for centuries, they went shopping in the international marketplace of ideas. Although Brazilians searching for the modern still turned to Europe, by the 1920s they increasingly looked to the United States as well. The United States was an inspiring economic, industrial (and increasingly, cultural) giant, yet like Brazil it remained dependent on European ideas. British and German genetic and eugenic theories, Italian criminological models, and French schemes for measuring intelligence were all consumed by an emerging class of scientists and social scientists concerned with establishing and managing a "natural" order to their society. Leading social scientists from the United States, such as educator John Dewey and psychologist Lewis Terman, synthesized theories and practices that Brazil's educational reformers devoured.[21]

During his tenure, Anísio Teixeira turned Rio's normal school into the Institute of Education, an institution modeled after the Columbia University Teachers College in New York, where he had just completed his master's degree. Teixeira's reorganization of the normal school brought together the Brazilian elite tradition of importing the ideas that shaped their institutions and the growing desire of elites and institutions in the United States to export their educational and social scientific thought. The Columbia University Teachers College was the primary destination in the United States for Brazilian educators. With the help of a $1 million grant from John D. Rockefeller, the Teachers College opened its International Institute in 1923 to recruit foreign educators for study in the United States.[22] The ambitions of this program were only one step removed from the imperialism of the beginning of the century. The International Institute's director, Paul Monroe, had assisted in the creation of the school system in the Philippines, while members of his staff had worked in the other recent U.S. acquisition, Puerto Rico, or in opening Christian schools in China. They projected training an international educational elite "destined to occupy strategic positions in their homelands."[23]

The International Institute facilitated the integration of foreigners into the programs of the Teachers College, while providing them with a panorama of education in the United States. Students took a Fundamental Course that included visits to public schools. Part of this program was a road trip to schools linked to the Teachers College in Baltimore, Washington, and the segregated South.[24] Between 1920 and 1959, eighty-six Brazilian educators studied at the Teachers College—more than from any other nation in Latin America. A dozen of these students were enrolled in the 1920s.[25] The vast majority of the students were single women, which reflects the degree to which teaching became a means for Brazilian women to assert their economic and professional independence.

The International Institute's endeavor to spread American educational methods and ideas overseas could not have been more effective than in its relationship with Anísio Teixeira. After Teixeira returned to Brazil and assumed the directorship of the Rio school system, he enacted a series of reforms modeled on his experiences at Columbia. Central to this program was the restructuring of the normal school as an Institute of Education modeled after the Teachers College. He developed an experimental elementary school at the institute like the Teachers College's Horace Mann School. In order to prepare candidates for the institute's Teachers College, Teixeira also organized a highly selective secondary school. Indeed, he was so shaped by his experience at Columbia that Lois Williams, an American he had recruited to direct physical education in Rio, told Teixeira, "you are, indeed, more American than I, and more up-to-the-minute?!" because of his enthusiasm for using the expression "swell."[26]

Teixeira completed the Institute of Education's makeover by luring educational psychologist Manoel Lourenço Filho to direct it. Lourenço Filho, Brazil's first educational psychologist, was a professor at the normal school in São Paulo, where he had just completed the creation of a test to determine the intellectual maturity of children entering school. This test allowed school officials to efficiently and scientifically place students within the educational hierarchy. Azevedo, Teixeira, and Lourenço Filho worked as a team, designing plans for their new school system and mounting national educational campaigns. They put up a broad political front that influenced the 1934 Constitution's articles on education, but also attracted a bitter reaction from the Catholic Church, which felt threatened by secular schools.

By 1932, the year Teixeira and Lourenço Filho's restructuring of the Institute of Education was completed, progressive educators had formed a loose association called the Pioneers of the New School and led a national progressive educational movement that reformed school systems across the country. They directed the largest and most influential school system in Brazil, and they had begun redesigning the practices and reach of the public school. The New School they created long outlasted their tenure in the Rio school system. Lourenço Filho's tests and measures were used at least until 1957. In 1958, Anísio Teixeira's reform of the Rio schools became the basis for national education legislation, the Law of Directives and Bases in Education (Lei de diretrizes e bases em educação). While this legislation was modified by the military regime to include more nationalistic and Catholic moral content, education remained largely unchanged. The 1958 law was restored by Brazilian legislature in 1996.

THE MARCH OF PROFESSIONALIZATION

When Azevedo, Teixeira, and Lourenço Filho brought definitive shape to the Institute of Education and to the patterns of teacher training in Brazil, they built on a rising tide of professionalization that had grown since the end of the nineteenth century, when most states established normal schools to train the teachers who staffed their nascent public schools. The initial importance to education of these normal schools was limited. They originally filled the vacuum created by the near absence of public secondary education left by the Empire (1822–1889), providing a classical secondary education supplemented by a few courses on pedagogy. At the beginning of the century, a high school degree was sufficient for teaching elementary school anywhere in Brazil.

As racial theorists shifted their analyses of the nature of race from biological to cultural foundations, teacher training gained greater urgency. Suddenly, degenerate Brazilians could be redeemed through health and education, or, as Teixeira expressed, "the school must give our people their certificate of health, intelligence, and character." Consequently, teachers became the potential saviors of the nation, leading Teixeira to add that "such a task . . . cannot be entrusted to anyone, much less a corps of men and women who are insufficiently prepared."[27] Because teachers would need to be capable of managing the redemption, they would need access to the most modern, technical, and professional resources. Beginning in the 1920s, new teachers would increasingly have the equivalent of a college degree earned through specialized study of social sciences like psychology and sociology, as well more explicitly eugenic fields of study such as hygiene and puericulture (the science of prenatal and postnatal care, based on the eugenic theory that special care during gestation can alleviate genetically accumulated deficiencies).

The first attempt to fortify teacher training was made in 1917 by one of the leading eugenicists, Afrânio Peixoto, when he directed the Rio de Janeiro Department of Public Instruction. Peixoto was one of the chief exponents of the field of legal medicine in Brazil, and he helped popularize the Italian criminological school of anthropology and the study of race. It is revealing that once racial degeneracy came to be seen as an acquired and remediable condition, a doctor and legal medicine pioneer would direct the nation's principal school system and a eugenicist would take the first significant steps toward the professionalization of teaching. Peixoto saw teaching, and therefore teacher training, as female responsibilities. Indeed, according to Peixoto, "having been a school system director, I never failed to disdain those rare men who matriculated in the normal schools. They are failures who have capitulated before life in a country in which masculine capacities are rewarded with masculine compensation. Women who aspire to become teachers, however, are the best of their gender."[28]

Peixoto's reform separated secondary education from pedagogical training in Rio's normal school and made pedagogy a postsecondary field of study. Antonio de Sampaio Dória, director of public education in São Paulo, applied this same reform to his state's normal schools in 1920. Dória also instituted the practice of student teaching and extended the pedagogical content of a normal education to three years. Over the ensuing decade, reformers in Rio,

São Paulo, Minas Gerais, Paraná, and Pernambuco delineated professional teacher training, which usually involved three years of study past the secondary level.[29]

The defining reform of normal schooling was carried out in Minas Gerais by the state's secretary of the interior, Francisco Campos, who soon gained national prominence as the chief ideologue of the Vargas government. Campos organized the Ministry of Education and Public Health in 1930, authored the corporatist Estado Novo Constitution in 1937, and implemented it as minister of justice until 1942. Shortly before being swept into national politics by the Revolution of 1930, Campos implemented a reform that elevated normal schooling to the equivalent of university study, modeled on the United States and Europe. He argued that normal schools should "destine themselves exclusively to the science and practice of pedagogical techniques."[30]

A curious aspect of Campos's reform is his heavy reliance on ideas from the United States, especially given his later flirtation with fascism. Throughout his preface to the reform, Campos relied on such untranslated English terminology as "training," "tests," and "syllabus," and he repeatedly cited U.S. journals. More surprising was his interest in John Dewey's progressive "New School" philosophy, given that a few years later Catholic nationalist allies of Campos would persecute and seek the imprisonment of adherents of Dewey by labeling them communists. Indeed, in the reform Campos referred to Dewey more than to any other educator.[31] Campos's reliance on U.S. pedagogical and social scientific thought illustrates the emerging intellectual and scientific dominance of the United States.

Campos imported Taylorist practices of observing and assessing teaching. He also instituted social scientific studies as the basis of teacher training, explaining that "normal schooling is not an intellectual exercise, a simple instrument of general education; it involves, above all else, the acquisition of techniques: psychological techniques, intellectual techniques, and moral techniques." This program included biology, broadly meaning puericulture and hygiene, the eugenic studies that were increasingly used to perfect the race. But the real bread and butter of the program was educational and child psychology. For Campos, to neglect psychology was akin to "not teaching future teachers the language through which they will understand their students."[32]

The Campos reform became the paradigm of teacher training that other projects in normal schooling in the Vargas years built on. Anísio Teixeira acknowledged Campos when he transformed the normal school of Rio de Janeiro into the Institute of Education. Campos's program definitively established teacher training as a form of higher education, grounded in the study of social science. The student teachers—mostly women—educated at the Minas normal school after 1930 were among the first Brazilians to receive formal training in psychology. What is more, they were perhaps the only people outside of the medical community who were trained to disseminate hygienic and puericultural education.

FROM THE NORMAL SCHOOL TO THE INSTITUTE OF EDUCATION

The normal school of Rio de Janeiro underwent reform between 1927 and 1934 at the hands of two of Brazil's leading educators, Fernando de Azevedo and Anísio Teixeira. The reform pushed professionalization beyond Campos's program in Minas Gerais, aiming not only to train teachers in the capital but also to serve as a model for the nation. The new institution was conceived as a filter between the public and educational policy: it restricted teacher training to an increasingly elite group of women and imbued them with the technical training and socialization needed to identify with social scientific paradigms rather than with the communities being educated. The new Institute of Education galvanized the obstacles faced by Brazilians of color in both education and employment.

When Fernando de Azevedo—a sociologist who was an early leader of the São Paulo Eugenics Society—began his reform of public education in the capital, one of his first initiatives was to move the normal school out of the city center to a sumptuous new building in the affluent district of Tijuca.[33] The building's location and its elaborate resemblance to a Jesuit college helped inaugurate a new image for the normal school as a facility most accessible to the elite (see figure 8). Simultaneously, Azevedo continued the institutionalization of pedagogical training as postsecondary study and initiated a curriculum in sociology influenced by John Dewey, Emil Durkheim, and Edouard Claparéde.

The most extensive transformation of the normal school occurred when Anísio Teixeira restructured it as the Institute of Education. He divided the

FIGURE 8. The neocolonial normal school building, completed in 1930. Augusto Malta Collection, MIS, Secretaria de Estado de Cultura e de Esporte do Rio de Janeiro, 127s/fo08971.

institute into an elementary school for student teaching, a university-level Escola de Professores (Teachers College), and a secondary school that prepared students for the Teacher's College. Teacher training included biology, pedagogy, sociology, and psychology, the latter instituted by Manoel Lourenço Filho. Teixeira justified: "It was not simply a question of elevating teacher training to the university level. . . . It was indispensable that over the scaffolding of general education be built the new professional and scientific culture of the teacher."[34]

The secondary and postsecondary curriculum included not only social scientific technicalization, but also reflected the new nationalism. Students studied crafts and nationalistic choral songs in order to gain a love for work and nation thought missing among elites: as Azevedo explained, "what matters above all is the cultivation of patriotic sentiments."[35] The concern for perfecting the race manifest itself in physical education, hygiene, and puericulture courses. Students learned eugenic norms so they could teach them: the courses would "imbue students with knowledge of supervising physical education within a plan based on continuous physical, mental, moral, and social betterment."[36] Azevedo, Teixeira, and Lourenço Filho shared the goal of creating a technical-professional class that could build a strong and racially sound nation.

Reformers imagined the new Institute of Education as a beacon of educational reform and research nationwide. Over the ensuing decade, the institute's program was adopted by the states of São Paulo, Pernambuco, Espírito Santo, Alagoas, Maranhão, Amazonas, Pará, Paraíba, and Sergipe. The institute attracted many of Brazil's leading educators to its faculty and funded sociological and psychological research, primarily with the aim of adapting foreign tests and procedures to domestic conditions. The institute also began publishing a journal, *Arquivos do Instituto de Educação*, and established a research library.

The journal and research library permit an intimate reading of the procedures at the institute, revealing four levels at which aspiring teachers of color might be marginalized. First, the three additional years of study placed the career out of the reach of poorer aspirants. Second, a battery of entrance exams based on rigid academic, physical, aesthetic, and psychological criteria established hostile standards for admission. Third, students at the institute were routinely evaluated by their classmates, placing members of a nonwhite minority at the subjective normalizing gaze of their white peers. Finally, less than half of the students graduating from the secondary school were admitted to the Escola de Professores, further narrowing the pipeline and reinforcing the professionalizing criteria for being hired as a city teacher.

There is no evidence that racial exclusion was deliberately intended by these policies. Nonetheless, Teixeira was clear about the agenda behind the series of hurdles presented by the institute: "The objective of preparing technical *elites* equivalent or superior to those of other countries . . . [has created the] need for a real talent search for privileged intellects." The institute's selection and promotion criteria continuously screened its students over the course of eight years. Students could only enter the Escola de Professores from the secondary school and could only gain admission to the secondary school in the first year. Transfers were not permitted. Teixeira sought to create a "fine flower" of educators, trained at the institute and specialized overseas, having come to believe from his years in New York that "the wealth of nations is now measured by their wealth of intelligence of their scientific and indus-trial *leaders*."[37] The very concept of elites he used to define his educational model was imported from the United States: in his text on the 1932 reform, Teixeira left "leaders" and "elites" untranslated from English and italicized.

The primary ritual of social engineering at the Institute of Education was the entrance exam. This was an immense public event in which commonly several thousand candidates presented themselves for admission to an enter-ing class of about two hundred. Although teaching had already largely be-come a female profession, the institute furthered the gender discipline by at first admitting no more than 10 percent of a class as male, and soon thereafter admitting only women. Anecdotal evidence suggests that the few males who gained admission had a hard time: according to one source, "we had one [boy in our class], but we teased him that he was a ballerina . . . he had to drop out because he was weak . . . he did not become a teacher."[38]

Admissions criteria narrowed the pool of candidates in other ways as well. Candidates had to be between twelve and sixteen years of age, placing admis-sion and a teaching career out of the reach of students who had interrupted their education to work or for other reasons. The academic portion of the exam was so rigorous that successful candidates often took a year-long, daily preparatory course at one of several private schools, again placing admission out of the range of the popular classes.[39] But high marks in the academic exams alone were not enough: these were applied to a formula along with the results of the Alfa Scale, a psychological exam developed in the United States to test army recruits for the First World War, and which for years served as "the prime source for studies of occupational, ethnic, racial, and geographic differences of ability in the United States."[40] Still, for Mário de Brito, who as director of the Institute of Education secondary school administered the ad-missions process, the intelligence tests would help select "only the most capable."[41]

Although the admissions process was composed of a barrage of academic and intelligence tests, the first stage of admissions was an eliminatory health exam. As Brito explained:

Since periodic health exams are not in the domain of common practice, even among the wealthy . . . we decided to initiate the selection process with a health exam that would therefore reach as many people as seek admission; the benefits of such an exam . . . will not therefore be restricted to the reduced number of students who pass the intelligence exams. The medical exams irradiate hygienic and sanitary education to thousands of individuals, since the exams have a propaganda value in passing these values to the families of the candidates.[42]

Brito's remark illustrates the extent to which eugenic concerns for public health and hygiene guided thinking about admission to the institute. It also reflects the assumption held by institute directors about the social class of candidates, noting that the exam and eugenic health norms applied even to the wealthy. Aside from defining the physical and health standards for future teachers, the exam was a public drama that projected the image of a medically meritocratic social hierarchy.

The medical exam was an elaborate ritual that celebrated eugenic norms of health. First, a *ficha*, or record, was created that included a photograph and thumbprint to confirm identity. The candidate's legal guardian presented a signed disclosure of the candidate's previous maladies and surgery. The exam began with a nurse's examination of the candidate's dressed appearance and the state of their skin. This was followed by the measurement of the candidate's height, weight, and chest capacity, which was conducted by not one but two nurses who verified and authenticated the judgment of the other "under the most rigorous personal responsibility." Following the measurements and examination of the candidate's appearance, one doctor examined the circulatory and respiratory system, while another evaluated sight and hearing, and a third checked the skeletal and nervous systems, as well as dental hygiene.[43] Figure 9 illustrates the execution of a similar set of biometric exams conducted at the women's vocational school, Rivadavia Corrêa.

Candidate weight and height norms were set at a narrow eugenic ideal. Some graduates from this period recall placing weights in their underwear or eating large quantities of butter as last-ditch efforts to meet the standards.[44] If Brazilians of color, or others, objected to the criteria used for admitting candidates to the institute, no record of their concerns remain. Still, members of the São Paulo Frente Negra did complain that height requirements comparable to those used at the institute were used by the Civil Guard, the city's police

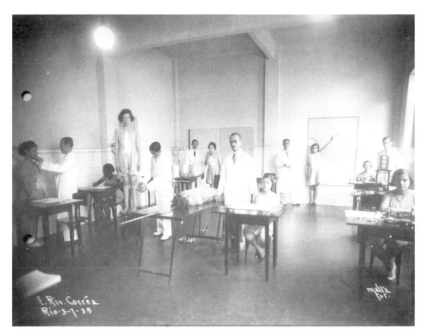

FIGURE 9. Biometric examination at the Escola Rivadavia Corrêa, 1935. Augusto Malta Collection, MIS, Secretaria de Estado de Cultura e de Esporte do Rio de Janeiro, 127j/f009154.

force, as an arbitrary obstacle used to keep candidates of color from joining the force. The Afro-Brazilian press in São Paulo decried the guard's unwillingness to admit candidates of color until the Frente Negra secured a promise from Getúlio Vargas himself to admit two hundred men of color into the force.[45] One Afro-Brazilian newspaper, *O Clarim d'Alvorada*, criticized the selection process for the guard by declaring that "the only conditions the government can demand for a man . . . to serve in the Civil Guard are: moral rectitude, physical robustness, and a regular education. Height is already a criteria worthy of criticism."[46] One Frente Negra militant recalled "they demanded a certain height, which we knew was just to keep us out."[47]

Altogether, each candidate was individually scrutinized by three nurses and three doctors, who recorded their observations on the admissions health exam form, which included the candidate's photograph and fingerprint, an echo of the criminological procedures that were increasingly being used by the authorities. Many of the judgments were aesthetic. The medical exam sought to screen out candidates who did not meet an ideal physiotype, and photographs of students from the 1930s and 1940s show a student body at the institute that was largely homogeneous in appearance (see figure 10). Whether candidates gained admission by meeting the rigid medical standards, or whether their consolation prize was to "irradiate medical and hygienic norms" in their community after a failed exam, their experience with the health exam reinforced eugenic norms.

But gaining admission to the secondary school alone did not guarantee entrance to the teaching profession. Of the two hundred students graduating from the secondary school each year, less than half would be admitted to the Teachers College. Those admitted did not just make the grade academically but were selected based on "consideration of their state of health, temperament, and intelligence." Health was measured by performance in physical education classes, where students underwent "periodic robustness examinations." Lourenço Filho explained that the ability to measure temperament and intelligence were the reason why secondary education had to be completed, from the outset, at the institute.[48]

Because the eugenic goals that these criteria satisfied generally equated whiteness with robustness, those few students of color who made it into the secondary school faced an additional obstacle to entrance to the Teacher's College. Photos of graduation balls during the 1930s and 1940s confirm this: graduates were, almost without exception, white and extravagantly dressed (see figure 2). The 1942 yearbook of the institute had photographs of 171 graduating teachers, of which only two were male. Only twelve of the graduating teachers (7 percent of the class) bore even slight afrodescendant phenotypic characteristics—that is, slightly darker skin or kinkier hair than their classmates. This percentage coincided with that of women who described themselves as *preto* or *pardo* public educators or public sector workers in the 1940 census for Rio de Janeiro.[49]

The selection process was so successful at defending the ideal qualities of the new teacher that Brito lamented that in 1934 the secondary school admitted fewer students than there were openings. Brito drew two conclusions from this situation. First, so many of the candidates were inadequate that the institute was forced to "resort to elimination on a grand scale," and that in future years conditions would be different as the "interested parties discover the futility of their efforts." Second, Brito thought that the school system

FIGURE 10. Students at the Institute of Education, 1943. *Revista de Educação Pública* 1, no. 2 (1943): 276.

needed to continue to promote the image of teaching as a career, "so that the institute attract only those candidates which meet the necessary conditions to have the desired success."[50] Indeed, the Department of Education and the institute went to great lengths to promote a professional, middle-class public identity for teachers.

TEACHERS AS A "DEFENSIVE CLASS"

In his annual report on the institute for 1933, Lourenço Filho described in glowing terms the participation of institute students in an array of civic and nationalist ceremonies. Physical education performances, for example, reflected "the overall discipline of the classes, and the positive attitude of the students."[51] Discipline, nationalism, and motivation were three of the bases of the new professionalism promoted by the institute, forming a crucial component to the acceptance of the educational reform by political elites. Consequently, a moment of impropriety during the end-of-the-year physical education demonstration was so scandalous that Brito offered his resignation over the incident, feeling that he had failed to sustain the public image of the institute.

According to Brito, the end-of-the-year ceremonies "revolved around physical education, not only to promote it, but also because it is the only way to make the project visible." The physical education performance showcased both discipline and the outcome of the eugenic movement to create a healthier "race." But on the day of the performance, everything went wrong. Because the performance was a public event, the school had requested the presence of the municipal guard for crowd control. But the contingent of guardsmen who arrived, two hours late, was described as "ridiculously small." The absence of police at the door resulted in an "invasion of the building by the popular classes." The institute was so overrun that "simple movement through the building was difficult."[52]

The lack of security and the lower-class crowds simply set the stage for controversy. The dance instructor, who Brito described to Teixeira as possessing a "slightly vulgar temperament, as you know directly," had the students perform a dance that was "judged inconvenient" by the official public at the event. In another performance directed by the same teacher, one of the Teachers College students (and a discipline monitor) improvised a scandalous routine. She performed an "agitated" dance judged all the more "inconvenient" by the fact that she was not wearing a brassiere.

There were two aspects of the dancers' behavior that generated scandal. The first was the image of inappropriately clad women dancing at the institute, which cultivated a stern image of propriety. The second was the "agitated" nature of the dancing, already seen as a concern with regard to the "somewhat vulgar" dance instructor. All this was set to the backdrop of inappropriate security and the "popular classes" mobbing the august institution. Brito's description is indirect and does not give a very precise account of the events that transpired, although from his letter of resignation it is safe to conclude that the perception of the event held by Brito and perhaps Teixeira was grave. On another level, Brito's meaning is abundantly clear: the description of sensual, agitated dancing by indecently dressed women to a backdrop of a mob of the popular classes seemed like Carnival. Regardless of the color of the people involved, the institute's image and therefore its mission were at risk of descending back into blackness.

The ensuing scandal created precisely the opposite effect of that desired of the performances. Institute officials wanted to showcase the harmony and discipline of the bodies of the students, molded by the ordered, hierarchical education they received in the halls of the Jesuit college-styled building. Instead, an overcrowded, rowdy mob watched a lewd show of ill-clad dancing girls. To make matters worse, this scandal unfolded barely two months after institute Director Lourenço Filho expelled an eighteen-year-old Teachers College student for distributing flyers from the Red Student Federation—"a renown communist organization."[53] Allegations that the women of the institute were communists or were being inspired toward communism strengthened the hand of Catholic nationalists who vehemently opposed the New School.

Performance of nationalistic choral music and disciplined physical education demonstrations fused New School progressivism with the broader nationalistic and disciplinary projects of the state. Such performances created the political space for other reforms. But year-end performances at the institute instead netted renewed accusations that the students of the institute were under the influence of communism. In a contentious national political environment amidst which the reformers were increasingly embattled with the Catholic Church, such incidents were ruinous. Catholic conservatives sought in the institute's practices evidence of subversive thought or behavior. The dance provided one such example, while the presence of leftist literature in the institute's library provided another.

Declaring that "one of the most impressive deficiencies of the institute is its library: almost all of its titles are works published before 1890," Anísio Teixeira embarked on an ambitious book-purchasing program. The new library acquisitions and their use reflected the changes in the institute's education project. Titles in psychology, sociology, and philosophy dominated acquisitions, while circulation of sociology titles leapt from 77 to 3,033 between 1932 and 1933. Many key texts were available either only in Spanish or in translations carried out by Lourenço Filho, Anísio Teixeira, and other Brazilian educators. Most of the books in Spanish were translations from English, which students found easier to read. Conspicuous among the patterns of library circulation was the decline of French influence. As Lourenço Filho explained, "the old French mold was definitively broken."[54]

But this extensive library acquisition program also meant that politically controversial books often surfaced as proof of the leftist subversion that Catholic conservatives charged the Pioneers of the New School with propagat-

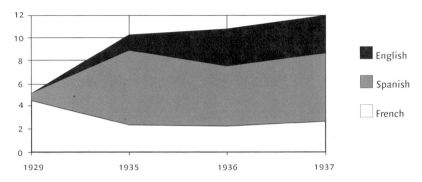

CHART I. Percentage of books in foreign languages circulated at the Institute of Education library for selected years between 1929 and 1937. Source: Diana Goncalves Vidal, "O exercicio disciplinado do olhar: Livros, leituras e practicas de formação docente no Instituto de Educação do Distrito Federal" (Ph.D. diss., FEUSP/Universidade de São Paulo. 1995), 158.

ing. In 1935, the institute received a set of books on the Soviet Union from the school system's central library. These included *The New Russia*, *Education in the Soviet Union*, and *Intellectual Culture in the USSR*. Careful to avoid controversy, Lourenço Filho personally asked the director of the central library to remove the books because "such works could not be part of the institute's library, and will not be catalogued." One of the institute's librarians, Margarida Castrioto, nonetheless used the brief presence of these books as proof of a conspiracy by communist professors at the institute to kill Vargas. In May 1936, she denounced to the Political Security Department (DESPS) what she believed to be communist meetings at a nearby cafe, which included Raja Gabaglia, director of the Colégio Pedro II; Afrânio Peixoto, director of the University of the Federal District; Delgado de Carvalho, sociology professor at the institute and the colégio; and Celso Kelly, director of the state of Rio school system.[55]

Despite the implausibility of these accusations, the DESPS began an investigation. Sensing the danger of these allegations, Lourenço Filho sought to preempt the DESPS by inviting the head of its bureau to install an office at the institute to investigate. Upon this invitation, investigators set up shop for a month in what became "an extension of the DESPS . . . [which included] the presence of Lourenço Filho, a stenographer, and two witnesses, members of the institute's staff were invited day after day to testify."[56] Lourenço Filho's strategy was to advertise as widely as possible that the institute, "under my tenure has been against communist ideas." In response to subsequent accusations of subversive activity, Lourenço Filho could assert that "the Chief of Political Security sent to the Institute an investigator of his choosing, who, for over a month, scrutinized everything. The same policeman conducted complete investigations of the lives of several professors, employees, and upon me."[57]

The only evidence of communist activity unearthed after a month of investigation was that the youth who operated the mimeograph machine once attended a meeting of the leftist National Liberation Alliance. There is no record of what action may have been taken against him, nor of the fate of the librarian who invented the host of accusations about many of the city's leading educators and her bosses at the institute.

Questions of nationalism and discipline cut both ways at the institute. On the one hand, they were tools wielded by opponents of the New School to question the loyalties of educators and sometimes of students. On the other hand, the institute's chief objective was the preparation of a professional teacher corps that would transcend politics, but that also would reflect a conservative set of class and social values. To this end, educators labored to create parallels between the work of teachers and of doctors, and to forge linkages between teachers and army officers. Both in and out of the institute, student teachers were prepared to assume the roles of defender of the race and defender of the social order. The relationship between teaching and medicine stressed the eugenic purposes of both disciplines: "Medicine and education are united by the same methods for addressing the same problems . . . all medicine and all education is being transformed into a hygiene of the body and spirit."[58]

Aside from bolstering the image of teaching through comparison with medicine, the social role and status of teachers was sustained by a pay scale matching that of junior officers and an array of activities designed to socialize teachers and officers. The Institute of Education and the national military academy, the Escola Militar, cohosted a number of civic and social events. Chief among these was a regular schedule of dances for the normal students and cadets. Indeed, through the 1970s, marriages between teachers and military officers were common. One of the few students of color to graduate from the institute in the 1940s, Umbelina de Mattos, was the daughter of one of the top-ranking army officers of the period, Baptista de Mattos. She recalled

FIGURE 11. Getúlio Vargas at the Institute of Education, 1943. *Revista de Educação Pública* 1, no. 3 (1943): 393.

opening seven schools in the Amazon while her husband, an army engineer also of color, worked on the Transamazon Highway project in the 1970s.[59]

Teachers were also targeted by magazines and journals promoting their status and refreshing their pedagogical techniques, and they were the intended audience of a daily regular radio program, the *Hour of the Teacher*, broadcast on the city's PRD-5 station. In all, considerable resources were invested in defining the role and identity of teachers. They were identified with medicine, one of the most prestigious male professions. They were taught to identify with the military and in their pay were given a social rank equivalent to junior officers, forging a "defensive class." Given the autonomy that teachers wielded in the classroom, and the importance read into education as the "means of public salvation," in the words of Getúlio Vargas, building a teacher corps that identified with official ideology and established values was elemental to nation building. Even Vargas himself would speak at the Institute of Education's graduation as well as make informal visits (figure 11).

During the Estado Novo, the linkages between the institute, teachers, and the military were strengthened by the appointment of military officers as directors of the institute. Students at the Institute of Education in the 1940s were often the children of officers, like Umbelina de Mattos. The arrival of military officers at the Department of Education and the Institute of Education shifted into military circles the patterns of patronage and promotion throughout the system. One normal school student recalled how the military patronage network worked to get her her choice of jobs. Beginning teachers had to teach for two years in the suburbs, but the normal school student declared, "I would have just died if I had to go to the rural areas." So her father, an officer, intervened, as she explains:

> Have you heard of Jonas Correia, professor at the Colégio Militar? He was secretary of education. Since the commander of the Colégio Militar was a friend of ours, he made the request, and I was placed immediately. . . .
>
> I was called to the department to talk with Jonas Correia and choose a school: "My commanding officer has recommended you. . . ." And I went to the school at Alto da Boa Vista in my father's car. Daddy had an official car. Such was the militarism. . . . And when the principal saw that car, with a soldier at the wheel, she came to the door. I was treated like you would not believe. I got along great with the principal.[60]

FINAL CONSIDERATIONS

What happened to the teachers of color? They lost ground to the rising tide of the social sciences, modernization, technicalization, and professionalization. Interestingly, the experience of teachers of color suggests that Brazilian social hierarchies became less flexible as public institutions became more rational and systematic. The public institutions and the social policies that were erected in the waves of nation building of the Republic and the Vargas years normalized social hierarchies. The creeping vine of technocratic policy fixed places and social roles along lines of race, class, and gender.

By writing social codes in technical and scientific language, educators and administrators avoided speaking of race. Their psychological, sociological, and medical language provided the crisp sounds of modernity and objectivity. The pernicious result of this uncritical faith in science and professionalism was the development of a school system that was increasingly exclusionary in its training and hiring practices and increasingly discriminatory in its handling of students. Noteworthy in these practices was the absence of explicitly racial language against which opposition could coalesce: the marginalization was cloaked under a veneer of professionalism and technicalization.

Were the Rio de Janeiro Department of Education and the Institute of Education racist institutions? The Brazilian definition of this term coincides with the U.S. concept of hate crime, implying that a deliberate and violent action of intolerance had taken place. Under this definition, the answer would be no. However, the actions of school system administrators were hostile to racial integration. Beginning in the 1920s, a color line descended over the school system that reflected more than the blindness of administrators to the effect of their policies.

Educators and administrators expressed uncritical confidence in the scientific and social scientific underpinnings of new policies. But these scientific truths were really just a new way of expressing old subjective judgments about race and class—judgments that were costly to the afrodescendant community: ostensibly technical and objective policies singled out Brazilians of color, resulting in a loss of professional opportunities for adults and in limited educational opportunities for children.

Reformers saw public education as the key to modernity, and they equated this modernity with whiteness. As Kim Butler explains: "The economic and political factors hampering Afro-Brazilians at abolition had social and cultural concomitants that proved equally disadvantageous. Stereotypes of African people and culture as 'savage' were antithetical to elite notions of progress and development based on European models."[61] Psychological testing of normal school candidates and schoolchildren provided empirical evidence supporting this belief. The more thoroughly reformers used new social scientific criteria to regiment the educational system, the more obstacles and subjective judgments stood in the way of Brazilians of color.

Within education, the equation of whiteness with modernity was simple: public schools would move Brazil ahead by helping children shed inherited habits that Fernandes called "anomie." Teachers of color, or of lower-class backgrounds, were perceived to be inappropriate mediators of this process. Because a growing pool of white and affluent women sought work as teachers from the 1920s onward, the school system simply had to meet the challenge of filtering socially undesirable candidates—the "common men and women" described by Teixeira. The elegantly dressed white women featured in photos of the Institute of Education graduation balls of the 1930s and 1940s embodied modernity triumphant. Meanwhile, students of color herded into classrooms for slow learners were scientific proof of the backwardness and degeneracy of afrodescendants.

The tools and techniques that made this division possible were borrowed from a racially segregated United States. Brazilian educators such as Isaias Alves were openly critical of the U.S. model of democracy, which he saw as promoting mediocrity. Others, like Anísio Teixeira, were uncritical of U.S. society or of democracy as interpreted by John Dewey, and they saw these systems as the model on which a modern Brazil must be built. But the United States they knew was far from democratic: while at Columbia, Teixeira and Alves toured segregated schools in the U.S. south, some of them developed under the direct auspices of the Teachers College.

Educators like Azevedo, Lourenço Filho, Alves, and Teixeira were—and through their work continue to be—widely respected intellectuals, especially for their range of vision. They were the educational leaders responsible for driving the organization and expansion of the public educational institutions of Brazil. But, as they interpreted U.S. society and sought to model their Brazilian institutions on North American counterparts, why did they fail to examine more explicitly the racial dynamics of the two societies? At least one South African student at Columbia did: he declared that the Teachers College's initiatives were "much too easily combined with the will to keep the Negro 'in his place.' "[62]

Although education reformers never specifically acknowledged the role of race in their policies, their policies nonetheless reflected prevailing racial values. The more systematic their schools and methods were, the tighter the web of modernist values became. Through the reformist vision, successful teacher selection and training meant the selection of white, middle-class women. Their training consisted of both an immersion in social scientific thought and their public socialization into a "defensive class." The extent to which whiteness came to be equated with the success of the Institute of Education in training teachers is further illustrated by an exchange that took place at the institute in 1995, when I was researching this material.

By 1995, the graffiti on the institute's walls, the broken 1930s-vintage furniture in the classrooms, and the black tarn that passed for a swimming pool belied the history of the institute as a home to generations of educators and social scientists who sought to transform and modernize Brazil. More than seventy years after the normal school was reorganized as the Institute of Education, Brazilian public education is firmly rooted in everything the reformers sought to erase. Teachers are poorly trained and underpaid. Middle-class and wealthy children as a rule attend private, often religious schools, and even parents living in favelas struggle to place their children in private schools. Educational resources are embezzled and misdirected to such an extent that, in some cases, drug gangs step in to pay for pedagogical materials. The public school system of Rio de Janeiro, like most others in Brazil, is a failure by any account. And although the Institute of Education still trains teachers, and its secondary school is still highly sought after as one of the only decent public secondary schools in the city, many of its students are of color, as are many of the city school system's teachers, who seldom earn more than $300 per month. Did the Institute of Education decline because of the entry of the poor and people of color? Or did the decline of the institute drive away its traditional cohort of wealthy, white students?

In 1995 I talked to a white teacher, who offered her answer as she stood by the photocopier near the courtyard of the institute. She pointed to a group of black girls playing in the schoolyard and said: "This institution really has fallen. It wasn't like this before. There are all kinds of people here who don't belong." For this teacher, whose identity was closely rooted in the Institute of Education—she taught there, she had studied there, and her mother had studied there before her—to blame lower-class afrodescendants for the institute's decline illustrates the extent to which her beliefs about race and class conflicted with her faith in merit and progress.

For the woman of color who operated the photocopier, the story was different: she recognized that the institute was a key to entering a professional world, and she saw the difficulties these students of color had to overcome in order to claim that opportunity. The photocopier attendant stood by in deferent silence, but when the teacher left she set the record straight: "That teacher doesn't know what she is talking about. Those girls have worked hard to be here. All of these students here have worked really hard for what they have." At least during this exchange, the values of merit and scientific objectivity remained at odds with the endeavor of racial integration in Brazil.

4

ELEMENTARY EDUCATION

Between 1931 and 1935, Anísio Teixeira carried out the most far-reaching education reform of the city of Rio's schools. Teixeira brought together the paradigms of eugenic nationalism, statistical analysis, professionalization, and scientific rationalism to create a formula for building and running a universal elementary education program in Rio de Janeiro. The racial, scientific, statistical, and professionalizing values discussed in this volume helped fuel the spirit of pedagogical optimism that gave rise to the reform. As the school system was expanded, these values helped make the new system work. The Teixeira reform rapidly expanded the number of schools, bringing health and education programs to the suburbs and striking at the perceived core of the nation's deficiencies—the state of degeneracy and of eugenic and moral unfitness that accumulated among the poor in the city's margins. Schools were more tightly tethered to an administrative "system," and the Department of Education was increasingly governed by the principles of scientific rationalism borrowed from industry. Following the new statistical outlook, the Department of Education began an expansion plan that brought a number of new schools to the rapidly growing suburbs. Hundreds of teachers newly trained by the Institute of Education in the most modern social scientific theories and practices were sent to these schools in order to meet the challenges of creating universal education.

While teacher training was heralded as the key to education reform, both the structure and operation of the system itself and, of course, the actual conduct of education and health programs were also transformed. The extent of Teixeira's reform, and his insistence in the laity of public education, attracted numerous critics. By 1935, Teixeira's opponents gained the political strength to purge him and many of his lieutenants from the school system. But even the succession of conservative clergy and military officers who came to direct the city school system in the ensuing decade continued to carry out Teixeira's blueprint of reforms, and they did so with surprisingly few alterations beyond the introduction of religious education. Although Teixeira began the reform it was concluded by his opponents, thereby reflecting a lasting consensus between conservatives and progressives over the technical and scientific paradigms that should govern education. Looking at the Teixeira reform means looking at mainstream twentieth-century Brazilian public education at the moment in which it was formed from the racial, nationalist, and scientific paradigms of the beginning of the century.

A SCHOOL AT A CROSSROADS

In 1933, the Department of Education opened a school on the fifth floor of a downtown Rio office building housing the newspaper A Noite. Escola Municipal Vicente Licínio was a short-lived, transitional institution. The creation of Escola Vicente Licínio marked the arrival of New School educational paradigms and the departure of the downtown residential population, which was being pushed into the northern and western suburbs. The practices reported to the Department of Education by the principal of Escola Vicente Licínio reflect the ways in which eugenic theories shaped public education. The experiences also illustrate the awkward intersection between policies reflecting norms of race, class, and gender, and the public toward which these policies were directed.[1]

As the city center's residential population was driven to the suburbs by urban reforms, the schools that served this population were shut down. The dwindling student body of three schools was consolidated into the A Noite building, and although the principal complained about the many inadequacies of the office space as a school, she also acknowledged that as the population it served diminished, this installation would go with it. Although the school represented a closing chapter in the history of the communities that lived in the city center of Rio, it was one of the first schools created under the New School guidelines introduced by Anísio Teixeira in the reform he commenced in 1931. In the report the principal illustrated the difficulties educators faced in the city's schools, as well as the paternalistic and eugenic tendencies that they wrote into school practice.

From the standpoint of staffing and material, Escola Vicente Licínio was a disaster. The school suffered from a shortage of teachers, and for the first two months of the school year (March and April), teachers were transferred in and out of the school as the Department of Education's teacher corps was allocated across the city. Consequently, the principal observed, "it was not rare for the school to be a simple depository of children."[2] Other difficulties included a shortage of desks—only 200 for the 557 students who were divided between the school's morning and afternoon sessions. Moreover, the desks were all the same small size, even though the students ranged in age from seven to fourteen. The principal also complained about the shortage of blackboards, stressing that some classrooms had less than one square meter of blackboard space.

When the school did function, it only taught students through the third grade. At best, the Escola Vicente Licínio's wards learned rudimentary literacy. Other than this limited pedagogical goal, the school focused on health and hygiene habits that were intended to make students eugenically fit. The principal explained that she sought donations from local businesses to buy toothbrushes, toothpaste, towels, soap, and combs for the children because it made little sense to teach these habits without the means to put them into practice. The Escola Vicente Licínio, like most others in the city, developed a "health brigade" of older students whose job was to monitor the state of hygiene of their schoolmates (see figure 12). These older students were also given responsibility for teaching the younger ones how to brush their teeth, clean their ears, and other personal hygiene tasks. Student responsibility for hygiene was typical of the New School approach to active learning. A student from each class was entrusted with recording the room's attendance on a chart in the hallway that read "attending school is a pleasure." The classroom that had the highest monthly attendance was awarded the school's Brazilian flag for the month.

Much of the principal's report dealt with parent-school relations. The prin-

FIGURE 12. Member of a school health brigade teaching students to wash their faces, 1931. Augusto Malta Collection, MIS, Secretaria de Estado de Cultura e de Esporte do Rio de Janeiro, 127m/f009282.

cipal saw a particular challenge in acclimating parents to the elevator of the fifth-floor school, describing the first days of the school year as swamped by anxious mothers who insisted on delivering their children to the classrooms in person. The principal reported that "I normalized the situation by explaining the principles behind elevators and giving practical demonstrations when necessary." The challenge of working with parents extended beyond the elevators. The principal reported deferring the creation of a parent-teacher association until she had created an appropriate culture about education through private meetings and through a weekly openhouse to "prepare them, educate them for a later parent-teacher organization." By the year's end, the principal declared, "Parents came to accept that the administration only wanted what was best for their children . . . the only problem I continued to have with parents came from the unalterably precarious economic situation of the family."[3]

The principal's report on Escola Vicente Licínio illustrates the convergence of three critical aspects of public education in Rio de Janeiro in the 1930s: the precarious nature of the expanding school system; the prominence of health and hygiene programs, which were an extension of racial and eugenic thought; and a relationship in which school officials treated parents as ignorant and unable to exercise basic decisions about their children's education without the school's tutelage. The principal justified this latter point about the unfitness of the parents by alluding to their poverty. As the school system expanded, the precariousness of public education diminished, giving way more fully to the racial and paternalistic tendencies that so dominated the report on Escola Vicente Licínio.

This chapter explores the relationships between race, scientific management, and paternalism in elementary education. Its analysis focuses on the Anísio Teixeira reform of 1931–1935, the educational project that most thoroughly defined public education and established lasting relationships between educational institutions, race, and paternalism. This analysis begins with a survey of the Teixeira reform and the circumstances it confronted. This reform can be divided into the three elements: expansion and systematic rationalization of the school system; implementation of psychological, eugenic, medical, and hygienic criteria for assessment; and the adoption of tracking criteria to move students through the expanding system.

PUBLIC EDUCATION IN THE 1920S

The school system whose directorship Anísio Teixeira assumed in 1931 was the largest in Brazil and had undergone a series of reforms at the hands of nationally renowned intellectuals, beginning with Afrânio Peixoto in 1917 and ending with Fernando de Azevedo in 1927. These reforms expanded the school system very little, and primarily addressed administrative reorganization and the professionalization of teaching. In 1931, the elementary school system had capacity for 85,000 students, with another 45,000 attending private schools. Public school capacity was actually slightly lower in 1931 than it

FIGURE 13. Inauguration of the Escola Municipal Uruguay, 1925. Augusto Malta Collection, MIS, Secretaria de Estado de Cultura e de Esporte do Rio de Janeiro, 127u/fo09741.

FIGURE 14. "A contingent of children from the Morro do Pinto who don't go to school? . . ." Augusto Malta's comment on his 1925 photo outside the inauguration of the Escola General Mitre. Augusto Malta Collection, MIS, Secretaria de Estado de Cultura e de Esporte do Rio de Janeiro, 127u/fo09742.

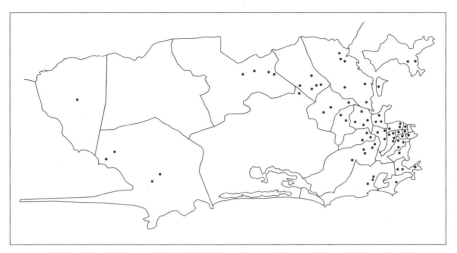

MAP 6. Location of city-owned school buildings in 1930. Source: Nereu de Sampaio, "Plano regulador das construcções escolares (Annexo ao relatório do Diretor Geral de Instrução Pública)," *Boletim de Educação Pública* 1, no. 1 (1932): 376.

had been in 1923.[4] Anísio Teixeira estimated the number of children aged six to twelve in the city at 196,000, meaning over 60,000 children (almost one-third) had no access whatsoever to public education, even with many schools running in morning, afternoon, and evening sessions.

Who was excluded? City photo chronicler Augusto Malta offered one perspective in an improvised criticism of the pattern of school expansion in the 1920s. In June 1925 Malta was sent to record the inauguration of the Escola General Mitre at the base of the Morro do Pinto favela near the city center. There he photographed an entirely white cadre of students, well dressed in starched white uniforms (see figure 13). Similarly, white and well-to-do teachers and school officials surrounded the students. But alongside that photo in the same folder in the Malta archive is an impromptu photo taken outside the Escola General Mitre after the inauguration. This photo shows poor afrodescendant children, many of them barefoot, standing outside the school and looking on with curiosity at the event. A note by Malta is written at the base of the photo: "A contingent of children from the [favela] Morro do Pinto who don't go to school? . . ."

The stark discrepancy between the color and class appearance of the students inside Escola General Mitre and those outside reflects the narrowness of educational opportunity up to the 1920s. Because the school was located near the city center, wealthy and poor and black and white were physically, though not socially, close to one another. Another way to look at the disparity in access is to see where city-owned school buildings were located. As map 6 shows, city schools were concentrated around the city center and in the wealthy districts due west and south of the downtown. In the sprawling suburbs where most of the city's inhabitants lived—those who were poor and often nonwhite—public schools were rare. They were nonexistent in the favelas until the 1930s. The school system also rented buildings to use as schools, although there is no record of how many or where they might have been located. Criticism of the rented buildings as mostly decaying *palacettes* (small mansions) rented by wealthy families to the city for usurious prices suggests anecdotally that these too were located in wealthier neighborhoods.

THE ANÍSIO TEIXEIRA REFORM

When Anísio Teixeira returned from his master's degree studies at the Columbia University Teachers College in 1931, Brazil's Republican political system had just been upset by Getúlio Vargas and the Liberal Alliance Party along with their nationalist supporters. A key player in the events leading to the Revolution of 1930 was the progressive doctor Pedro Ernesto Batista, who was rewarded with an appointment as interventor (federally appointed administrator) of Rio de Janeiro.[5] Pedro Ernesto, as he was known, inaugurated a reformist government that distinguished itself in the attempt to develop political autonomy for the city (which had been under the tutelage of the federal government); the development of a populist political base; and the extension of social services such as schools and community health clinics (see figure 15). Pedro Ernesto was the first mayor to attempt to integrate the impoverished suburbs and favelas into the fabric of social services and political organization. In 1931, on the recommendation of the nationalist author Monteiro Lobato (who had written the Jeca Tatú stories that helped popularize the environmental model of racial degeneracy), Pedro Ernesto hired Anísio Teixeira and gave him a broad mandate to reinvent the city school system.

A few months later, Teixeira introduced his plan for reforming the public school system of Rio de Janeiro. He consolidated past gains in the profession-

FIGURE 15.City Councilwoman Bertha Lutz and Mayor Pedro Ernesto inaugurating a school in the favela Morro de São Carlos, 1934. Augusto Malta Collection, MIS, Secretaria de Estado de Cultura e de Esporte do Rio de Janeiro, 127p/f009442.

alization of its teachers, embarked on an ambitious school construction program, and introduced a series of innovations drawn from his experience in the United States. The reform plan presented in early 1932 was based not only on John Dewey's progressive educational theories but also on Fordism and Taylorism as means to rationalize teaching and administration, as well as Lewis Terman's intelligence testing in order to arrange children in teaching groups.

Fordism is the term employed to describe activities and worker flows that followed the assembly-line system pioneered by Henry Ford. Taylorism is a philosophy of industrial production based on "scientific management" conceived in the United States by Frederick Winslow Taylor. Taylor's ideas were first published in 1911 under the title *The Principles of Scientific Management*, which, according to Peter Winn, by the First World War "had become standard practice in the modern industrial sector of the United States, adopted as a strategy for reducing labor costs and controlling the work force."[6] Under Teixeira's plan, the school system would reach all the capital's children by applying "systematic rationalization" to public education.[7] Teachers would be trained and supervised under scientific methods, and schools would be located according to studies in statistical demography. Students would be classified and grouped homogeneously according to their performance on intelligence and maturity exams.

Like Dewey's social philosophy, popularized in Brazil by Anísio Teixeira, Taylorism and Fordism became buzzwords of modernity. The emergence of scientific rationalism as a social philosophy championed by public institutions took place almost simultaneously in the Rio de Janeiro school system and among São Paulo business leaders. As Barbara Weinstein has discussed, the powerful Federation of Industries in the State of São Paulo (FIESP) embraced educational and social programs "aimed at rationalizing the industrial milieu both within and beyond the factory."[8] Psychologist Lourenço Filho, who directed the Institute of Education and established the maturity and intelligence tests used to track students in Rio schools, also participated in labor rationalization projects and was a member of the influential Institute for the Rational Organization of Work (IDORT) in São Paulo.

In addition to expanding the school system and rationalizing its administration, Teixeira sought to turn the school system into a beacon of progressivism and social scientific innovation for the rest of Brazil. He converted the normal school into an Institute of Education modeled on the Columbia Teachers College. In addition to his responsibilities as the reformist secretary of education, Teixeira taught sociology at the institute and promoted Dewey's works, which he also translated into Portuguese and published. Teixeira also instituted a scholarship program for teachers to study abroad as Dewey had recently done. A journal called *Boletim de Educação Pública* was created to broadcast the Rio reforms across the country.

One of the most far-reaching of these innovations was the creation of the Institute for Educational Research (IPE), with particular emphasis on its Orthophrenology and Mental Hygiene section, directed by anthropologist Arthur Ramos, and its Antropometry section, headed by Bastos D'Avila. Together the departments of the IPE employed many of the leading scholars on race and stood at the vanguard of racial studies, and the institute's activism helped keep anthropological, medical, and psychological theories and practices—the backbone of eugenics—thoroughly interwoven with the Department of Education's programs. Throughout the Teixeira reform, the nationalist eugenic concept of health was firmly wedded to the public school: "The school must give our people their certificate of health, intelligence, and character, which is indispensable for modern life," Teixeira declared.[9]

Anísio Teixeira's 1932 reform followed the brand of Brazilian nationalism espoused by Alberto Tôrres. Teixeira's language echoed Tôrres's criticisms of Brazilian society: the existing school system served only to weed out a few students for inclusion in a parasitic semielite that was ruining the country. The academic preparation students received in school either drove them out or prepared them to become sterile bureaucrats. Teixeira rejected the aspirations of social mobility that brought people into the schools, arguing that they should make do with the class they were born into rather than be "attracted to bourgeois appearances—to the ornaments of a lettered life."[10]

So what did Teixeira believe the schools should teach? They should teach children to "live better." This meant, first, learning about health and hygiene (after all, there was nothing more important than perfecting the race); becoming a motivated and efficient worker; and developing self-improvement habits such as reading and critical skills. The obstacles to this program included not only the existing curriculum but also parents, who dreamed that their children might one day become doctors. "Parents live rudely . . . their jobs, domestic culture, society, their very worldview prevents them from considering the options for personal improvement *within* their class," Teixeira declared.[11]

For Teixeira, as for the principal of Escola Vicente Licínio, parents were an obstacle to their children's education. Consequently, he envisioned a school system that resisted popular pressures and administered public education through the scientific and technical principles he brought with him from the United States. Decisions would be made by statistical analysis of intelligence tests, medical exams, and demographic surveys. The new school system was divided into four departments: Curriculum; Enrollment and Attendance; Tracking and Advancement; and Buildings and Material. These departments answered to Teixeira, who defined for himself the role of "organizer, conductor, and rationalizer" of the administration, setting its political orientation, and guiding and correcting the administration of schools and the tracking of children.

In Teixeira's new system, statistical knowledge would increase administrative control over schools because, with city-wide information processed at a central office, city-wide policies could be applied in a "school *system* and not an agglomeration of schools that function independently." But building a statistical profile of the city's educational system and its students took time. In his 1932 report, Teixeira lamented that the Matriculation and Attendance Service (or SMF) experienced trouble building its statistical map because "data before 1932 were incomplete and fell short of letting us reach the inductive conclusions that should constitute our principal guiding force." Teixeira also alluded to resistance to the centralization of administration based on statistical induction. He reported that the SMF's project "would show even greater results once we have completely vanquished the obstacles to the need for centralized direction still attached to the old order."[12]

BUILDING MORE SCHOOLS: THE BUILDINGS AND MATERIAL SERVICE

When Teixeira took office, nearly a third of the city's children age six to twelve were not attending school. This was not a personal choice: the public and private school systems were saturated. As Teixeira observed, many of the existing schools were a worse venture than not having a school at all. Few of the seventy-nine city-owned buildings had been designed as schools. Almost one hundred other schools operated in rented buildings. Rented or owned, most of these buildings were former residences. The city assumed them as a political favor or because of the need for a school in a specific area rather than because of their adaptability as schools. As Teixeira indicated, the decision to acquire these homes was made based on "individual requests, accepted with no other motive than the warmth and persuasive insistence of the solicitors."[13] Classes were held in cramped spaces that had once been bedrooms. Many lacked adequate illumination or ventilation (characteristics that were deemed essential to the hygienic environment that schools were intended to provide).[14]

Teixeira charged Nereu de Sampaio, director of the Buildings and Materials Service (SPAE) to develop a plan for rebuilding and expanding the school system's physical base. True to the technocratic orientation of the new administration, Sampaio introduced his plan by demonstrating that it was statistically grounded. Indeed, the plan's text began with the neatly boxed section header "statistics," and was introduced with the remark: "The development of a regulatory plan for the construction of schools can only be based on statistics."[15] The report went on to "technically" evaluate different sets of demographic data to determine the need for schools in the city's districts and estimate the rate of growth in the school-aged population.

Sampaio outlined a plan for condemning almost half of the seventy-nine city-owned schools, and for building seventy-four new schools over the course of a decade. The plan recognized the high cost of building all the schools at once, and was presented as a blueprint for succeeding administrations to use to continue to expand the school system as resources permitted. Echoing Teixeira's concern that the program be shielded from public pressure, the technocrat Sampaio stressed that "for this formula to work it is essential that the plan carry the force of law and be protected by . . . a commission for the defense of the plan."[16]

Sampaio confidently declared that, "with the defense of this plan, all of the technical problems will be solved, such as distribution of students, management of attendance . . . and efficient organization of physical education and health programs."[17] During the Teixeira administration twenty-nine new schools were built, and these schools transformed the face of education in Rio. Most of the schools were constructed in the poorer neighborhoods of the northern and suburban zones, and the schools that were built in wealthy neighborhoods such as Copacabana were also intended to serve the poorer residents. In Copacabana, the thousands of children of housekeepers and others employed in the service sector were served by two schools in small rented spaces, which reached a combined enrollment of 850 students only by teaching in three shifts. As Sampaio noted, the shortage of schools for these children was even greater than it was in the suburbs.[18]

As map 6 shows, prior to 1930 the majority of schools were concentrated in the city's central area.[19] By contrast, map 7 shows the way Teixeira spread schools into the poorer and more proportionately afrodescendant neighborhoods. These were the neighborhoods that grew the most rapidly between the wars and were also the places where city services were most scantily allocated. This program of school closings and new construction netted a steady rise in

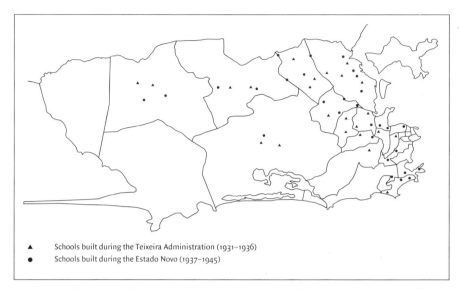

MAP 7. Schools in Rio de Janeiro prior to 1930. Sources: Azevedo Lima, "O problema do prédio escolar no Distrito Federal," *Cultura Política* 1 no. 5 (1941): 80; J. C. Da Costa Sena, "Observações estatísticas sôbre o ensino público municipal," *Revista de Educação Pública* 2, no. 4 (1944): 697.

the number of spaces available, which were quickly occupied by children who had no previous access to schools. Between 1932 when the program began and 1935 when Teixeira was purged enrollment grew from 84,539 to 106,707 (see chart 2).[20]

Enéas Silva, Teixeira's chief architect, summarized the design of his schools in three words: "health, hygiene, economy."[21] Schools provided health services, broadcast messages about health and hygiene through students to their families and neighbors, served as civic centers for nationalist rituals, and conveyed an architectural message to all those who passed by them, let alone walked through their doors. During the Estado Novo, the plain but modern styling of schools echoed the businesslike and aloof political style of the regime—the unadorned walls of the exterior provided no cultural forms of reference, no images that would give a passerby a sense of possession and therefore control over the building.

By contrast, the highly stylized art deco appearance of the cookie-cutter schools Teixeira built were rich in symbolic messages to students, teachers, and the general public. Their curvacious deco appearance was written in the

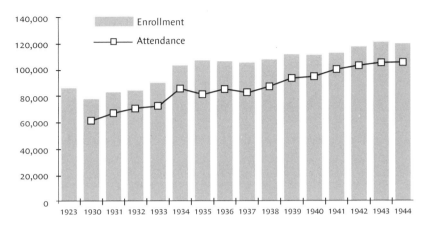

CHART 2. School enrollment and attendance in Rio de Janeiro for 1923 and 1930 to 1944. Source: Azevedo Lima, "O problema do prédio escolar no Distrito Federal," *Cultura Política* 1, no. 5 (1941): 80; J. C. Da Costa Sena, "Observações estatísticas sôbre o ensino público municipal," *Revista de Educação Pública* 2, no. 4 (1944): 697.

cosmopolitan and modern visual language of Hollywood films. The buildings were internationalist and yet served as a visual break with the past. Designed to vaguely resemble the most modern transatlantic cruise ships, with their porthole-shaped windows and prowlike frontpieces, the school buildings invoked dreams of Brazil's industrial future (figure 16).[22]

As Teixeira often argued, the city of Rio was at the vanguard of Brazil's modernization, and it was the schools that would build this modern Brazil. The architectural language of the schools conveyed these convictions. School buildings evoked the future that was being created within their walls. In context, the deco style of the schools set them all the more apart from earlier schools because Teixeira's predecessor, Fernando de Azevedo, had chosen the neocolonial style for the schools built during his administration, and the schools that preceded these were designed in neoclassical or even Tudor styles.

But more than setting these buildings apart and echoing the modernist message of Teixeira's educational program, the schools incorporated elements that facilitated management of students, classrooms, and teachers, and propagated images of discipline and hierarchy. Windows were large enough to allow ample daylight and fresh air into the classroom, but were too high to

FIGURE 16. Escola Municipal Fonte da Saudade, 1934, showing construction typical of the Teixeira administration. Augusto Malta Collection, MIS, Secretaria de Estado de Cultura e de Esporte do Rio de Janeiro, 127u/f009706.

allow students to see out of the room. Attention was thus fixed on the teacher or classroom activities. Hallways were designed to facilitate Taylorist observation of classrooms: "without dead space, without wasted space . . . down to the least detail these school buildings offer a level of economy and comfort expressed in the following percentage of efficiency [in terms of the volume of school space used for teaching], never reached by any other schools in the world: instruction: 68 to 72 percent."[23]

School architects echoed Teixeira's near-fanatical adherence to statistical logic, designing buildings that were statistically efficient in their cost, educational output, exercise of authority, and conditions of health and hygiene. For example, windows were oriented so as to admit "between 20 and 30 candlepower per foot."[24] These schools were an exercise in control. The modern Brazil their exterior promoted was to be achieved by asserting centralized, planned authority over every instant in the school, from the statistically quantified volume of natural light to the ritualized observation of teachers and students to the obsession with hygiene.

In 1932 Anísio Teixeira created a Tests and Measures Service (STE) charged with formulating tests to select students and divide them among the city's classrooms according to their perceived potential. He explained:

> The [STE] was created by force of the modern need for systematized studies and the application of technical processes, above all *tests* of intelligence and scholastic aptitude. . . . In a great organization of "mass education" there are classes which need greater homogeneity, others that need to be accelerated, and others retarded in the pace of teaching. The whole complex of measures destined to adjust teaching to the individual, demands the extensive application of centralized and systematic control.[25]

With this declaration, Teixeira inaugurated Brazil's age of testing and measurement. Psychological and physical exams similar to those used to classify criminals, the insane, and other "degenerates" would now be applied outside the clinic to determine the place of each student in school. In doing this, Teixeira gave rise to a complex legacy of dealing with a diverse student body through race- and class-coded scientific measures. After Teixeira was purged in 1935, the tracking system continued to grow in sophistication. Through the 1940s, educators continued to experiment with and apply the means of measuring and dividing students. Alongside the psychological exams used to track new students, educators applied medical and hygienic standards. Together, these criteria closely followed the prevailing eugenic theory that environmental factors accumulated as hereditary deficiencies.

The principal instrument for classifying entering students was the ABC Test developed by Lourenço Filho. This test, used extensively in Rio and São Paulo, was an instrument of "differential psychology," meaning the study of differences in mental aptitude. The test measured students' readiness to learn reading and writing, defined as "educational maturity." Essentially, students who could already identify and write the words for a group of objects in a chart—car, key, cat, hand, and radio, for example—and who had developed the motor skills to draw geometric patterns, were classified "mature." The test favored students whose parents were literate and had the capability to teach them their first letters at home. Among these students, those for whom the first words might be the names of luxury goods like car, radio, or apple, placed highest.

The class-coded ABC Test served as the backbone not only of the system of tracking that segregated city schools but also of extensive scientific studies to explain poor performance. Lourenço Filho's own lectures given at the Institute of Education stressed that the differences in "educational maturity" were linked to hereditary and environmental factors.[26] Lourenço Filho believed that these tests made the school system democratic because each student was given the opportunity to demonstrate aptitude. Yet faith that a child's capacity for learning could be empirically measured was based on sciences still heavily invested in an ongoing endeavor to understand and contend with the perceived racial inferiority of Brazilians of color.

Through these tests, the school system achieved two fundamental, although seemingly incongruous goals. On the one hand, exams differentiated among students, bestowing educational privilege on some while applying the dystrophic labels of unhealthy, unruly, unintelligent, or immature to others. Testing and tracking policies reified belief in the inherent and hereditary difference between individuals. On the other hand, educators attended to those students whom they classified as unfit, weaving them into the nation's cultural, social, and economic fabric by attacking these differences. Ultimately, no matter how progressive their endeavors were, educators perpetuated social inequalities by institutionalizing class- and race-based assumptions. School policies simultaneously integrated and segregated students.

Differential psychology was new to Brazil. While such gauges of intelligence as Binet's I.Q. Scale were presumably known to the wider medical and scientific community, there was little experience with psychological assessment outside of psychiatric clinics and the legal medicine establishment. Some of the earliest experiments in Brazilian differential psychology were conducted in São Paulo in 1928 by Lourenço Filho, who subsequently published the rationale and guidelines to his ABC Test, making it the most extensively used measure in Brazil for decades. Yet outside of the small team of psychologists working with him at the normal school in São Paulo, only a handful of educators, many of whom had studied at the Columbia Teachers College, had any understanding of how to implement or evaluate such measures.

Outside of Rio de Janeiro and São Paulo, there were two other centers in Brazil where intelligence testing was attempted. In Recife, psychologist Ulisses Pernambucano organized a Psychology Institute within the school system in 1925, with the aim of creating measures of intelligence. Through the Psychology Institute, Pernambucano developed an intelligence test to screen candidates for the state normal school, as was done with the Rio Institute of Education in the 1930s.[27] Francisco Campos's reform of Minas Gerais public education also included a department of applied psychology that experimented with intelligence tests. In 1929, he invited Russian emigré Helena Antipoff, a researcher in Edouard Claparéde's Psychology Laboratory at the University of Geneva, to head the program. Before leaving Russia after the revolution, Antipoff had developed a theory of "civilized intelligence," which held that children were influenced by their environment. In Minas Gerais, she developed a system for measuring intelligence in order to divide students into "homogenous classrooms" based on their abilities, as was done in Rio de Janeiro and São Paulo. Antipoff also proposed "mental orthopedics" for children who tested poorly, and she introduced the use of the term "exceptional" in place of "retarded" to describe children with learning disabilities.[28]

In Rio de Janeiro, Anísio Teixeira began the most extensive experiment in intelligence testing and tracking by recruiting Lourenço Filho to direct the Institute of Education and Isaias Alves to direct the new STE and teach psychology at the institute. Alves, who studied alongside Teixeira at the Teachers College, set about adapting different intelligence and maturity exams, ranging from Lourenço Filho's ABC Test to the Terman Group Test and the Binet I.Q. Scale. Notably, the word used universally by Alves, Lourenço Filho, and others for the psychological exams they instituted was *test* (or sometimes *teste*). This transliteration illustrates the extent to which both U.S.-trained educators like Teixeira and Alves and Brazil-trained educators like Lourenço Filho and Campos relied on pedagogical theories imported from the United States. Of the seventy citations in the instructions to Lourenço Filho's ABC Test, forty-five came from U.S. sources.[29]

As the director of the STE, Alves saw as his responsibility shoring up an eroding social order by grounding it in science: the school system should be organized to recognize "the social value of brilliant children."[30] Alves thought differential psychology would mitigate the exaggerated egalitarianism that he perceived during his time in the United States. He explained:

> If democracy should be the form of government for the society . . . it must be based on a new educational order that gives the more capable the opportunity to rise to positions of leadership.
>
> The grave problem that democracy offers is the false notion of equality . . . that was so important to the political and educational history of the United States through the course of the nineteenth century.
>
> In that country, the government always resulted from suffrage borne by the majority of its citizens, formed on the *frontier*, where the boss and worker, husband and wife, given to fighting the Indians and the dangers of the wilderness seeded with typhoid or malaria, and the struggle for gold, could not think about the social selection that is evidenced still today in French society, so stable and so cultured. . . .
>
> In consequence of this, the school promoted mediocrity, or rather, the leveling of all capacities to the middle ground.[31]

Alves offered his "frontier" thesis to build his case that "all human groups contain a normal distribution of individuals, of extremely differentiated intellectual capacity that demand special organs in our educational systems." Through science, he could define that natural differentiation, and the school system could then apply a scientific order to the burgeoning population of the federal capital.

Alves conducted an experimental test in 1932, repeating Lourenço Filho's 1928 ABC Test on 1,879 students, as well as the Terman Group Test on 7,060 students. Alves tabulated and analyzed the results by race and class, which Lourenço Filho had resisted doing in his research in 1928, explaining that "[because of] a lack of sufficient data along the various age groups of black children, we did not find differences between black, white, and mixed students in our initial research." To the contrary, although Alves's sample also included few children of color, he did not hesitate to draw broad conclusions about the "significant differences between the scores of white and black groups."[32]

Results of the Terman test by racial category are shown in charts 3, 4, and 5. Of the students who took the ABC Test 14 percent were mulatto and 8 percent were black. Of 7,060 students who took the Terman Group Test, only

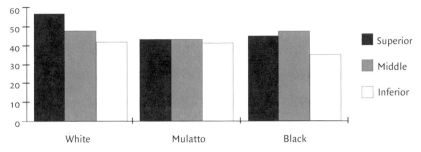

CHART 3. Rio de Janeiro Terman Group Test scores, 1932. (Note: "Superior," "Middle," and "Inferior" refer to the class background of the students. Higher scores are better.) Source: Isaias Alves, "Testes collectivos de intelligência (Terman Group Test) e a sua applicação nas escolas públicas," *Boletim de Educação Pública* 1, no. 1 (1932): 421.

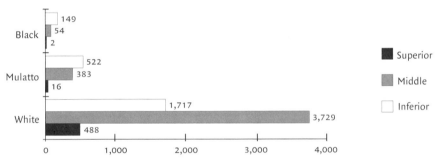

CHART 4. Racial background of students tested in the 1932 Terman Group Test. Source: Isaias Alves, "Testes collectivos de intelligência (Terman Group Test) e a sua applicação nas escolas públicas," *Boletim de Educação Pública* 1, no. 1 (1932): 421.

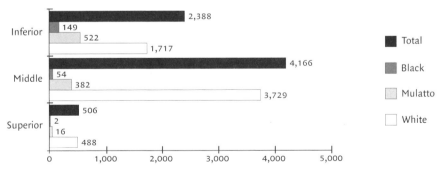

CHART 5. Class background of students tested in the 1932 Terman Group Test. Source: Isaias Alves, "Testes collectivos de intelligência (Terman Group Test) e a sua applicação nas escolas públicas," *Boletim de Educação Pública* 1, no. 1 (1932): 421.

3 percent were black and 13 percent mulatto. The reason Alves had so few students of color to evaluate is that his tests were conducted at the elementary school of the Institute of Education and the Escola Argentina, both in the affluent Tijuca neighborhood. Of the 7,060 students, 2 were classified as black and wealthy and 16 were classified as mulatto and wealthy. By contrast, 487 whites met this standard.

By 1934, a new director of tests and measures, J. P. Fontenelle, began the annual application of the ABC Test on all students entering the first grade. Fontenelle was a doctor who had been active in the public health and sanitation movement during the 1920s. His tests, applied to 22,400 students, confirmed the trend set by Alves two years earlier: white students scored highest (with 3.5 points), followed by mulatto students (3.4), and finally blacks (3.3).[33] Alves and Fontenelle showed little reluctance in using race as a category of analysis of their measures, and the scores of both their ABC Test and Terman Group Test mirrored the stratification of Brazilian society. In the Terman Group Test, wealthy and white students performed almost twice as well as poor, black children (57 points compared to 35 points), while the ABC Test placed whites on top, blacks on the bottom, and mulattoes as an intermediate category.

When Alves wrote of the "extremely differentiated intellectual capacity" of students, he defined difference through race and class. The color of a child's skin or the polish of wealth only confirmed what the tests showed. For educators like Alves, standardized tests established differences among students that mirrored broader differences in Brazilian society. They thought of race and class as similar social conditions, and they used them almost interchangeably to define deficiencies. Alves and Fontenelle employed definitions of class and race in order to define the innate differences that the testing programs they designed would gauge: being either poor or not white explained developmental handicaps.

TRACKING AT THE ESCOLA GENERAL TROMPOWSKY

A 1935 principal's report from the Escola General Trompowsky shows how testing and tracking were applied in schools.[34] Over the course of Anísio Teixeira's four-year reform, schools were rearranged to accommodate separate "homogenous" classrooms. Homogenization, the term educators used for tracking, divided students along lines of aptitude measured through testing. But in this report, the principal at Escola Trompowsky explicitly showed how measures of social class were conflated with test scores to arrange students. The school ran two sessions, each with three sections of first grade students that the principal defined as "well off," poor, or very poor. The expectations teachers held of these students, and the ways the students were taught, varied by their classroom and class.

The wealthy students were divided into the two advanced classes. These children were young, typically six to seven years old, and were on a fast track. Because all had placed well in the ABC Test, teachers taught them to read. At the end of the year, these students' performance was described as "very interesting—all are reading." Their performance was not surprising: these were model students, receiving Escola Trompowsky's model education.

At the other end were students classified as "very poor." They were all more than nine years old and all were repeating the first grade, many of them for the third time. They were described by their low-to-average I.Q. and by their poor behavior: they were "very unstable and aggressive." One of the classes did well: the teacher reported that the majority had learned to read. The other teacher described her students as "mediocre, with poor results." In both classrooms of very poor students, the principal reported that the students "should have had a lot of training in manual tasks, but the school is only being equipped for these courses in the current year." The "very poor" were problem children, and were repeatedly characterized by their inability to advance from the first grade. The principal stressed the need to place these children in vocational classes, revealing expectations for the future of these children, and the educational path they should follow (figure 17).

As the two classrooms with "poor" students show, it is hardly surprising that lower-class students were unstable and consistently repeating. The poor students entered school at the same age as the wealthy children, six to seven years, but they were not taught to read. Instead, their teachers saw their first year as a time for adjustment to the school. As one of the teachers declared, the class objective was "facilitating adaptation to school life. There was no concern with teaching." Naturally, these children would need to repeat the first grade because they were given nothing to learn in their first year of school.

FIGURE 17. Students manufacturing figures of black servants in the manual tasks course, 1929. Augusto Malta Collection, MIS, Secretaria de Estado de Cultura e de Esporte do Rio de Janeiro, 127m/f009299.

Because teachers devoted little energy to teaching these children to read when they began school, their assumptions trapped the poorest students in the first grade, where they became restless and either left school or finally learned to read in the time it took middle-class children to pass third grade. If they stayed in school, they were out of place and stigmatized as slow learners and problem children. Teixeira's New School approach called for the school to adapt to the "social reality" of its community, but this reality was defined through unquestioned assumptions about race and class.

With tracking practices like those of the Escola General Trompowsky applied to students throughout the school system, the number of poor students progressing to the higher grades was low. In 1932, throughout the Rio public school system, more than half of the children classified as poor were in the first grade, as chart 6 shows. Chart 7 shows the low rate of children advancing through school. There were virtually no indigent children in third grade. While the fourth grade had less than 10 percent of the first grade's poor children, it had almost half as many of the middle-class and wealthy children as entered the first grade. Wealthier children were far more likely to continue

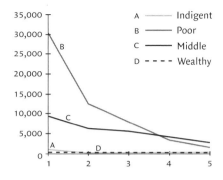

CHART 6. Students in the Rio de Janeiro educational system, by social class. Source: Anísio Teixeira, "O sistema escolar do Rio de Janeiro, D.F.: Relatório de um ano de administração," *Boletim de Educação Pública* 1, no. 4 (1932): 324.

in school long enough to enjoy the fruits of their education. Poor children commonly did not pass the first grade, and only rarely did they make it to the third or fourth.

The ABC Test, whose use was illustrated by the principal at Escola Trompowsky, was applied annually to all students entering the school system, and it was used to divide students between classrooms and sometimes between schools. In 1943 the director of the Orthophrenology Service, Ofélia Boisson Cardoso, took to the airwaves to give a series of lectures on administering and assessing the ABC Test on the *Hour of the Teacher* program on the city radio station, PRD-5. The radio lectures, which elaborated on the written instructions for the test that would be administered to newly matriculating students, offer a sense of the school system's philosophy in differentiating between students.

In her first radio lecture, Cardoso explored the relationship between natural intelligence and meritocracy. She began by stressing that testing must be understood "under the light of the *equality of men* before the law, and the recognition that every citizen has the same rights and responsibilities, a concept based upon Christian morals and followed by we Brazilians." Yet she conceded that it was necessary also to consider difficulties in adjustment based on "the hereditary baggage of each of those elements more or less influenced by environmental factors."[35] In other words, all were equal except for the deficiencies they might have inherited.

Cardoso went on to explain how test results should be used to organize homogenous classrooms. Reflecting the maturity and sophistication that the tracking system attained over its first decade, Cardoso rejected as rudimentary

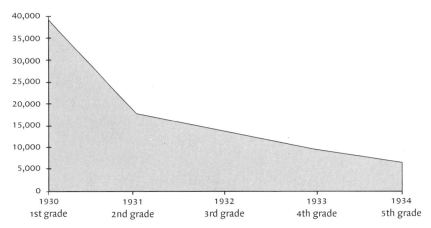

CHART 7. Number of first graders in 1930 that advanced to later grades. (Note: this graph reflects the students who spent only one year completing each grade. In later years, the school system's rate of retention improved, but only slightly: in 1930 fifth graders constituted 4.6 percent of elementary students and in 1935 they constituted 6.3 percent.) Source: Anísio Teixeira, *Educação pública: Sua organização e administração* (Rio de Janeiro: Oficina Gráfica do Departamento de Educação do Distrito Federal, 1934), 131.

simple I.Q. and social class judgments. She acknowledged that at the age children entered school, a child's intelligence was too complex to be measured so simply. Instead, a child's "intellectual maturity," as defined by the ABC Test, would be correlated with his or her level of nutrition and rate of growth, as assessed by an index employed by the Anthropometry Service. Together, these would determine the "mental level" of the child.

Why did children underperform? For Cardoso it was because "nearly all of these children come from economically inferior social groups. The poor performance of these groups is largely caused by poor nutrition . . . as well as unhygienic living conditions which give rise to anemia, pre-tuberculosis, adenopathies, and malnutrition." Aside from the medical problems, poverty "exposed children, in the bluntest promiscuity . . . to all of the brutality of life, unleashing psychic problems and perturbations of character." She concluded her lesson by stressing that there was no single cause, but rather a "complex of causes . . . which originate in society and in heredity."[36] Like other educators, Cardoso conflated race and class through the eugenic theory that degeneracy was both hereditary and accumulated.

While the principal at Escola Trompowsky and the director of the Ortho-phrenology Service stressed social class in the division of students, the re-searchers in the Anthropometric Section of the IPE favored race in their analysis of student development. In 1935—the same year as the Escola Trom-powsky report—Bastos D'Avila, director of the Anthropometry Service, re-ported the implementation of a *ficha antropométrica*, or "anthropometric file" of each student's physical development. This record permitted the Depart-ment of Education's biometricians to measure the "differences in develop-ment from individual to individual" and allowed the service to study the relationships between race, ethnicity, and environment among the city's chil-dren.[37] For at least the next decade, this research formed the basis for applying medical-pedagogical criteria for tracking that were used alongside tests of psychological aptitude.

Over the course of the 1930s, the classification that Teixeira introduced expanded from the ABC Test to include other eugenic criteria. In 1936, Bastos D'Avila explained the ways these criteria related in the measurement of stu-dents by describing the ways in which the three sections of the IPE (An-thropometry, Orthophrenology and Mental Hygiene, and Tests and Measures) worked together. According to D'Avila: "The Anthropometry Section studies students' *habits* (their physical development), determines the type in which they can be catalogued, and provides reliable information about their *tempera-ment*. It leaves to the Orthophrenology Section the part that regards *character*, and to the Tests the part that pertains to *intelligence*. Thus the student is studied, completely and harmoniously, through the four facets conceived by Pende."[38] Nicola Pende was a leader of the turn-of-the-century Italian school of criminology. D'Avila's assessment showed how the school system's mea-surement of students was rooted in legal medicine.[39]

Alongside the ABC Test and I.Q. test scores, a student's record included the "anthropometric file" measuring their physical and phenotypic develop-ment, as well as an "orthophrenology and mental hygiene file" created by the section headed by anthropologist Arthur Ramos. In a text similar to D'Avila's report on anthropometry, Ramos explained that the "orthophrenology file" was modeled after the records used in psychological clinics in the United

States and Germany—records assembled at the zenith of Mendel-based eugenics in those countries.[40]

A student's educational development and potential were gauged through a set of records based on a broad collection of medical and social scientific measures. These ranged from the Terman Group Test to the Binet I.Q. Scale, Lourenço Filho's ABC Test, Pende's facets of human character, and mental hygiene and orthophrenology frameworks adapted from Nazi Germany. These measures reflected the extent to which educators borrowed from the United States and Europe: all of the analytical tools were foreign, with the exception of the ABC Test. These measures also reflected the shape of eugenics as practiced in Brazil: physical development, character, intelligence, and temperament could be quantified and manipulated—they were ways of gauging deficiencies and charting paths for addressing them.

Hygienic, sociological, and psychological visions of race, a statistical worldview, and scientific rationalism combined to create a public school system that was managed from top to bottom along modern paradigms. These values combined a common origin in debates on racial ideology and national identity with a European and North American sense of technicalization, they combined and worked together easily within the school system. What is more, these modern practices brought the original discourse on race and identity to bear within educational policy and school practices. The day-to-day life of Rio schools, beginning with the decision as to where to place a student and culminating within such everyday and private activities as brushing teeth and cleaning hands, were carried out within a logic soundly rooted in discourse on race. Different practices within the schools themselves, and within the system as a whole, reinforced each other in their expression of racial values.

An essay written during the Estado Novo in a Department of Education publication captured the synthesis of race, medicine, rationalism, and nationhood by explaining the need for and feasibility of a student orthodontics program. The essay profiled an elementary school student's orthodontic treatment, and introduced her as: "Djalma de Carvalho—Escola Manoel Bonfim—10 years old, white, 1.32 meters, weight 26 kg, poorly nourished and poor. General condition, notwithstanding, good. Brazilian. Bad dental occlusion."[41] The author detailed Djalma de Carvalho's condition, a seriously occluded

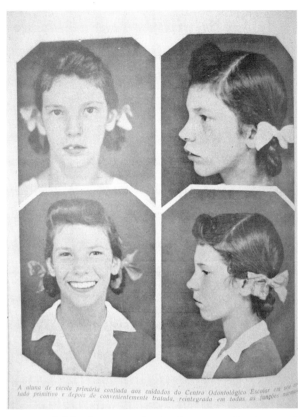

A aluna de escola primária confiada aos cuidados do Centro Odontológico Escolar em seu estado primitivo e depois de convenientemente tratada, reintegrada em todas as funções normais

FIGURE 18. "The elementary school student entrusted to the care of the School Orthodontic Center in her primitive state after being properly treated, reintegrated in all her normal functions." Comment on a photo from *Revista de Educação Pública* 1, no. 1 (1943): 42.

front tooth, and the cost-effective treatment she was given, proposing that the type of service she was provided might be economically applied more generally to students with grave orthodontic problems. There is no record that this became a widespread practice during the Vargas era.

What is significant about this case, however, is the language employed to define the student's situation and the role of the school system in remedying it. Although it had no explicit role in her medical case, the medical-record-format of the description of the girl included a mention of her color, her place of birth, and her social class. Together, these observations made the report into a statement not simply on Djalma de Carvalho's personal condition, nor that of city schoolchildren, but on the nation. That she was white did not prevent her from falling into degeneracy, which accumulated because she was poor, malnourished, and had been raised by her father since her mother had died. The text of her photo caption made the case of her degeneracy even clearer when it referred to her "primitive state." The medical process gave her "normal" teeth, which allowed her to be "reintegrated." The essay reported the final outcome as Djalma being able to have the "normal, happy life of a girl her age."

The school system could be made to work on the shortcomings of Brazilians, bringing medical and social science to bear in rational and cost-efficient ways. Although Teixeira created the blueprint for this system and brought its various parts together, it would gain its fullest cohesion—and Djalma de Carvalho would gain her state-provided, exemplary orthodontics—at the hands of military officers during the Estado Novo.

5

ESCOLA NOVA NO ESTADO NOVO:
THE NEW SCHOOL IN THE NEW STATE

November 1935 was a month of insurrection and repression in Brazil. Nationalists who had fought together in the 1920s and in the Revolution of 1930 had drifted into increasingly antagonistic camps, anchored at their extremes by the Brazilian Communist Party and the fascist Ação Integralista Brasileira (Brazilian Integralist Action). When leftist junior officers struck out in rebellion in Rio and in the northeast, sparking a Soviet-guided uprising on the morning of 27 November, the right-wing state security apparatus had already been tipped off and it moved swiftly to repress the insurgents. Immediately afterward, leaders of the Left and suspected communists throughout Brazil were imprisoned or deported. In Rio, the Political Security Department (DESPS), headed by Nazi-sympathizer Filinto Müller, jailed university professors, union leaders, and other perceived leftist sympathizers. Getúlio Vargas assumed extraconstitutional authority and operated with a free hand. Within two years, Vargas would establish an authoritarian Estado Novo modeled on Mediterranean (Italian, Portuguese, and Spanish) fascism. Vargas would rule with the support of the military, suppressing civil liberties and political parties.

In the months following the communist uprising, Anísio Teixeira and part of his team were purged from the Department of Education. Some were jailed. Francisco Campos, who had been the organizer and first minister of the Ministry of Education and Health (MES), was appointed to succeed Teixeira. Because Campos was the most powerful right-wing ideologue in Vargas's circle, populist mayor Pedro Ernesto Batista chose him out of hopes that it would help save his government from the anticommunist crackdown. Francisco Campos spent his tenure drafting the corporatist authoritarian constitution for the Estado Novo, and after its proclamation in November 1937 he assumed the Ministry of Justice in order to put the document into practice.

By February 1936 Paschoal Lemme, director of vocational education for the Department of Education, had come to believe he had survived the wave of persecution, his appointment having been confirmed by Francisco Campos. But as the circle closed around Mayor Pedro Ernesto, vocational courses offered by the Department of Education to the mayor's union supporters became another way of framing charges that Pedro Ernesto held communist sympathies. Lemme became a target. As he recollects, after a long day of interviewing candidates for a position in the Department of Education, Lemme turned to receive the last person sitting on the benches outside his office, a man who identified himself as an inspector from the DESPS. Their meeting began pleasantly: the DESPS agent said that because he saw Lemme was busy, he would wait until the end of the day to speak to him. When that time came, the agent asked Lemme to go on a short walk down to the DESPS headquarters to answer some questions. Tired, Lemme suggested instead they take a taxi, and in his memoirs he noted the irony of paying for his ride into police detainment. He was questioned about the vocational courses for unions and subsequently held in a series of political prisons for the next sixteen months.[1]

Although heretofore this narrative has focused on meaningful moments in the creation of racialized politics and practices below a largely smooth process of education reform, Paschoal Lemme's experience and story in this chapter invert this perspective. The transition from progressive to right-wing and largely military leadership of public education in Rio was, on the surface, one of the most turbulent moments in the history of Brazilian education. But beneath the political and ideological controversies the policies dealing with race, rationalization, science, and professionalization remained largely intact. The internal significance and influence of race was not challenged or renegotiated. Indeed, the fractious politics of education unfolding after 1935 further reinforced the eugenic nationalist and technical model of education by forming lines of battle between progressives and conservatives that lasted for more than a half century but that skirted meaningful debate over the role of race in public education.

Within this political space, the persecution of Lemme assumes an even more significant irony than his bitterness about paying for the taxi. Unlike other educators, after his time in jail Lemme became an open critic of technicalization, the unquestioned embrace of U.S. values, and the disregard for the racial implications of educational policy. Lemme recalled that after studying at the University of Michigan in 1939, he began to perceive that Dewey's progressive education privileged a homogenous middle-class vision that ignored "the violent historical experience of Indians, of blacks, of immigrants, and the labor movement."[2] Lemme also came to see intelligence testing as an unfair system aimed at developing social hierarchies. These critiques were formed subsequent to the educational reforms and to Teixeira's departure from the school system. The only contemporary dissent in regard to Teixeira's technicalization that Lemme noted was a resistance on behalf of some professors at the Institute of Education to the excessive importation of English-language terminology.[3]

While Lemme's criticisms of Teixeira's reform appear to have been unique and postdated the reforms themselves, they cut to the heart of the racialized implications of Teixeira's program. This critique was not at all the subject of debate in 1935 or during the Estado Novo, and Lemme was imprisoned instead for his participation in educational programs designed for labor unions allied to Mayor Pedro Ernesto. After he was released from prison, Lemme worked as a schools inspector for the state of Rio de Janeiro, and in 1938 he became a researcher for the then newly formed National Institute for Pedagogical Studies (INEP). According to Lemme's biographer, Lemme left INEP in 1942 because he disagreed with the technicalization of Lourenço Filho's educational vision. Radicalized by his experience as a political prisoner (after 1945 Lemme became active in the Brazilian Communist Party) and dissenting from the U.S.-influenced technicalization that shaped Brazilian education, Lemme became isolated and largely forgotten. He regained prominence in the field of Brazilian education only in the 1980s, when the field itself embraced Marxist pedagogical currents.[4]

The battles between the Church and progressive educators, as well as the educational programs carried out by the military officers who held all of the leading posts in the Department of Education during the Estado Novo, show the failure of consensus on certain areas of education policy. But more strikingly they show the remarkable continuity of racially influenced ideas and practices. The faces changed, but the Teixeira reform remained in place. The new administrators continued to build from Teixeira's blueprint (which already included many of the nationalistic and disciplinary measures embraced by the Estado Novo) with only two exceptions: the introduction of religious education in the schools and the reintroduction of a paternalistic practice of responding to popular petitions for favors and intercessions within the school system. The latter was a practice that ran directly contrary to the scientific rationalism, technicalization, and professionalization championed by the progressives, but that nonetheless placed the school system more functionally in touch with the dominant currents of populism and the paternalism of contemporary social politics and, in a limited sense, made schools more responsive to the public.

What did the Estado Novo change in the lives of Brazilians, or in the organization of the country? What did this historical moment mean in terms of the institutionalization of racial discourse? The Estado Novo embarked on institution building but, at least in the case of education, the regime only gave a new face to Brazil's eugenic nationalism. Even the aspects that most characterized the Estado Novo—such as ebullient nationalism; the mobilization of youth in public ceremonies, which echoed those of European fascism; and the implementation of public policies that precluded both popular mobilization and political participation—all had their roots in the years between Vargas's rise to power in 1930 and the advent of the Estado Novo. Was the Estado Novo a turning point in Brazilian history? Certainly it brought greater visibility to the practices and ideals that had emerged in the previous decades, and it continued the expansion and consolidation of these practices. Hence, the public school system of Rio became more paternalistic, the role of race became more fixed, and the links between education, race, and nationalism more evident.

The often violent political changes that swept the country between December 1935, the month of the failed communist uprising, and November 1937, when the Estado Novo was inaugurated, had a significant influence in determining who would lead the institutions that emerged from the interwar processes of state building. The Church, in particular, wanted a broader hand in education. The military also saw itself as a manager of education. Between 1935 and 1937, the administrative leadership of the city government and the educational system narrowed. The Church and the military invoked language that permanently redefined public debate on education. Charges that progressive educators were communists surfaced repeatedly, not to question programs but to challenge leadership. Indeed, there is very little in the educational projects brought forward by Teixeira, Azevedo, or Lourenço Filho that could be considered communist. Nearly all of their innovations came from mainstream practices in the United States.

The significance of this period lies in the patterns through which the Church and the military ratified and continued the technical aspects of public education while forging a lasting antagonism to the politics of progressive educators. The Church and military replaced Teixeira and others, but continued to nourish both the spirit and direction of public education established by these educators, and in doing so these institutions transformed the New School educational policies into the educational status quo. Church and military leaders were important in cementing racial values because of the ways they defined their opposition; that is, setting up a duality between conservative and progressive education and drawing attention away from the technicalization elements that were most directly shaped by racial thought.

This chapter looks at patterns of continuity and change during the Estado Novo. The musical education program led by composer Heitor Villa-Lobos illustrates the continuity in visions of race and in the values of discipline and nationhood. The battles between Anísio Teixeira and Catholic conservatives, on the other hand, reflect the political and ideological backlash the progressive educational project generated. But a look at the Estado Novo itself, and the administration of Interventor Henrique Dodsworth, reveal a great deal of continuity with New School paradigms and programs. Education reflected the intense political battles of the period. More important, though, the school system reflected the continuity of values, especially those of race and of popular participation.

At Rio's Vasco da Gama Stadium—the largest in Brazil—forty thousand students in blue and white uniforms sang in one, two, or four voices, hymns about the fatherland, about the race, and about Vargas: "We are little soldiers / Strong in the struggle to find / The conquests and destiny / That we offer to our fatherland / March little soldier, content and happy / Be guided on your journey by your love of your Nation."[5] These youth mobilizations dotted the nationalist calendar: for example, Day of the Race (September 5), Independence Day (September 7), Proclamation of the Republic (November 15), and Proclamation of the Estado Novo (November 10). The stadium scene, evocative of the rallies depicted by Leni Riefenstahl in her documentaries of Nazi Germany, was the tip of an iceberg—the songs were learned in the regular musical curriculum, the assemblies were drilled for weeks, and smaller performances dotted the calendars of individual schools.

The sight of this youth mobilization, the idea of a multitude singing in one voice, and the nationalist themes and the calendar they supported are elements that forge one of the most immediate images of the authoritarianism and protofascism of the Estado Novo. Paradoxically, while these mobilizations became the grist of Estado Novo imagery and culture, they originated in the progressive educational project of Teixeira, under the leadership of composer Heitor Villa-Lobos. Villa-Lobos began his musical education career in the Rio school system in 1933. Nationalist, disciplinary, and pedagogically modern, Villa-Lobos's musical education program bridged both the educational aspirations of progressives like Teixeira and the authoritarian vision of the Estado Novo.

Beginning with Teixeira's 1932 reform, nationalist choral song became one of the cornerstones of public education in Rio, and Teixeira recruited Villa-Lobos to develop this program. The hymns Villa-Lobos wrote, such as "Hymn to the Sun of Brazil," "Brazil United," and "Hymn to President Vargas," were nationalistic even by the high standard of the 1930s.[6] Gustavo Capanema and Getúlio Vargas were regular guests at these civic commemorations, and after the proclamation of the Estado Novo, the performances became one of the cornerstones of Vargas's cult of personality. Such choral presentations were put together for key historical dates or for the visit of important foreign

FIGURE 19. "Magnificent view of the Vasco de Gama stands during the choral assembly of 7 September 1942—Day of the Fatherland—in which 30,000 public elementary school students from the Federal District participated." Comment on a photo from *Revista de Educação Pública* 1, no. 2 (1943): 179–80.

dignitaries, such as U.S. Coordinator of Inter-American Affairs Nelson Rockefeller in 1943.

Villa-Lobos envisioned the choral song program as a socializing agent: "With its enormous cohesive power, it creates a powerful collective organism, it integrates the individual within the social patrimony of the Fatherland."[7] Nationalistic songs and practices were seen as a means of social discipline. As Villa-Lobos explained, "there is no *liberty* without strict and severe control of *consciousness*, of the ability to differentiate between right and wrong."[8]

But alongside discipline and nationalism, any attempt to define and enforce a musical culture was rife with racial implications. Stated plainly, Villa-Lobos saw his musical program as an instrument for the European acculturation of non-white students, and for the preservation of social discipline in schools where students from different races increasingly came into contact. The presumably white student imagined by Villa-Lobos learned not only "the good teachings of their professors, but sometimes certain habits and customs from rebellious children, generally influenced by environment or heredity, even thought the school should be a temple for developing the soul, cultivating a love of beauty . . . focusing on the qualities and virtues that human progress depends upon."[9]

Villa-Lobos counterposed whiteness—defined by progress, beauty, and virtue—to blackness, which embodied rebelliousness, bad habits, and problems of heredity. His musical program was an educational, disciplinary, and nationalistic allegory of the journey away from blackness, through mixture, into whiteness. One of the traits Villa-Lobos believed had to be left aside was the "obstinate" and "unconscious" rhythms performed during Carnival. He bemoaned the fact that that enthusiasm was not projected into the singing of the national anthem. But Villa-Lobos believed that the transition from street rhythms to forcefully sung civic hymns could be achieved through the "constant exercise of marches and martial songs," which not only sharpened the musical capacity of the population, but "awaken a greater civic interest for things patriotic."[10] Choral songs were the bridge between an undisciplined African past and a white and ordered Brazilian future.

A short hymn composed by Villa-Lobos in 1937 illustrates the musical and cultural march of progress he envisioned. The hymn, titled "The Rejoicing of a Race," was composed of two choruses, one identified as African, the other as mestiço. The African chorus could not have been simpler or less sophisticated. It was three syllables, continuously repeated: "A - - iu - - ê / A - - - - - iu - ê." The mestiço chorus was more complex but still repetitive: "Chumba Tuma á - ê - ma, Chumba Tuma á - ê - ma / Chumba Tuma á - ê - ma, Chumba Tuma á - ê - ma / Can-ja can-jê - rê tu-ba! Can-ja can-jê - rê tu-ba!"[11] Lyrics became increasingly sophisticated as the cultural voice transitioned from African style toward European, but they remained primitive in their simplistic repetition.

Writing of the "race now being created," Villa-Lobos explained: "This is a task of preparing the child mentality to, little by little, reform the collective mentality of future generations."[12] Villa-Lobos endeavored to create a new national aesthetic which, among other things, was hostile to Afro-Brazilian culture. Villa-Lobos did not try to erase Brazil's African and indigenous cultural expressions—to the contrary, he gained fame specifically by celebrating Brazilian "folklore" and weaving African and indigenous elements into his classical compositions. But the structure he brought to musical education assumed the vantage of a white man looking on African and indigenous cultures as folk artifacts and vestiges of the past.

Beginning with the Teixeira reform in 1932, students of the Rio school system typically spent six hours per week in the musical education curriculum put together by Villa-Lobos, who was head of the Musical Education Service. As early as 1934, top federal officials including President Vargas attended Villa-Lobos's choral assemblies. Such was the appeal of these gatherings that in 1938 Minister Capanema invited Villa-Lobos to organize and direct a federal Musical and Artistic Education Service (SEMA) within the MES. During the balance of the Estado Novo, the SEMA trained music teachers in order to spread the program of choral song to other regions. These choral gatherings took place as many as eleven times per year and included as many as forty thousand students, according to a report prepared by Sylvio Salema, who succeeded Villa-Lobos once he went to the federal ministry.

How did students react to these assemblies? In some cases, parents prevented their children from participating, arguing that the process of assembling so many students from around the city was too chaotic. In the absence of specific evidence that there was a moral or political opposition to the events and their messages, one may choose to read such rationales for evasion as veiled distaste. On the other hand, the account of these events given by Norma Fraga, a woman of color who participated in them in the 1940s, suggests that the political and nationalistic messages were lost on at least some of the participants. Norma Fraga adored the events: they were a time to be out of school and in the street. All her classmates participated, everyone sang—"it was lovely," she recalled.[13]

According to Norma Fraga, Day of the Race was thought of as commemorating youth: "It meant 'race' in quotation marks, because what 'Brazilian Race' is there? . . . It is a totally erroneous concept, there is no race to it, but they called it Day of the Race. . . . It was just in the heads of the Estado Novo ideologues, with their fascist models." Instead, for Fraga it was a day of youth because of the musical assemblies at Vasco da Gama Stadium, which counted on the presence of Vargas, "Chief of the Nation." Fraga loved the events for the music and the multitudes: "I thought it was a great deal, going to Santana Field to learn to march, [it was] something that really attracted me as an adolescent. What did I care about what race was? If it was race, if it was white, if it was black? What I wanted was to participate." Still, she conceded that some of the students "must have detested the events, particularly since they were mandatory."[14]

Table 5. Nationalist Musical Assemblies, 1932–1942

Date	Location and Event	Number of Students
Oct. 24, 1932	Fluminense Football Club (F.C.) Stadium	18,000
Nov. 19, 1933	Russell Field (Flag Day)	2,000
Nov. 26, 1933	Fluminense F.C. Stadium (Music Day)	9,000
Sept. 7, 1934	9th District Schools (Day of the Fatherland)	8,238
Sept. 7, 1934	Russell Field (Day of the Fatherland)	7,000
Sept. 7, 1934	São Christovão Field (Day of the Fatherland)	7,238
Nov. 8, 1934	Muni. Theater (Culture and Friendship of Nations)	800
Nov. 15, 1934	Botafogo Stadium (Proclamation of the Republic)	1,500
Nov. 19, 1934	Russell Field (Flag Day)	3,000
July 7, 1935	Vasco da Gama Stadium (Educational Congress)	30,000
Aug. 16, 1935	Institute of Education (Educational Concert)	1,200
Aug. 22, 1935	Institute of Education (Educational Concert)	1,300
Aug. 29, 1935	João Caetano Theater (Educational Concert)	1,200
Sept. 7, 1935	Castelo Esplanade (Day of the Fatherland)	30,000
Sept. 15, 1935	Pan-American Red Cross Conference	2,000
Oct. 10, 1935	João Caetano Theater (Educational Concert)	700
Nov. 19, 1935	Russell Field (Flag Day)	3,000
July 19, 1936	Homage to the President of the Republic	1,500
Sept. 7, 1936	Castelo Esplanade (Day of the Fatherland)	25,000
Sept. 24, 1936	Audition for exchange with Vienna Children's Choir	1,200
Oct. 10, 1936	João Caetano Theater (Festival of the Child)	1,200
Oct. 17, 1936	Muni. Theater (National Education Crusade)	1,200
Nov. 19, 1936	Castelo Esplanade (Flag Day)	8,000
Nov. 27, 1936	Praça Mauá (Reception for President Roosevelt)	2,000
May 13, 1937	Muni. Theater (Presentation of the Student Theater)	1,000
Sept. 7, 1937	Castelo Esplanade (Day of the Fatherland)	35,000
Oct. 10, 1937	Muni. Theater (Week of the Child)	1,400
Nov. 11, 1937	Inauguration of Statue of Marshall Deodoro	1,200
Nov. 27, 1937	Russell Field (Festival of the Flag, and mass)	1,500
Nov. 17, 1938	Institute of Education (Educational Concert)	1,000
Nov. 19, 1938	Russell Field (Flag Day)	900
Nov. 30, 1938	Educational Concert (No location mentioned)	800
Sept. 7, 1939	Vasco da Gama Stadium (Day of the Fatherland)	30,000
Apr. 19, 1940	School 20–13 (Birthday of the President)	—
Sept. 7, 1940	Vasco da Gama Stadium (Day of the Fatherland)	40,000
Nov. 10, 1940	Presidential Palace (Aniv. of Estado Novo)	10,000

Table 5. (continued)

Date	Location and Event	Number of Students
Sept. 5, 1941	Day of the Race	5,000
Sept. 7, 1941	Vasco da Gama Stadium (Day of the Fatherland)	30,000
Sept. 5, 1942	Santa Ana Park to Tiradentes Palace (Youth Parade)	4,000
Sept. 7, 1942	Vasco da Gama Stadium (Day of the Fatherland)	30,000
Oct. 12, 1942	Grounds of the Presidential Palace	7,000

Source: Sylvio Salema Garção Ribeiro, "Documentação das grandes demonstrações civico-orpheônicas realizadas pela Secretaria Geral de Educação e Cultura," Revista de Educação Pública 1, no. 2 (1943): 184–85.

COMMUNISM AND CATHOLICISM

Beyond the continuity in the racial and nationalist components of education, serious political and philosophical disputes simmered. The principal one of these was the conflict between the Pioneers of the New School and advocates of the resurgent Catholic Church over the place of religious education in public schools. For the pioneers there was no place for religious instruction within secular public institutions. For Catholic activists of the 1930s a public school without religious instruction was one that failed to educate. This disagreement, which surged over the articles on education in the 1934 Constitution, escalated into a bitter political feud in which Catholic activists successfully accused New School educators of being communists and counterposed their own program of religious and moral education as a safeguard of the "social peace" of Brazil.

What were the roots of Catholic opposition to lay education? Maria Yedda Linhares, who twice directed the Rio de Janeiro municipal school system during the 1980s and the state school system in the early 1990s, began her career in education in the capital in the late 1930s. She worked closely with Anísio Teixeira when he returned to the national education policy scene after 1945. Linhares interpreted Catholic activism in Brazil as a vestige of European anticlericalism in the nineteenth century. After France's defeat in the Franco-Prussian war it expelled its religious orders, closed the religious schools, and instituted universal, free, secular public education on a national level. Many of the expelled orders settled in Brazil. In some cases, wealthy individuals who had previously sent their children to be schooled in Europe financed the immigration of members of the religious orders. The sisters of these religious orders opened schools for elite children. These schools were meant to rival those of Europe and, naturally, taught in French.[15]

The arrival of these religious orders and the creation of elite religious schools coincided with the zenith of anticlericalism in Brazil. The Republican 1891 Constitution stripped the Catholic Church of its status as the official church of Brazil, and it established the legal basis for the creation of secular public schools. By the 1930s, the Catholic Church and its conservative lay allies embarked on a campaign to restore the Church and its values to Brazilian public life in general, and to public education in particular. Beginning with Cardinal Sebastião Leme's intervention on behalf of Vargas in the Revolution of 1930, the Vargas regime maintained an open door to the Church and its activists. In particular, Minister of Education Capanema saw his position as stemming from Church support, and national educational policy reflected his gratitude. At the local level, the Rio de Janeiro city council during Teixeira's administration counted one demagogic priest and several Catholic conservatives. Because of the Church's interest in education, some of the city's leading educators, such as Isaias Alves and Jonathas Serrano, were closely allied to the Catholic campaign.

The Church and Catholic activists encountered trenchant opposition from many of the Pioneers of the New School. Sociologists Fernando de Azevedo and Anísio Teixeira in particular stood fast against the introduction of religious education in public schools. Despite their Catholic roots—Teixeira had once entered a Jesuit seminary on the road to the priesthood—they saw religious education as dogmatism. They viewed the Catholic Church as a predator which exploited the supposed ignorance of students. Increasingly, Teixeira saw his purportedly modern and scientific schools as a seawall standing between an immature public and a Church that represented "superstition and outright obscurantism."[16] Consequently, Teixeira made it his mission to obstruct rather than to accommodate the growing Catholic interest in emerging public education institutions. This line in the sand made Teixeira a convenient scapegoat for Catholic nationalists.

The pioneers saw the 1933 constitutional convention as an opportunity to write their reforms into national educational policy. A 1932 "Manifesto of the Pioneers of the New School" laid out their agenda. Teixeira and Azevedo saw to the distribution of the manifesto in every state of the nation, and from their respective bases in Rio and São Paulo they promoted it in the press in order to create an "environment" for their ideas.[17] The manifesto achieved two of its goals: the New School educational philosophy became known, at least to a limited extent, across Brazil, and nearly all of its principles were included in the education articles of the new Constitution. Yet the costs of these victories were high. Many Catholic supporters of New School educational philosophy left the movement, religious education was written into the constitution, and a highly politicized educational battle was begun.[18]

Teixeira resisted instituting religious education in the Rio school system. He read the constitutional mandate loosely, creating a program of optional instruction in which parents could submit a written request for religious education and receive after-school instruction by a teacher employed by the school system rather than a Church-designated priest or lay instructor. This half-measure brought attacks by city councilmen and made Teixeira one of the principal targets of the national campaign to define the Church as the bulwark against communist subversion.

From the ratification of the 1934 Constitution onward, Teixeira, Azevedo, and other progressive members of the New School found themselves increasingly isolated within a hostile political environment. Catholic conservatives seized on elements of their programs—in particular the failure to institute a more extensive religious education program—as evidence that the Pioneers of the New School were communists who were undermining Brazilian culture and society. Although Catholic attacks on the New School focused on religious education, this issue and accusations that Teixeira and others were communists were part of a broader effort on behalf of Catholic leaders to carve a new political role for themselves as the defenders of the social order.

Alceu Amoroso Lima, director of the influential Catholic lobby organization, the Dom Vital Center, wrote to Minister Capanema in 1935 to demand the removal of Teixeira and to outline the relationship between church, state, and social peace that Catholic conservatives proposed. "Could the government allow," Amoroso Lima asked, "that a new generation be impregnated with ideas that are completely contrary to Brazil's true traditions and to the true ideals of a healthy society? . . . I write to inform you of the great uneasiness among us, and what we expect from the patriotism of our leaders for the defense of Brazil's moral patrimony and its future as a Christian nation." Amoroso Lima went on to demand the replacement of Teixeira by men of "total moral confidence and technical capacity (and not socialists like [Teixeira]). . . . The government must do these things immediately and indefatigably, because upon these tasks depends the stability of our institutions and the social peace."[19]

One curious aspect of the letter is that it was directed by the lay Catholic leadership to the federal Minister of Education to attack a local school system. The decision to retain or remove Teixeira was in the hands of the city's Interventor, Pedro Ernesto, not Minister Capanema. Local opposition grew as well from city councilmen representing the Catholic Electoral League, in particular from Olimpio de Mello, a demagogic priest from the western suburb of Bangú. One of the leaders of this movement, Átila Soares, introduced a bill in May 1935 requiring implementation of religious education. The dispute over this legislation quickly merged with the broader political confrontations that had surged between the Right and Left. Teixeira and other progressive New School advocates found themselves increasingly isolated politically, as well as more frequently accused of practicing communism.[20] In the heat of the city council debate on the measure, Soares telegrammed Teixeira, declaring "condolences on your nefarious Bolshevizing actions at the Department of Education. The Brazilian nation cannot be at the mercy of such insidious enemies as yourself, whose objective is to dismantle and spoil its most valued possession—the social peace."[21]

Opposition surged even within the school system's leadership. Isaias Alves, who had developed the program of intelligence testing in the Rio school system after studying at the Columbia Teachers College, also accused the New School leadership of being communist. In a 1937 attack on Institute of Education director Lourenço Filho, Alves charged that "Bolshevism is difficult to find in educators, even though it exists, but educators are Bolshevizing involuntarily every time they weaken the sentiment of patriotism, of religion, of domestic order, of social discipline."[22] Between 1934 and 1937, Alves participated in the fascist Integralist movement, and during the Estado Novo he directed the state of Bahia educational system. Although he had been the author of one of the most important elements of the Teixeira reform in Rio, his accusations nonetheless offer the clearest argumentative link between opposition to religious education and the propagation of communist ideology.

The leaders of the New School—Azevedo, Teixeira, and Lourenço Filho—defended themselves through different strategies. Lourenço Filho was the most successful at remaining in a position of leadership: a reading of the political currents led him to introduce religious education at the institute, and despite accusations by rivals that he was a communist, Lourenço Filho advanced to the head of the federal government's educational research institute, I N E P. Lourenço Filho wrote in his annual report on the institute for 1936 that "religious education has been carried out at this institute in conformity to the instructions of the director of education, without difficulties and in perfect harmony with the aims of the Church." Parents had the option of not enrolling their children, but 84 percent of students enrolled in the classes. Perhaps because religious education reflected the class values of the students who gained admission to the institute, or because they understood the significance of religious education to the faction ascendant in national educational politics, virtually all of the *normalistas*, or normal school students, of the institute's Teachers College enrolled in the program.[23]

In addition to his discussion of religious education, Lourenço Filho also expanded his discussion of nationalist and civic programs at the school. He even appended the text of a letter from José Duarte, secretary of the National Defense League, describing the institute's secondary school students' participation in the Flag Day activities of 19 November. Duarte wrote: "The Institute's students assembled in great numbers, they were well disciplined, and they marched gallantly in their white uniforms, radiating their optimism and the purity of their love for Brazil."[24] Reprinting this letter about the disciplined, patriotic behavior of the institute's students was the finishing touch to a report that emphasized the religious, disciplined, and nationalistic programs of the school.

In his report for the following year, Lourenço Filho again stressed the participation of institute students in nationalist events. These included Flag Day and Independence Day parades, performance of nationalist hymns for the visits of dignitaries from Italy and Uruguay, as well as demonstrations of physical education and nationalist chorus. Although such demonstrations took place during the Teixeira years and before, they took on heightened importance in the corporatist social environment of the late 1930s, when they illustrated the imagined bonds between the Vargas regime and the Brazilian soul. By meeting heightened expectations about participating in these events, Lourenço Filho and the Institute of Education kept their autonomy in other areas of policy and practice.

Although Fernando de Azevedo worked alongside Teixeira in the leadership of the progressive New School movement, he was spared the brunt of the political persecution Teixeira suffered. In large part, his work as director of the normal school of the city of São Paulo distanced him from the center of political pressure. Still, the issue of religious education was used by opponents to undermine his progressive education program. Writing "brother to brother as a soldier who takes advantage of a moment of calm in the trenches," Azevedo described the backlash in a 1933 letter to Teixeira. He explained: "You have seen the undeniable signs of a conservative backlash . . . that has the ends of a 'return to tradition' (reaction against the Lourenço Filho and Fernando de Azevedo reforms). . . . I have heard that the actual director [of the São Paulo school system] has the expressed aim of instituting religious education in the schools, introducing a discipline of religion in the normal schools and promoting a reaction not only against anti-Catholic but even un-Catholic or suspicious thought."[25] Azevedo pointed to the coded language of "a return to tradition" as a means of attacking the progressive educational projects. This language resurged frequently in both newspaper reporting and school system records during the Estado Novo.

Anísio Teixeira received the brunt of the Catholic backlash. As historian of political populism Michael Conniff has suggested, Teixeira was a "lightning rod" for a series of reasons. He was "pedantic and disdainful to politicians," he failed to perform the political favors asked of him by other influential elites, he was intransigent on the question of religious education, and he became an outspoken defender of Mayor Pedro Ernesto as his governing coalition fragmented and radicalized. Teixeira was not a gifted politician, but the root of his difficulties also lay in the importance of the Rio de Janeiro school system. Because it was the school system of the federal capital, it was directly linked to national politics. Like Teixeira, Catholic conservatives saw the school system as a model for the nation.[26]

One example of Teixeira's intransigence was his rejection of press baron Assis Chateaubriand's request that Teixeira appoint one of Chateaubriand's protégés as a fourth grade teacher. She held a teaching certificate but had not yet completed the teaching time required for appointment to the fourth grade. Teixeira replied to Chateaubriand's request: "I regret to inform you that it was impossible to attend to your request of hiring Ermelinda Mendes . . . since she has only 451 days of service, placing her nowhere near the first 500 places. . . . I hope to be able to serve you on another occasion."[27] The records do not suggest that another opportunity arose. Refusing favors to such powerful men as Chateaubriand may have helped the processes of professionalization and systematic rationalization, but it certainly did not alleviate Teixeira's mounting isolation.

Teixeira brought this intractability to his struggle with the Catholic Church, which he referred to as the "Inquisition."[28] The former seminarian saw his mission as protecting his students from the superstitious dogmatism that the Church represented. He reflected: "Paradoxically, modern anthropological and sociological studies have given new impetus to the philosophic and religious prejudices that we believed ourselves free of. In this time so shaped by science . . . how do we explain the resurgence with such acceptance or even aggressiveness, of so many systems of superstition and outright obscurantism?"[29] His steadfast refusal to consider religious education gave the Church a target in its endeavor to shape its role as the defender of the "social peace," and it cost him the directorship of the program he had painstakingly organized.

From 1933 onward it was increasingly clear to those around him that Teixeira's position as head of the Rio school system was becoming politically inviable. Federal statistician Freitas sought an exit for Teixeira by splitting the director positions of the educational and agricultural statistics services, both of which Freitas held. Under this bargain, approved by Minister of Agriculture Juarez Távora but rejected by Minister of Education Washington Pires (1932–1934), Freitas would direct the agricultural statistics service while Teixeira would direct the educational statistics program. Freitas explained the plan later to Azevedo: "When I learned Anísio's position was becoming untenable at the Department of Education, I tried to get him transferred to another line of work, less visible, certainly, but where his powerful presence would nonetheless irradiate victoriously throughout the educational life of the Republic."[30]

Freitas emerged as the interlocutor between the increasingly conservative and authoritarian federal government and progressive educators. Although his bid to rescue Teixeira failed and left him "seriously threatened, reduced to either immobility or taking my leave," Freitas continued to bridge the increasingly distant tendencies. On one hand, he was deeply invested in public education. On the other hand, he believed in a strong state and embraced the drift toward authoritarianism. Although he failed to save Teixeira from "unsavory and painful surprises," he succeeded in luring Lourenço Filho to direct the INEP in 1938, and he persuaded Fernando de Azevedo to write the classic *Brazilian Culture* as the introduction to the 1940s census. As late as 1936, after Teixeira had been exiled to his family estate in Bahia, Freitas wrote: "I have not lost hope, if not of replacing myself with Anísio, at least drawing him into the field of statistics, where he will shine with greater tranquility, and without ceasing to serve national education."[31]

Despite the increasingly acrimonious political environment, Teixeira pushed forward with his reforms and stood his ground on religious education. But the link drawn between secular education and Bolshevism by Catholic conservatives served as the pretense for the removal of Teixeira and his team after the failed communist uprising of November 1935. Within days of the uprising, Teixeira submitted his letter of resignation and fled for the safety of his family estate in Bahia. He explained that he had tried to avoid the class conflicts created by urbanization and industrialization, resolving the "tremendous perplexities of the historical moment in which we live." He asked rhetorically, "what other alternative is available for the pacification and conciliation of the spirit?"[32]

With Teixeira's departure the school system lost many of its most talented intellectuals and administrators. Some, like Paschoal Lemme, were arrested. Some left of their own will. On 1 December, a group of Teixeira's coworkers resigned in protest of his dismissal. Their resignation was accompanied by a letter that stated: "Dr. Anísio Teixeira maintained himself far away from any political ideologies subversive to the constitutional order, devoting himself exclusively to national culture, for education and only for education."[33] Although others, like Lourenço Filho and J. P. Fontenelle remained in place, the concentration of New School educators who attempted to create a model school system based on merit, democracy in access, and modernist pedagogy ended at the same time Brazil took a decisive step toward authoritarian dictatorship.

From exile in the state of Bahia, Teixeira corresponded with a U.S. diplomat, asking for his help in ending the "dulled fascism" that was the Estado Novo. He described the "experiment of democracy through education in Brazil which has been tried not very successfully in Rio de Janeiro," and lamented that: "You have seen the real face of modern Brazil—a corrupted and most degrading . . . fascism which is giving life and form to our most objectionable potentialities."[34] Meanwhile, the school system Teixeira reformed received Francisco Campos as its new director. As Pedro Ernesto tried to placate his critics, he chose an individual whose Catholic and nationalist credentials and whose proximity to Vargas were above reproach. During his nearly two years as director of Public Education, Campos was largely absent from the challenges of school system administration, focusing instead on the task of drafting the constitution of the Estado Novo.

THE DODSWORTH REFORM

After the tumultuous battles over control of the city government, which resulted in Pedro Ernesto's arrest in May 1936 and a brief and unstable tenure by Padre Olympio, Getúlio Vargas chose Henrique Dodsworth, an obscure administrator, to run the city. According to Conniff, Dodsworth was "chosen by Vargas largely to stabilize and if possible depoliticize local administration while the Estado Novo conspiracy ran its course."[35] Although Dodsworth had held anti-Vargas stances in the past—his file with Filinto Müller's DESPS described him as "a revolutionary in 1932, on São Paulo's side"—he was a long-time city councilman who identified with the more economically conservative factions of the city.[36]

Dodsworth had a long career as a doctor and educator, serving as a schools inspector, physics and chemistry teacher, and eventually director of the Colégio Pedro II. Dodsworth graduated from the Rio de Janeiro Medical School in 1916, and like many of the leading eugenicists, he balanced careers as educator and doctor. For example, in 1920 he was sent to Europe by the Ministry of Justice to study secondary school methods and programs, and in 1925 he was the Brazilian delegate to the Third South American Conference of

Microbiology, Pathology, and Hygiene in Buenos Aires. On his return from Buenos Aires, he became a chaired professor of physics at the Colégio Pedro II and served as director of the day school from 1931 through 1933. His tenure at the colégio was characterized by the introduction of a nationalistic choral song program; the creation of a position of health inspector who maintained health and hygiene records of the students; and the establishment of a policy that students' behavior outside the school also came under the jurisdiction of the colégio's disciplinary codes.[37]

Dodsworth's original interest in education rested primarily in secondary schooling, which was largely administered in private schools, almost exclusively serving the children of wealthy families. His orientation as an educator resembled his overall administration—it was characterized by increasing the efficiency and reach of the system, rather than revising the theoretical or pedagogical orientation of the schools. His educational philosophy seems to have been largely shaped by his trip to Europe and by his inspections of schools. In his 1920 report to the Ministry of Justice, Dodsworth contrasted European and Brazilian education:

> Let us consider the Brazilian case. Primary education is subordinated to the city, its schools are attended primarily by the poor. Primary education exists more for the sake of freeing parents during the day than educating the children. Once students have absorbed to commemorate the civic dates and know how to sing the national anthem, they leave the school and never return. Children from privileged classes who go on to secondary and higher education attend academies that are unregulated by the government and fail to provide a thorough primary or secondary education, favoring instead the remunerative business of "training for the official exams."[38]

Dodsworth saw parallel problems. Private education was geared to providing students with the talismans demanded by superior social standing: "Children don't learn: they get tested." Meanwhile, public schooling trained poor students to be seen and not heard—to perform the national anthem and appear in disciplined formations during civic parades. But in either case, schools failed to teach.

The Henrique Dodsworth reform, issued in 1944, was the first substantial reorganization of schooling in Rio since Teixeira's reform more than a decade earlier. Yet unlike previous reformers, Dodsworth did not significantly revise the educational philosophy of the school system. Instead, he strengthened vocational training and institutionalized the moral values championed by Catholic conservatives. Aside from these changes, the Dodsworth reform continued the expansion and pedagogical orientation of the school system introduced by Teixeira. The new vocational structure divided primary education into two stages of three years. The first stage "seeks the wholistic education of the child." This meant developing literacy and basic skills as well as a nationalistic consciousness. The second stage was prevocational, providing "preparation for work, following the economic needs of each region."[39]

The reform echoed Alberto Tôrres's call for an organized, trained, and positively disposed workforce: "One of the most imperative needs of national education is doubtlessly to awaken in new generations consciousness of the value and dignity of manual labor," explained the director of primary education, Colonel Jonas Correia.[40] Dodsworth's emphasis on "spiritual values and national traditions," however, departed from the work of Teixeira and Azevedo. Rhetoric about tradition, Azevedo argued, was language coded against the modernist, social reformist aspects of the New School.[41] Newspapers eulogized the reform as an "expression of modern social pedagogy," reaching "ends" adapted to social reality through "means" developed by Azevedo and Teixeira.[42] Indeed, the press stressed the connection between the Henrique Dodsworth reform and Teixeira and Azevedo's reforms: "Mr. Jonas Correia did not breach this tradition, even when reforming, he knew to respect the structure that is being consolidated and slowly expanded."[43]

This was a New School without Teixeira's polemical laity. Still, it preserved the New School's technical and pedagogical innovations: it built upon and resembled the educational philosophy of Lourenço Filho. In fact, news reports in both the *Jornal do Brasil* and *A Noite* alluded to the reform's adherence to educational psychology. What is more, *A Noite* reprinted an interview with Lourenço Filho, who expressed "great satisfaction" at the reform and compared it with his own work.[44]

EDUCATION BY *MILITARES*

Dodsworth's education reform, like his management of the city, was pragmatic. He avoided bold initiatives, made existing systems function more efficiently, and kept city politics out of the national spotlight. Dodsworth chose military officers to succeed Francisco Campos as director of education and Lourenço Filho as director of the Institute of Education. The military men who filled the top administrative posts in education lent the school system the disciplinary and nationalistic tone of the Estado Novo. But on the whole these officers did not fundamentally shift the school system from the direction it was given by Teixeira and Lourenço Filho.

After Francisco Campos completed work on the Estado Novo constitution and left the Rio Department of Education, Dodsworth appointed Colonel Pio Borges to direct the school system. Among Borges's reforms was the abolition of classical education at the city's vocational secondary schools. This was an innovation by Teixeira that offered some students of the city's few vocational schools a degree equivalent to that of the private, classical secondary schools that prepared elites for the universities. Classical curricula had been implemented in only a few of the vocational schools before Teixeira's dismissal—interestingly, two of the three were girls schools, which, coupled with the Institute of Education, had given female students an enormous proportionate advantage in educational opportunities.[45]

Closing these programs eliminated the only public classical education opportunity outside of the Institute of Education and the Colégio Pedro II. In the wake of this move, the secondary school of the institute was renamed the Colégio of the Institute of Education. The name change resolved the inconsistency of having only one public secondary school conferring university-recognized diplomas. By renaming the school the Colégio, it became a publicly maintained private secondary school.[46]

Borges also restructured the school system administration by creating the Department of Nationalist Education (DEN) in 1940. The DEN consolidated physical education, choral song, and moral and civic education. This rationalized the administration of the most openly nationalistic, eugenic, and disciplinary elements of the 1932 Teixeira curriculum. Headed by another offer, Lieutenant Colonel Moacyr Toscano, the DEN's job was to prepare "a generation whose civic spirit, moral sentiments and physical vigor are capable of maintaining Peace, preserving the conquests of science, and guaranteeing the life and progress of Brazil."[47]

Under Borges's tenure, yet another officer, Colonel Jonas Correia, directed primary education. Correia, formerly a teacher at the Colégio Militar, stream-lined the nutrition, health, and hygiene programs of the schools, coordinated medical and dental care systemwide, and studied students' nutritional levels to adapt school lunches. Jonas Correia replaced Pio Borges as director of the school system in 1942. His administration brought the wartime mobilization to the schools. Brazil's entrance in the Second World War provided an oppor-tunity to promote nationalism among, and demand discipline from, students. For instance, schools repeated Vargas's call that all citizens must contribute to Brazil's victory through their "Discipline, Diligence, Discretion, and Unity."[48] In the schools, the war was a vehicle that conveyed the Estado Novo's lessons. And under these circumstances the presence of military officers in civilian school administration underscored the nationalist and disciplinary demands of the era.

Correia turned eugenic programs into a coherent system that not only looked after the healthy development of children but used judgments about their health to determine the student's academic track, much as standardized testing was intended to do, creating the "medical-pedagogical" orientation of student placement.[49] The medical-pedagogical philosophy was carried to the extreme of segregating these students or removing them from the schools altogether. The pretense that sick children could jeopardize the health of healthy children separated wealthier, whiter children from their poorer, often darker counterparts. Health now accompanied intelligence and maturity test-ing as the bases on which schools were segregated in Rio. Poor students were commonly "recognized as sick (syphilis, parasites, adenopathy, anemia), anti-social in their behavior for hereditary or cultural reasons, and indifferent to education."[50] Systematization of these judgments as the basis for the distribu-tion of students skirted explicit differentiation by class or race but had the same effect.

Using health rather than age as the criteria for admitting children to schools served to restrict access to the schools by the poorest children. This was the first moment in the process of expansion of the school system at which a barrier to the most destitute was imposed. Throughout the Vargas era, the city's educational system expanded. The type of student that Teixeira and later directors wanted to draw into the schools was the child of the working poor. The patterns of school construction show special energies dedicated to education in the suburbs, including a program commenced in 1945 to build schools along the Leopoldina rail line.[51] But the system did not cater to the poorest children. The criteria of "school health" further distanced these children from the schools.

Over the course of the Estado Novo, analyses of race, health, and educational performance accompanied the testing and tracking program. The results of these analyses were shared with educators in Rio de Janeiro and across Brazil through the *Revista de Educação Pública*. These essays revealed a consistent trend of equating poor educational performance with poverty, malnutrition, cultural inadequacy, and race. The analytical frameworks adopted by these researchers revealed the extent to which an educational system based its measures of performance and merit on norms established by the eugenics movement, which in turn depended on prevailing hierarchies of race and class. Ultimately, the school system dressed the prevailing social stratification in scientific clothes.

The military officers continued the testing and tracking programs, and as these programs reached maturity educational researchers began to examine the patterns of failure that the tracking system revealed. One question captured their attention: Why were students—like the nine year olds still in the first grade at Escola General Trompowsky—repeating grades to such an extent? Their data showed that of the 100,000 students in public schools, 33,000 were being held back each year.[52] This problem dominated the agenda of educational researchers of the 1940s. Some groups of students consistently measured lower on tests or underperformed in school. What was the cause of this reduced performance? Was it poor nutrition? Poor health? Environmental factors? Was it cultural? Or hereditary?

The consensus of the national Medical-Pedagogical Conference, held in São Paulo in 1941, was that grade repetition was a symptom of illness. Following the eugenic correlation between health and intellectual capacity, the educators sought medical solutions to academic problems. Colonel Pio Borges, the city's secretary of education during the early years of the Estado Novo, divided the school system into fifteen Medical-Pedagogical Districts (DMP). As the director of elementary education, Colonel Jonas Correia, explained, "the problem as it is posed is medical-pedagogical. The student carrying disease, suffering from cavities, or otherwise infected, will always learn poorly in school."[53] He boasted that the Rio school system was the most complete expression in Brazil of the combination of education and medicine. The new network of DMPs analyzed and treated the biological, hygienic, and medical reasons for failure.

Students were evaluated not only on their academic performance, but on their state of health and nutrition, what Correia called the "educational condition of the student." He pitched the medical-pedagogical approach as "a Brazilian solution to a Brazilian problem." The problem lay in the ability of sick children to gain admission to the city's schools. These "innumerable sick children afflicted by extremely serious maladies are able to enroll in our schools, constituting at once a health threat to their colleagues and an object of scorn for their companions."[54] Low school performance was equated with illness. Students who tested poorly were sent to the DMP doctor.

In 1942, students from the 5th DMP, which covered the neighborhoods of the south end of Rio, were divided into categories of promotable, barely promotable, and unpromotable. The unpromotable students were sent to the medical clinic located at the Colégio Cócio Barcelos in Copacabana, along with their psychological records and their mothers. There the student underwent a medical evaluation that included assessment of their mental hygiene and social environment. If the mother did not accompany the child, the school secretary visited the home "to collect data relative to the home, the way of life, the degree of poverty, of hygiene, and the 'modus vivendi' of the family, etc., indispensable data for assessing the causes of the child's maladjustment."[55]

Each of these students was then given a special "Problem Child" record, registering the diverse treatments they were administered, as well as their living conditions, nutritional habits, and family life. According to Antônio Maria Teixeira and E. Corrêa de Azevedo, authors of the report on the 5th DMP, an analysis of these "Problem Child" records revealed that the majority of maladjusted children were malnourished. They explained that the principal reason for their malnutrition was the "poverty + ignorance dialectic."[56] A vicious cycle seemed to exist: because students were too malnourished to learn, they grew to be ignorant like their parents, who in turn did not know how to feed them properly. Behind the fortified milk these students received lay a complex of assumptions and judgments that laid blame on family poverty and ignorance for their deficiencies.

If the doctors of the 5th D M P were identifying malnutrition in the fashionable and affluent neighborhood of Copacabana, conditions in poorer parts of the Federal District were considerably worse. In a 1944 report titled "Cephalic Development and Sub-Nutrition," Joaquim Thomaz of the Anthropometry Service described the state of malnutrition of students in the far western, semirural region of Guaratiba. These were children of poor, uneducated farmers and, as a rule, carriers of the parasites endemic in the region. According to Thomaz, half of the children were malnourished and, by consequence, stalled in their learning. He described them as "accomplished grade repeaters who spend five, six years in the first grade, with low fatigue indices and subnormal I.Q.'s."[57]

Thomaz reached a curious conclusion about the role of race in contending with malnutrition and endemic diseases. He explained that, as in other studies by the Anthropometry Service, the evaluation of these students revealed a greater degree of malnutrition among white children than blacks, with an intermediate number among "mestizos." Thomaz suggested that all things being equal, black children "have greater resistance to environmental factors, adversity, poor nutrition, etc."[58] By arguing that blacks were better suited to poverty, Thomas implicitly equated blackness with misery. What is more, this analysis—like many others by the Anthropometry Service—disqualified the higher level of educational performance by students of color by reducing it to a better adaptation to misery.

ESTADO NOVO AT THE INSTITUTE OF EDUCATION

Even the Institute of Education was headed by an army officer who continued the trajectory initiated with the 1932 reform. In 1939, Colonel Arthur Rodrigues Tito, an instructor at the Escola Militar, was appointed to replace Lourenço Filho when he left to direct I N E P. Like the other military officers in the school system, he had no pedagogical training but had built a career in military instruction. The official biography of Tito in the 1954 history of the institute described him as "energetic but affable, he maintained admirable discipline without resorting to Prussian methods, and the students had great sympathy for him."[59] Having officers heading the school system meant more than placing loyal, conservative men in key posts. It introduced military and nationalistic values. One former student recalls that "reveille was played and everyone assembled."[60]

Within the Institute of Education itself, militarization and the nationalistic, disciplinary air of the Estado Novo worked themselves into the daily experience. A 1941 publication by the Institute of Education Literary Society, *Instituto*, reveals the extent to which the political phenomena that was the Estado Novo wove itself into school culture. Between the photographs of white normal students standing in military formation and holding flags were articles eulogizing Vargas and discussing the "moment of national effervescence."[61] Only the first edition of the magazine is preserved in the institute's library, and it is unclear whether additional editions were ever published. Also unclear is the degree to which it reveals the culture of students at the institute, or reflects only the ideological demands of the regime. Whichever the case, *Instituto* echoed the official ideology that prevailed in the school system and institute administrations.

One article discussed the rewriting of the institute's hymn. On instructions by Colonel Tito, Theobaldo Recife, a professor of moral and civic education at the institute, stripped the 1886 hymn of its original wording. Recife added new words reflecting contemporary values and a tone more appropriate to the great civic commemorations of the day. The last refrain of the song epitomizes the new meaning: "From the purest civic spirit comes the spark / That illuminates our Institute / And the greatness of the Fatherland is mirrored / In the divine splendor of our doctrine."[62] Recife described his inspiration in composing the new hymn: "They are words that my heart dictated while I thought of the magnificent presence of students studying, dutiful and applied, future teachers, precious collaborators that they will be in the moral and spiritual perfection of the Brazil of tomorrow."[63]

Like the school hymn, the Flag Day that had been commemorated by students in Rio for decades acquired new symbolic language evocative of fascism. *Instituto* described the 1941 Flag Day in the following way: "Giving homage to the Flag of Brazil, sacred symbol of our land, blessed by God, we feel within our chests, beating with greater fervor, an intense desire to reach for the pinnacle of the glory of the Fatherland that we so worship." The director of the institute, Colonel Tito, as well as the secretary of education, Colonel Borges, were present, along with other "figures of prominence in the government." The highest-ranking dignitary, Colonel Borges, raised the Brazilian flag, followed by "the act of incinerating the school Flag, realized by students of the Benjamin Constant Civic Center, whose president led the lit torch to the pyre, where other students had deposited the old flag of the Institute of Education."[64]

When students at the institute burned their school flag they reenacted a 1937 ceremony in which Getúlio Vargas presided over the burning of the country's state flags in a pyre as the Brazilian national flag was raised. Enacted in the aftermath of the proclamation of the Estado Novo, the ceremony on Russell Field (where the larger student choral presentations took place) symbolized the end of federalism under a regime of national unity. As historian Daryle Williams explains, "when Vargas's civilian, military and ecclesiastical allies watched the symbols of regional sovereignty go up in flames, they lent their support to the state's attack upon elements of Brazilian society deemed threatening. Unbending regional elites, communists, liberal republicans, Jews and unacculturated immigrants would bear the brunt of a broader assault on groups that did not conform to the regime's vision of Brazilian society."[65]

As indicated by the ceremony bringing the national flag-burning ritual down to the Institute of Education terrace, the institute remained a model for national education, but not quite in the way Teixeira, Azevedo, and Lourenço Filho had conceived. Vargas appropriated it as a stage from which to address the nation about issues of education. In 1943, Vargas was the graduation speaker at the institute. His presence elevated the prestige of the teachers college and of teachers and made its graduation ceremonies a pulpit from which to discuss social values. Referring to teaching as a "priesthood," Vargas spoke about how teachers will "teach the meaning of the Fatherland, the Family, and the Society; instill civic courage, and establish the healthy normative values of work and discipline."[66]

Vargas commended Dodsworth for building twenty new schools. He also addressed women's roles, contrasting the ideal of the domesticated woman performing services in the home with such jobs as nursing, teaching, farming, or factory labor. Vargas declared that women accompanied men in building the modern society, concluding: "We must still triumph over tremendous obstacles. But whatever they may be, we must not neglect education, where women find dignified permanent occupation."[67] Finally, he promised to one day hold a national teachers congress. The graduation speech was not only directed at the graduating teachers, it was also recorded by P R D-5, the school system's radio station, and distributed to schools throughout the country.[68]

Vargas's speech in 1943 represented the peak of nationalist authoritarianism within the institute. Just one year later, Secretary of Education Correia gave a graduation speech that reflected a deep ideological shift. He reminded Vargas of his unfulfilled 1943 promise for a national teachers congress. More surprisingly, he used the word democracy four times in his brief speech. Correia quoted British Minister of Education Butler's educational reform: "If the ends of democracy are making each member of the community richer and more filled with potential, it is evident that each must receive the best and most complete education that the government can offer." Describing the role of education in democracy, Correia underscored the importance of teachers in effecting the transition. Much as teachers were a "silent but important support of the government," at the outset of the war Correia told teachers that they now must come together in building the ideas of "justice and liberty, peace and progress."[69]

When Vargas was deposed in August 1945, the government of Rio quickly fell with him. By December, Dodsworth and all of his appointments in the school system were out of office. The school system swung back to the footing that had been established in the Teixeira years. In December, the new federal interventor, Philadelpho Azevedo, appointed Fernando Antonio Raja Gabaglia secretary of education. Raja Gabaglia had been a professor of geography at the Institute of Education and director of the Colégio Pedro II during the Estado Novo.

At the ceremony installing Raja Gabaglia, Colonel Jonas Correia spoke of the effort of his administration to reorganize the school system "on modern bases and with respect for Brazilian traditions."[70] But these ideas resonated as epilogue to an era that had passed. That same month, Colonel Tito was replaced as director of the institute by Francisco Venancio Filho, a philosophy professor there who for years had been identified with the most progressive wing of the New School. One of the first events he hosted at the institute was an homage to Fernando de Azevedo, at which a portrait of Azevedo as the Pioneer of the New School was unveiled.[71]

These new appointments closed a cycle that framed the politics of education in the city of Rio de Janeiro through to the present and that shows all the evidence of continuing for the foreseeable future. The New School reforms by Teixeira, Azevedo, and Lourenço Filho established the progressive terms of the debate. The nationalistic, authoritarian, and disciplinary extremes reached during the height of the Estado Novo reflected the demands placed on education by the Catholic Church, the military, and conservative segments of the community.

But these extremes were not incompatible. It was the progressives who created many of the nationalistic and disciplinary mechanisms employed during the Estado Novo. Without the base of choral song, physical education, hygiene programs, and tracking systems, the architects of the Estado Novo could not have rallied the school system to its colors as fully and in so short a period of time. The eugenic, psychological, medical, and hygienic assessments and classifications institutionalized by Teixeira were also continued largely intact. The only significant change in this area was the placement of physical education programs under the administration of the DEN, a move that reflected the importance of "perfecting the race" to the process of national development.

On the other hand, under the tutelage of military officers the Rio school system expanded the pace of school construction initiated by Teixeira, and placed special care in building schools in the poorer reaches of the city. These schools also continued to serve as access points for social welfare programs in areas where the reach of public policy was the weakest by providing nutritional lunches and, at least on a limited basis, medical and dental care. Indeed, the school system was so committed to meeting the demand for education that it repeatedly raided the Institute of Education for teachers, hiring students before they graduated. In 1945, when there was a shortage of fifteen thousand spaces in the public schools, the system raised Cr$1,688,000 (US$101,686) from the federal government to place the children for whom there was no space in public schools into private schools.[72]

POPULAR STRATEGIES AND PUBLIC EDUCATION

The tutelage of public education by military officers was consistent with one of the central aspects of the Teixeira reform—the perceived importance of shielding educational programs from the influences of parents and the broader public. Parents were deemed unfit for judging what was best for their children's education, and the school system was seen to function as a well-tuned, rational, scientific, and professional organism. Indeed, the authoritarianism of the Estado Novo rested substantially on the assumption that the best and most technical solutions for national problems could be carried out through the exclusion of politics and dissent, and this assumption had already been at work within the progressive education projects of Rio de Janeiro and São Paulo.

Still, the Estado Novo rested on authoritarian measures as well as on more traditional clientelistic appeals to the popular classes. Getúlio Vargas invited the poor to write to him directly with their grievances. As a result, letters flooded in and were attended to by his aides, each request forming a file that worked its way around the appropriate ministries. Some of the petitions to Vargas made their way to Henrique Dodsworth's office, others were addressed to Mayor Dodsworth directly. Successful or not, the petitions generally resulted in official inquiries: the mayor's office would send the petition down the administrative ladder until it reached the responsible authority, whose opinion on the petition would work its way back up the administrative hierarchy. Not surprisingly, the process usually took months. The administrative files that were opened to attend to these petitions remain preserved in the Henrique Dodsworth Collection of the Rio de Janeiro city archive.

Demand for public education consistently outstripped supply, so it is clear that parents and students valued and accepted their education to some extent. Perseverance in education did vary considerably, though. Because students were tracked in patterns that resembled the distinctions between race and class, the most privileged students received the most privileged education. At the other end of the spectrum, fewer than half of the city's students made it past the third grade. Seemingly, although parents and students saw some value in public education, those pushed to the lower rungs found the experience unrewarding.

These patterns of demand and desertion represent the boundaries of public acceptance of the educational programs in Rio. Between these extremes lay an array of strategies by which parents and students sought value in the schools that were being installed in their communities. Letters preserved in the Henrique Dodsworth archive testify to some of the types of strategies used by parents and children to appropriate or, more usually, simply gain access to the city's educational opportunities. As a rule, efforts to influence school or school system policy failed. By contrast, people who accepted the administration's authority over educational affairs and petitioned for favors or exceptions rather than changes often succeeded. These transactions between parents and the school system administration followed the centuries-old pattern of patron-client relations.

These petitions are especially remarkable for the language employed by the authors. The letters invariably began with a statement of the humility of the author and his or her smallness before the authority addressed: "I am a humble . . . father, railroad employee, maid, retired sergeant." Then, the petitioner would state a request, such as space in a school for their child. The petitioners contextualized the request within what they believed were the government's goals. These were usually health and hygiene, discipline, the strength of the economy, and the greatness of the nation. Their desires were presented as complementary with the aims of the authority they addressed, thus the letters stand as testimony to popular understanding of the regime's agenda and bear witness to public strategies for taking advantage of that agenda.

The petitions are a curious source, because they both include the agenda of the author, as well as their use of the rhetorical strategies that they imagined would result in the granting of their request. Consequently, the letters do not necessarily indicate what members of the public believed about public education. Instead, they offer a sense of what this public thought they were supposed to believe. As Joel Wolfe explains in his analysis of workers' petitions to Vargas, the texts reveal "the ways in which workers attempted to turn components of the regime's rhetoric—as well as Vargas' political problems—to their advantage."[73] Given the ways in which the petition writers manipulated political rhetoric to attain their ends, there is little evidence in the letters of public rejection of educational policies. In this sense, the petitions resemble the criminal records analyzed by Sueann Caulfield, who observes, "I find little evidence that individuals who testified in court rejected the moral values or gender norms defended by the law. Yet their 'strategic repetition' of these norms and values, to borrow Judith Butler's phrase, did not replicate the law exactly."[74] Similarly, these petitions gently coaxed school system administrators into changing policies or bending them to accommodate the author's request.

Most of the unsuccessful petitions were from parents or communities requesting that a school be built in their neighborhood. In 1944, for example, 180 residents of the northwestern rail-line neighborhood of Senador Camará signed a petition to Dodsworth requesting the construction of a neighborhood school with a capacity for 700 students. They complained that the nearest schools were two to three kilometers away and had "insufficient and precarious sanitary conditions." These schools did not have space for all the children of Senador Camará who wanted to attend school, so some children had to travel even farther to a school in Bangú, while confronting the "difficulties of the weather: the cold, the rain, and the scorching sun."[75]

The residents of Senador Camará did not approach the mayor's office empty-handed. Their campaign to obtain a school dated at least as far back as 1940, when they secured a donation of several adjoining plots of land from the developer of the suburb, Cristóvão Vieira Alves, "great landowner and friend of the people of this picturesque locale."[76] Although there is no further information on how, specifically, the residents gained the grant of land, the language with which they describe Alves suggests that they resorted to traditional paternalist appeals. They proposed turning this land over to the city as the site for a school that the city would own—unlike the two nearest schools, which were located in buildings rented by the city. The residents had already solved the most difficult problem facing the city in building new schools: the unavailability of undeveloped land in population centers. To put the final touch on their request, one of the residents even got Minister of Labor Marcondes Filho to send a supportive telegram to the mayor.

The Buildings and Materials Service (SPAE), the department responsible for school construction, rejected the proposal. In his response to the mayor, SPAE director Raul Penna Firme argued that the plot of land was unsuitably small, and that two adjoining plots—not owned by the petitioners nor by landowner Vieira Alves—would need to be purchased. As the map he submitted shows, the school building would have occupied a smaller area than the original plot, but because of the design of the building (consistent with the homogenous plan for new construction during the Dodsworth administration) it would exceed the boundaries of the available site (see map 8).

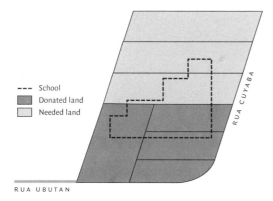

RUA UBUTAN

MAP 8. Map of the proposed school in Senador Camará. (Note: gray area designates the land acquired by residents for the school. Two adjacent plots [top] were projected as needed for a school using the design shown.) Source: Letter from Raul Penna Firme to Henrique Dodsworth, 25 May 1944, Henrique Dodsworth Collection, AGC, Box 108—"Education, 1939–1945," (07596).

A similar fate befell a petition by a worker's mutual aid society, the Companhia Confiança Industrial, to have the city rename an existing school in memory of Carlos Alberto de Menenzes, a labor organizer. In a 1944 letter to Dodsworth, the society justified its request on the basis of its support of the school. The society explained that it had provided both the land and the building where the school was located, and since its opening in 1938, they had furnished all of the school uniforms, meals, and other materials. Although this may have seemed a persuasive argument, the administrator who handled the petition replied that the school was already named Virginia Pinto Cidade after the first normal school graduate in Rio, and it would not be renamed. The city had no interest in having one of its schools named after a labor organizer, even if it was a labor group that had been responsible for the school and its upkeep.[77]

While efforts to change the way the school system did things generally failed, petitions asking for an exception or a special favor sometimes succeeded. One example is a petition by a housekeeper, Felicidade Rodrigues, to Getúlio Vargas asking that her two sons be interned in a vocational school. Rodrigues was illiterate, so she dictated the letter to a friend. Like other petitioners, Rodrigues stressed her extreme poverty—she and her two sons lived in a single room in a Larangeiras boardinghouse, and she could not afford to place them in any school. Consequently, although her children were eleven and nine years old, they were still basically illiterate.

Rodrigues's strategy was to argue that without an education the children would be a detriment to the society. She explained that while she worked all day the children "perambulated through the streets," a state of affairs that "could not continue since they will be *encaminhados na malandragem* [given to being hoodlums]." Illiterate and given to vice, these children would not only be a shame to their mother, but "prejudicial to the Nation, because once they became grown men they would certainly not be productive elements, and only by grace of God would not become criminals."[78]

The solution, Rodrigues suggested, was interning the children in a vocational school. This would "safeguard the sacred interests of the Country: those being to create a new generation prepared and apt to face the difficult contingencies of life, and to work for the grandeur of Brazil." Vargas's office forwarded the letter to Dodsworth, who in turn sent it to the school superintendent. The director of vocational education allowed the children to be interned in the Colégio Cardeal Leme. Felicidade Rodrigues succeeded in getting her children into school by appealing to the state as a patron, a strategy employed in dozens of letters within the Dodsworth archive.

In one case the petitioners were not outsiders but rather the teachers of one of the city's vocational schools, Escola Orsina da Fonseca. They bypassed the school superintendent and went straight to the mayor with a petition to expand their school into the vacant first floor of the city building whose second floor they used. The vocational school taught both elementary courses for young children and vocational courses in typing, stenography, and needlework for women. It was located in the downtown area, and most of the students were the children of Syrian immigrants.

The teachers stressed the school's pioneering role in educating women: "When it was founded by that illustrious battler, Professor Leonilda Daltro, in 1910, there did not exist in this country, perhaps in all Latin America, another such institution dedicated to women, with its technical, professional, artistic, and scientific characteristics." Yet more room was needed because the floor occupied by the school was unhygienically cramped, adding to the difficulties faced by the young, working-class women who studied there. Sending this petition directly to the mayor meant that it worked its way down the administrative ranks faster than it may have worked its way up. Maria de Lourdes Cardoso, the district superintendent, endorsed the idea and passed it onto the building inspector.[79] The inspector reported that the first floor was in dismal condition, but that the unhygienically cramped space of the second-floor school was the more serious problem: expansion would be a net benefit to the school. Finally, the director of the SPAE approved the idea and returned the request to the mayor's office with notes of approval from all the applicable administrators. The request made by teachers faced a more friendly reception from the school superintendency than did requests from parents or neighborhoods. Their request, however, foundered on the shoals of one final evaluation. The mayor's office sent the approved request to the office in charge of the urban renewal plan. The city engineers who were busily laying plans to clear the center of the city to build Avenida Presidente Vargas reported that the entire building where the school was located "is affected by the plans for building the avenue, and will be demolished."[80] Escola Orsina da Fonseca would not only not get the additional space but was on the verge of being torn down, unbeknownst to the teachers.

Education remained a scarce resource through the end of the Estado Novo, despite sustained efforts to expand capacity. The terms of access to public education were tightly controlled by administrators whose broad autonomy was first encouraged by Teixeira's positivism and later by military authoritarianism. But in public education, as in any system, there was room for negotiation. The public responded to technocratic authority with negotiating strategies that had worked for centuries. Relying on the transcript of patron-client relations, people seeking access to education petitioned technocrats. Their appeals acknowledged the power gap between themselves and the authority they approached, and identified an aspect of the official interests or agenda that their request served. The petitioner cast the favor as a way of strengthening or perpetuating the powers they humbly appeared before. Administrators often reacted favorably to these requests, and for a moment the system benefitted everyone involved.

These petitions show a system whose basic features had become a fact of daily life for over one hundred thousand students, thousands of teachers, and their families. Regardless of how these features were judged by participants, the window opened by the Dodsworth and Vargas petitions shows a tacit acceptance of the landscape of public education as a space governed by health, hygiene, nationalism, discipline, and work. The petitions uniformly cast the school system as a set of resources and reflect attempts to gain or increase access to them. The same strategies were also evident among the elite of public education, the students at the Colégio Pedro II. The petitions also reflected a step backward in the technical management of the school system. While the school system did not submit itself to popular will, it did bend to accommodate the politics of granting favors. This was the most profound change within educational policy between the Teixeira period and the Estado Novo, one which, despite the ostensible technicalization of the dictatorial regime, brought educational policies into greater conformity with the paternalistic and populist politics of the period.

6

BEHAVING WHITE: RIO'S SECONDARY SCHOOLS

On the morning of Wednesday, 13 November 1940, three students of the Colégio Pedro II made a big mistake. While their classroom was unsupervised, they rushed to the window to jeer at a corps of cadets from the Escola Militar marching down Avenida Marechal Floriano. The Escola Militar's commander stopped the corps in the street in front of the school and burst into the colégio director's office to protest the offensive indiscipline of the students. With no warning, a conflict had erupted between the Escola Militar, the prestigious academy that trained the "armed classes," and the Colégio Pedro II, the federal model school that for over a century had represented the zenith of the classical secondary education.

According to Wilson Choeri and Aloysio Barbosa, who were both students at the colégio in 1940, the jeers directed at the cadets had their origins in an embarrassing moment involving one of the cadets while he was on a date. The cadet, dressed in his gray uniform and imposing cape, took a young woman to the movies at the MGM theater, which at the time was the biggest, most modern, and most air-conditioned of the city's theaters, to watch *Gone with the Wind*, just released in Brazil. Once the lights dimmed, the couple began making out, and at one critical moment the woman inadvertently tore into a sensitive area of the cadet with a fingernail. The cadet screamed in pain and collapsed into the aisle, prompting the theater manager to turn on the lights and expose their act. Because there was perhaps no place more public than the MGM theater, students at the colégio heard of the scandal immediately. When the cadets from the Escola Militar passed, the students from the colégio hung out of the windows and yelled "gone with the wind" and "the nail, the nail!" mockingly imitating the cadet's scream.[1]

During the Estado Novo, then in full stride, the cadet's disgrace and the students' derision were magnified into an act of treason. Although the tenth graders somehow failed to register this fact, it was not lost on the director of the school, Fernando Antonio Raja Gabaglia. Raja Gabaglia negotiated the Estado Novo's treacherous political waters with remarkable skill. He was much more adept than Anísio Teixeira at soothing relations with important political figures, occasionally ceding sought-after spaces in the colégio as favors, and playing his political hand with confidence befitting his personal friendship with the Vargas family.[2]

Raja Gabaglia immediately recognized the parade incident as one of the greatest crises his school had faced in the decade since the Revolution of 1930. He must have known that within hours Minister of War Gaspar Dutra would hear of the incident, and that the sun would not set without a telephone call from Minister of Education Capanema, expecting steps to resolve the conflict between the two branches of the "national state." His long-term success as director rested on his recognition and deft manipulation of the school's prominent symbolic role.

Raja Gabaglia acknowledged the commander's concerns and promised punishments commensurate with the gravity of the insult. By the end of the week, he issued the most severe punishments listed in the colégio's "Register of Disciplinary Penalties." The three students who called from the window were expelled. The other nineteen students in the classroom were suspended for six days, and the incident was recorded in their permanent files in order to make sure that "such a thing will never happen again, for the good of the traditions of education and civic spirit of our students and the esteem and respect that we all owe to these young and brilliant Cadets."[3]

To soothe the tensions that had erupted between the Ministry of Education and the Ministry of War, Raja Gabaglia reported the following Monday to Minister Capanema, where he detailed the school's punitive measures. Capanema forwarded the report in a letter to Dutra, who in his reply stated that although he considered the incident closed, he wanted to repeat that the incident had been "deeply shocking." Moreover, he added that "we lament that these students were so misguided in their lives that on the occasion of a parade of the armed force of the Army, bearing the National Flag, instead of awakening a resonating enthusiasm and respect, generated a response of scorn or inattention revealing the premature civic disdain of their empty hearts." He ended his letter with the ominous remark that he considered the matter "symptomatic of the veiled corrosion afflicting the school."[4]

This incident amounted to more than a matter of the simple indiscipline of schoolchildren. At stake were the reputations of two of the most important educational institutions of the Estado Novo. By extension, the image of the Estado Novo as an agent of nationalism and order was also undermined. During the Estado Novo, a parade of the cadets of the Escola Militar was a public performance intended to evoke the sentiments of nationalism and respect for authority. Meanwhile, the Colégio Pedro II was the only school in the country directly administered by the federal government, and it served as a model for secondary education nationwide. Its students received a highly prestigious diploma, and they were trained as future leaders.

For students of the Colégio Pedro II to be the authors of such an act of indiscipline implied the failure of the Estado Novo to instill respect for order and hierarchy among the very youth who would one day hold privileged roles. A model school demanded model behavior. Insulting the students of the Escola Militar undermined the political harmony and unity of purpose that were the self-promoted virtues of the Estado Novo. Such incidents were rare at the colégio. The entire ten-year stretch of punishments recorded in the "Register of Disciplinary Penalties" witnessed only one other expulsion of a student. The record of the expulsion was vague, but intriguing: the student was dismissed for using "inconvenient language" in his "History of Civilization" final exam.[5]

The incident drew unwanted attention to the colégio. One of the three students, Alda Waksmann, was Jewish. This was not uncommon because many of the students at the colégio were children of recent immigrants from Europe and the Middle East. Their parents, often employed in commerce, could not afford the expense of private secondary schools and depended on gaining admission to the Colégio Pedro II as their means of social advancement. This trend was reinforced by the proximity of the colégio to the hearts of the Jewish and Middle Eastern communities—Praça Once and the SAARA.

Just a month after the three students were expelled, and possibly because of the Jewish name included among them, Minister Capanema demanded from Raja Gabaglia a list of all the Jewish students at the school. What is more, he rescinded the director's policy of not scheduling exams during Jewish holidays such as Yom Kippur. The school's tolerance of a non-Christian calendar stood against the Estado Novo's policy of cultural homogeneity. Henceforth, only officially sanctioned holidays were to be observed at the model school. Although the documents regarding Capanema's order and Raja Gabaglia's response do not address Capanema's motives for building a list of Jewish students at the colégio or for banning accommodations to Jewish holidays, the timing suggests the possibility that Capanema attempted further to placate the military and create an impression of firmness with the colégio.

Raja Gabaglia objected to Capanema's crackdown on Jewish students and non-Christian holidays at the colégio. He replied that there was no way to provide a list of Jewish students because the school kept no record of students' creed. Instead, he gave Capanema a list of students with "Jewish-sounding" names, which amounted to little more than 5 percent of the students. The majority of the names were Portuguese—for example, Monteiro or Carvalho—and thus implied that many prestigious Brazilian families had Jewish origins. In his letter, Gabaglia argued that the presence of Jews and the accommodation of Jewish holidays in no way undermined the brasilidade (Brazilianness) of the colégio. He cited a recent visit and praise from the archbishop as proof that "the Catholic traditions of Brazil in no way suffer in the Colégio." Finally, he listed distinguished Jewish graduates of the school, including an army general. Raja Gabaglia was always able to defuse challenges to his or the school's loyalty to the regime, and this incident was no exception. After his rebuff of Capanema there is no record of further ministerial action about the presence of Jewish or foreign students at the colégio.[6]

The incident with the Escola Militar and the Ministry of Education's crackdown on Jewish observances were stronger than normal reactions to situations that were probably commonplace in the Vargas era. The Vargas regime was different from its predecessors in that its social policy involved more than the police. Institutions like the new Ministry of Labor and the Ministry of Education and Health, as well as the Department of Press and Propaganda, realized Alberto Tôrres's aspirations by setting the government on a footing that managed the social relations, vitality, and economic integration of all classes and regions. The federal government used these resources to guide and instruct Brazilians on models of behavior and interaction, and the Colégio Pedro II played exactly this role.

Both New School educators working for the city school system and the directors of the federal model school Colégio Pedro II strove in their own ways to erode the dichotomies of educational opportunity. The Colégio Pedro II was a public high school administered directly by the federal government as a model to guide the nation's private high schools. Historically one of the most prestigious and exclusive secondary schools in Brazil, the colégio redefined its educational mission and became a model for popular secondary education. The school doubled in size by creating an evening session, starting to admit girls (and educate them with the same curriculum as boys), and waiving its modest fees so that all who showed merit and motivation could attend, regardless of means. These changes made the colégio a unique institution for its time and the model on which the nation's public high schools were to be built.

Under the direction of Anísio Teixeira and Joaquim Faria Góes—both graduates of the Columbia Teachers College and both inspired by the U.S. secondary education system—vocational schools also aimed for the middle ground. Teixeira intended to add a classical curriculum on par with the colégio's to each school. This way, students had a choice between classical and vocational education, and vocational students still received an academically strengthened education. What is more, elements of North American high school culture, such as extracurricular clubs, student newspapers, and self-government were introduced.

Teixeira's project failed. A lack of space and resources prevented the classical courses from being introduced in all but two of the schools—and the schools where it existed charged tuition for the classical programs. Funds for school system expansion were directed toward primary education, so only one new secondary school was built. Capacity increased only modestly, and by the end of the Vargas era only a few thousand students were enrolled in the city's secondary vocational schools. Finally, the aspects of North American student culture that were introduced, especially self-government, were abandoned amid widespread criticism for inciting anarchy, class struggle, and communism. By the end of Teixeira's administration, little had been accomplished to build a public secondary school system in the city.

The lesson to be drawn from the reforms of the 1930s was that efforts to elevate the prestige, status, and power of lower-class institutions, such as vocational schools, were rejected by conservative segments of the society as subversive and anarchic. By contrast, efforts to expand access to elite institutions, such as the Colégio Pedro II, were lauded. What was at stake were rival conceptions of the flow of power in a democratic society. If democracy meant transferring power to subaltern groups, it was unacceptable. On the other hand, allowing subaltern groups to share in the existing social order strengthened and validated the nation's hierarchies. Indeed, youths from the city's growing working-class and poor neighborhoods competed aggressively and applied themselves feverishly to take advantage of the opportunity the colégio offered to share in managing the social order. The record of student participation in the school reflects the endeavor of thousands of youths attempting to profit from the resources made available by the regime. Students at the colégio endorsed the dictates of social discipline, nationalism, and ethnicity propagated during the Vargas era because they believed those dictates were the key to admission into the cadre of elites. An examination of student culture at the colégio reveals a collective embrace of the regime and its promise of growing opportunity.

"SEMINARY OF NATIONHOOD"

Founded in 1837 in the building of a former Franciscan orphanage, the colégio was one of the jewels of the imperial crown. It was a finishing school for the nation's nobility and a recruiting ground for the imperial bureaucracy. It also was a favorite haunt of Dom Pedro II, who not only attended its graduation ceremonies but at times even sat in on its classes. With the advent of the Republic, the school's mission changed. It remained an elite men's school, but under the federal education reform authored by Benjamin Constant it became a model school for the nation's private secondary schools—secular and parochial alike. In order to receive accreditation for their diplomas, secondary schools had to adopt the Colégio Pedro II curriculum.[7]

During the Empire and Republic, the school educated many of Brazil's leaders. Its graduates included presidents Rodrigues Alves, Nilo Peçanha, Hermes da Fonseca, and Washington Luis.[8] A diploma from the colégio was a first step for many of the most important politicians, military figures, and businessmen. Its prestigious role as model school made the Colégio Pedro II one of the preeminent places to teach in the country. Being a chaired professor meant guiding instruction in a given field throughout the country. Moreover, salaries were good—usually kept at parity with the salary of army colonels. Teachers were classified into three ranks: *catedráticos*, or chaired professors; *livre-docentes*, who were permanent faculty; and *assistentes*, who were hired on fixed-term contracts. Competition for a *cátedra* was fierce.

Counted among the *catedráticos* were some of the top educators of the era. In the late 1920s and early 1930s the school's faculty included Jonathas Serrano, Henrique Dodsworth, Raja Gabaglia, Carneiro Leão, Francisco Venancio Filho, and Delgado de Carvalho, who in 1927 was a professor of English who organized and held the first chair of sociology at the colégio and was the school's director during the Revolution of 1930.[9]

Jonathas Serrano authored some of the most widely used high school history books, *History of Civilization* and *Epitome of Brazilian History*. He was also a leading member of the Historical and Geographic Institute and was a member of the National Schoolbook Commission, which in the 1940s reviewed each high school text in print in Brazil to compile a list of MES-recognized books. He was also influential in Catholic circles, and he served as one of the rare bridges between the Church and the New School.

Henrique Dodsworth was a math professor who directed the school from 1931 to 1933 and later became interventor of Rio. Carneiro Leão, a prominent *escolanovista* (adherent of Dewey's—and Teixeira's—New School) who directed and reformed Rio's school system between 1922 and 1926, taught French. Francisco Venancio Filho, yet another *escolanovista*, taught philosophy and directed the Institute of Education at the end of the Estado Novo. Venancio Filho, Delgado de Carvalho, Carneiro Leão, and Raja Gabaglia all also taught at the Institute of Education. The institute and the colégio were the two most important schools in not only the city but the nation. These educators had a keen sense that their work served as a model for the nation.

Textbooks written by professors at the colégio were almost guaranteed success. Given the cost of printing and the small number of secondary schools, books adopted by the colégio often became the only texts available. Most textbooks from the Republican era bore the phrase "Adopted by the Colégio Pedro II" under the title. This was sometimes substituted with the phrase "of Colégio Pedro II" under the name of the author, a usage that in the 1930s was restricted by the colégio and the MES, allowing only *catedráticos* to use the school's name on their publications, and denying the host of visiting, substitute, or assistant professors the prestigious—and remunerative—title.

This situation changed almost immediately after Vargas came to power. The new MES assumed responsibility for the national secondary school curriculum. Course requirements were developed by Minister Francisco Campos in the 1931 reform that bore his name, then submitted to congress to be made into law. The Campos reform skirted most of the nation's educational system by affecting only classical secondary schools. It replaced the staid emphasis on the classics that had endured since the Empire, and it placed a new stress on the sciences to prepare elites to meet the technical and technological exigencies of the modernizing nation.[10]

Thus with Vargas's rise to power the Colégio Pedro II jumped into yet another role. It remained a model school but the meaning of that model changed. Stripped of its role in guiding the national curriculum, it instead became the symbolic model of what a school should do, how its students should behave, and what they should aspire to. As the director of the school during the Vargas years, Raja Gabaglia professed at the school's 150th anniversary ceremony in 1937 that the Colégio Pedro II was the "seminary of nationhood."[11]

The colégio's new role characterized politics during the Vargas era, especially in its authoritarian years. In the corporatist political environment of the 1930s and 1940s, the students of this school represented the students of all schools, and the school symbolized all that could be achieved with the educational resources of the era. It boasted the best faculty in the nation, and the school's diploma remained the standard to which all others were measured. The minister of education never missed the colégio's graduation exercises, and its halls were a stage for major speeches about education policy, nationalism, or the race.

The inherently political role of the colégio was not lost on its students and faculty. Motivated and disciplined, they nonetheless reacted to the broader political currents of the era. For instance, in 1932, during the constitutionalist revolt that pitted São Paulo against the federal government in a bitter siege waged over demands for constitutional democracy, students of the colégio raised the São Paulo flag from the corner window of the school, overlooking the busy Avenida Marechal Floriano. Periodic incidents of antagonism by colégio faculty toward the regime were recorded by the MES, which kept a tight grip on the school.

Characteristic of the national security state that Vargas presided over after 1934, Filinto Müller's DESPS and the MES both had informants among the students and faculty of the colégio. According to one student, "the colégio was spied on widely."[12] In 1941, for instance, Captain Batista Teixeira of the DESPS informed Raja Gabaglia about an impending student demonstration against matriculation fees for the city's vocational secondary schools and the Colégio Pedro II. Teixeira told Raja Gabaglia that the DESPS believed that "the student movement is secretly guided by communist elements," and ordered Raja Gabaglia to prohibit students from participating in the demonstration. Raja Gabaglia loathed such interference in his school. He replied that his students were not responsible for the demonstration and insisted that "at the Colégio . . . perfect discipline reigns. There does not exist any perturbing element . . . the students are all guided by the most elevated civic principles as they have been set by the distinguished Chief of the Nation."[13]

While motivated students like those at the colégio could easily be disciplined into serving as a model for the nation, the autonomy of catedráticos was troublesome for the MES. An unsigned document sent to Capanema discussed the existence of an anti-Vargas faction within the school's faculty. As the anonymous informant charged: "The Colégio Pedro II is currently a hive of discontent with the government. Within the school, people speak out loudly and extensively against the regime of Brazilian renovation, of its leaders, and especially against President Vargas and his dignified wife. . . . It is sufficient to spend a few days among the faculty of the model school . . . to immediately feel the repulsion they feel toward everything related to the government." The informant wrote that the recent Escola Militar and Jewish holiday episodes characterized the disdain that the school's chaired faculty exhibited toward the regime's priorities. He insisted that the only solution was to hire faculty on "a contract lasting only as long as they serve appropriately."[14]

Faculty and student autonomy came from several factors. Secondary education remained primarily an elite space, so greater intellectual freedom was tolerated. Raja Gabaglia's presence was also an important bulwark of the school's autonomy: he repeatedly confronted not only institutional and ideological crises but also all nature of personal attacks—accusations that he was a pederast or a reptile or a fascist or anti-Catholic.[15] By surviving these attacks, he showed a strong hand over the school's sensitive political situation. When necessary, he invoked his proximity to the Vargas family. But the defense that he invoked most frequently was his insistence that the students of the colégio were a veritable paragon of discipline and nationalist feelings. The behavior of students at the colégio was a fundamental reason that the school enjoyed such a rare degree of institutional autonomy so close to the foci of political power. Acts of indiscipline were rare—and when they occurred they were sternly punished. Student culture reflected a spirited acceptance and endorsement of the Vargas regime's political and ideological agenda, witnessed in student newspapers, school activities, and extracurricular endeavors.

EYE ON THE PRIZE: STUDENTS AT THE COLÉGIO

The existence of a student body at the colégio that had so much to gain from the Vargas regime was symptomatic of broader transformations in Brazilian society that preceded the Revolution of 1930. The school's shift reflected an evolution in the role of education underway since the 1920s. When the school was organized as the "model school" at the end of the nineteenth century, 80 percent of Brazilians were illiterate. Secondary education was a privilege available only to a small elite. Mario Augusto Teixeira de Freitas's 1946 study of twenty-four year olds showed that across Brazil only 4 percent had finished secondary schooling.[16]

In the 1920s, changes in the meaning of education were etched into the school's enrollment. The colégio began accepting women and catered to a more popular audience. Both public and private education became more prevalent, and the growing network of private secondary schools absorbed an increasing number of elite children. Unlike the public school system, many of the private schools were quite conservative. In 1933, during the debate over education in the constitutional convention, for example, the conservative Syndicate of Brazilian Educators lobbied against the "propaganda of misdirected schoolteachers . . . [and acted] against the pernicious elements that until now have been tolerated in important government positions." This attack, directed against the Pioneers of the New School, counted with the support of thirty-nine private schools, many of them Catholic.[17]

As the elite student body of the colégio migrated to private schools, their spaces were taken by middle-class and working-class children. Their families took advantage of the school as an affordable path toward the social advancement of their children, enrolling them in the Externato, or day school of the colégio, which also maintained the Internato, or boardingschool. The Externato was the main campus and model-school component of the twin schools. The Internato shared the same faculty and curriculum, but it was smaller, remained all male, and catered as much to students from outside Rio as it did to students from the city. The Internato's choice to remain all male characterized the growing division between the schools.

The Internato's students changed from being the children of families wealthy enough to send their children away to the capital for their education to being something of an orphanage for children of elite families who had lost one or both parents. This was a much smaller change in the nature of the student body than took place in the Externato, which became a large, urban, and coeducational high school increasingly catering to the popular classes. The Internato was a more conservative institution whose identity and pedagogy changed little over the course of the century, a difference that became more pronounced until the Internato was closed after its building burned down in the early 1960s. By this time, the Internato remained a small boys' boardingschool, while the Externato had expanded to four campuses across the city.

The 1936 yearbook of the Internato reflects the conservative, elite culture that the school retained in the Vargas years (see table 6). Half of the students were at least partially orphaned, and nearly half (44 percent) were from Rio. A majority of students wanted to pursue military careers.[18] Students were described in such terms as "passionately loves Brazil," "is an exalted patriot," "will become a great scientist," or "imagines himself to be Captain Blood." The yearbook also records the regrets of two students who did not go into the military because of poor eyesight or "adverse circumstances."[19] Students were

Table 6. Internato Graduating Class, 1936

Student	Place of Birth	Parents	Career
Aloisio Nobrega	Rio de Janeiro state	Both dead	Law
Albano Gouvea da Rocha	Rio de Janeiro state	Doctors	Medicine
Alberto Chanon	Federal District	Father dead	Military
Egas Moniz A. de Barros	Minas Gerais	Live in Rio	Medicine
Ernesto Bandeira de Luna	Federal District	Father dead	Military academy
Eurico de Oliveira Assis	São Paulo	Father dead	Industrial chemist
Fernando R. de Alencar	Rio Grande do Sul	Admin.	Military academy
Germano Valente	Rio de Janeiro state	Living	Naval academy
Hervé Berlandez Pedrosa	Rio de Janeiro state	Living	War college
Jesus Bello Galvão	Maranhão	Father dead	Military academy
José Benedicto de Oliveira	Minas Gerais	Living	School of mines
José Maria Pinto Duarte	Federal District	Both dead	Military
José Marques Nogueira Filho	Federal District	Living	—
Luis Felipe A. de Barros	Minas Gerais	Live in Rio	Military academy
Luis Fernado G. Labouriau	Federal District	Dr. father dead	Agronomy
Luiz Edmundo C. Marcondes	Rio de Janeiro state	Doctor	Naval engineering
Marcondes G. de Oliveira	Minas Gerais	Father dead	Military
Moyses Chanon	Federal District	Father dead	Military academy
Muricy Alves Peçanha	Rio de Janeiro state	Father dead	Agronomy
Nelson de Barros Galvão	São Paulo	Father dead	Engineering
Nelson Ranucci Peres	Federal District	Living	Naval academy
Nelson de Salles Pereira	Rio de Janeiro state	Father dead	Industrial chemist
Newton de Oliveira Ribeiro	Federal District	Living	Military engineering
Olindo Mury Knust	Rio de Janeiro state	Living	Industrial chemist
Orlando Pereira do E. Santo	Federal District	Father dead	Military academy
Thryso da Silva Gomes	Itararé, SP	Doctor father	Military academy
Zilmar Pontes Ramos	Paraiba	Doctor father	Naval engineering

Source: "Turma de 1936—Colégio Pedro II, Internato." Colégio Pedro II Archive, São Cristovão Branch.

tracked into military careers by the directors of the Internato. As Director Clóvis Monteiro indicated in his report on the school to Capanema in 1943, the Internato's students "are ready to leave for public service, for commerce, for industry, to higher education and above all to our armed classes."[20]

Only one of the students in the yearbook had clearly identifiable African features. Aloisio Nobrega, an orphan, was described in the most glowing language used for any student. His description read: "Aloisio is the most noteworthy personality of our class. Endowed with a brilliant intelligence and a rare level of general culture, he has long held the respect and admiration of his classmates. He is a great soul, a dreamer, with great kindness and patience, destined to live in a better world than this one. . . . Throughout the secondary program, he was the most distinguished student in the class, obtaining the highest grades in all exams."[21] The exuberant language Aloisio's classmates used to describe him gave reason to those among them who denied the existence of racial prejudice within the school. That he was the only one of twenty-seven graduating students who was black points to the continued role of the Internato as a school for elites. Although barriers to the admission of afrodescendant children to the Internato may not have existed, plenty of barriers prevented them from entering the social ranks from which students of the Internato were drawn.

By contrast, over the course of the 1920s the Externato increasingly played the role of a large public high school. Tuition was low compared with private schools. In the early 1930s, the colégio charged an annual fee equivalent to the monthly minimum wage. All but the poorest families could afford the school, and for those who were too poor other measures were available. Many students paid tuition in monthly installments. Many others received tuition waivers. Raja Gabaglia expanded the number of waiver students and personally interviewed each admitted student who requested the waiver, assessing their financial need and paternalistically distributing the benefits. He also sought donations from businesses for an endowment that paid for uniforms, shoes, books, and supplies for the poorer children.[22] One student who received the waivers and materials recalled that the assistance was given discreetly in order to avoid stigmatizing the students who received it and thus minimize the significance of social difference within the school.[23]

The colégio increasingly became one of the few mechanisms of social mobility through education available in the city. The school embraced this role, expanding class sizes and offering night courses. By 1933, the school had exhausted the physical capacity of its ancient building, having already divided the students into morning and afternoon sessions. This left room for expansion to meet the growing demand only by opening a night session. As Director Henrique Dodsworth explained, "since the Colégio Pedro II is the

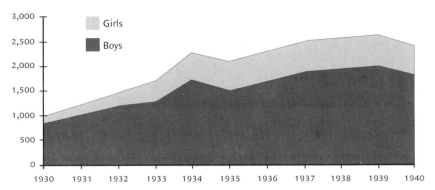

CHART 8. Enrollment in the Colégio Pedro II, Externato, 1930–1940. Source: "Relatório sucito de ocorrências e atividades verificadas no *Externato do Colégio Pedro II*," 1940, Gustavo Capanema Collection, CPDOC, 35.10.18g (130).

secondary institution that has the lowest tuition, and offers the best education—the demand for the third session is already guaranteed." The night classes boosted school enrollment from 1,457 to 1,947. By the end of the decade, the colégio would pack over 2,500 students into its cramped classrooms.[24] In these years, the colégio transformed itself from a small, elite men's seminary into a coeducational institution of mass education.

At the time of the Revolution of 1930, 14 percent of the Externato's students were women. By 1934, this number climbed to about 25 percent, where it remained through 1940 (see chart 8). While women continued to constitute a minority of students, the institution was plainly coeducational. Except for premilitary and physical education classes, the students were integrated in the classrooms and the curriculum. The Colégio Pedro II, which had been founded on the principle of training future leaders, provided the same training to both boys and girls in the Vargas era.

Matriculation records of the 1931 fifth-year class and the 1932 second-year class reveal the diversity of students at the colégio. The fifth-year class, which would have begun its studies in the last years of the Republic, characterized the transformation of the school into a more socially and economically representative institution. Students from the suburbs, areas that were almost entirely poor and working class, comprised 25 percent of total students. What is more, a third of all students studied for free, not even paying the small token tuition. Most of the students who attended for free were not even from the suburbs—they were the working poor who lived in such affluent neighborhoods as Tijuca, Botafogo, and Copacabana.[25]

Together, students from the suburbs and poor students from primarily affluent areas constituted almost half of the students at the colégio. This trend toward a poorer and more suburban student body accelerated over time, as the 1932 survey of the students who entered at the time of the Revolution of 1930 reveals. The number of students from the suburbs increased from one-quarter to one-third of the class. One student, Odette Ferreira da Silva, was from the Morro do Pinto favela. When she was born in 1917, the idea of a girl from a favela attending the Colégio Pedro II must have seemed impossible. Indeed, the Morro do Pinto was the site of photographer Augusto Malta's commentary about children who had no access to schooling (see chapter 4). What is more, her family paid the full tuition. The colégio was perhaps not proportionately representative, but its socioeconomic diversity was extraordinary for its time.[26]

The fact that students from all parts of the city, and therefore from all social classes, attended the colégio did not mean that the school was easily accessible. In Rio, only a tenth of children who enrolled in elementary school completed their elementary studies. Among those who completed elementary school, few went on to secondary school because of the scarcity of affordable public schools. Those who wanted to attend the Colégio Pedro II had to pass rigorous entrance exams to compete for scarce seats. Each year the school grew in size, but could not keep pace with demand. In 1933, for instance, of over 1,000 candidates, 717 were admitted.[27]

For many, the difficulty of attending the colégio only began with admission. For students traveling from the suburbs, a lengthy train ride on the Central do Brasil or the Leopoldina rail lines was a daily ritual that could take more than two hours. In the rainy season, students from areas such as Jacarepaguá, Bento Ribeiro, and Bangú had to negotiate flooded dirt roads on foot from their homes to the train station, and only then begin the two-hour train ride to the city center. Even today, asphalt roads with modern drainage are washed out completely by rains that in the 1930s completely cut off entire neighborhoods from the rest of the city.

Despite the ordeals they endured on the way to school, once these children arrived their uniforms and appearance had to be neat, clean, and disciplined. What is more, the school's disciplinary code applied uniformly to students whenever and wherever they wore their uniforms. The simple difficulty of going to school may explain why, in 1942, two students attacked a trolley conductor. Newton de Oliveira, a second-year student was immediately caught by the police and released to the school, while Nelson Romar was later identified in school by the trolley driver. Raja Gabaglia suspended both of them for six days for behavior "that was damaging to the good name of the Colégio Pedro II."[28]

Acts of indiscipline were rare. Each year a few incidents were reported in the "Register of Disciplinary Penalties." These were mostly minor incidents such as the suspension of night-student Euler Cruz for "blocking students and preventing them from entering their classes."[29] In all, the students were self-disciplined and took full advantage of the educational opportunity they were offered. Most stayed in school to complete their degree because at this stage the tangible rewards of the degree were a powerful lure. The students of the Vargas era came from economically mixed backgrounds but shared a common intention to profit from their education.

RACE AT THE COLÉGIO PEDRO II

Despite the endeavors by directors of the colégio to expand access to the school, the obstacles students of color faced within city elementary schools meant that few made it into Pedro II. Norma Fraga, a woman of color who attended the colégio between 1942 and 1947, recalled the presence of only one other student of color in her class, also female. All of the teachers were white, although a few of the discipline monitors and some of the school staff were of color, she recalled.[30] The fact that the Colégio Pedro II was an almost totally white institution does not mean that race was not significant in the functioning of the school or school culture. Nor does it mean that the meaning of race was experienced only by those occasional students of color who attended the colégio. To the contrary, as an elite model institution the colégio's culture reflected the relationships between race, nationhood, and discipline that characterized citizenship and social ascension in the Vargas era.

Issues of two student newspapers show how some students at the colégio reproduced elite ideology about eugenics and the creation of the "race." The October 1932 edition of the newspaper *Pronome* was dedicated to "Anti-Alcohol Week." Beginning October 3, the "Anti-Alcohol Week" was a national campaign to draw attention to the evils of alcohol and to agitate for adoption of a "dry law," bringing the prohibition of alcohol from the United States to Brazil. As the editorial board of *Pronome* expressed: "The editors of *Pronome* did not want to pass up the opportunity to cooperate with the eugenics of our race, which will never go forward if we do not achieve the abolition of sales of alcoholic beverages in our country."[31]

Each article detailed the pernicious effects of alcohol not only on the drinker but on their progeny and the race. The issue was shot through with imagery, metaphors, and theses appropriated from the hygiene and eugenics movements. It linked alcoholism with tuberculosis, and it repeated leading hygienist Belissário Penna's declaration that alcohol was the "demon of humanity." Tapping the language of eugenics, the paper argued that "in all respects: physically, morally, psychologically, alcohol destroys and degrades man. Its malevolent action does not only manifest itself in the individual: it is transmitted to the Species."[32]

The first issue of *O Arauto*, which appeared in April 1931, brought the same perspective to a broader array of topics. The names of the editors of the paper, Lycio de Carvalho, Seme Jazbik, Alfredo Tranjan, and Jacob Goldberg, embodied the foreign and Jewish influences that alarmed Capanema, yet the newspaper's content would have reassured the minister. For instance, the newspaper helped shape a corporatist identity for students complementary to the school's role as model: It was "destined to defend the interests of the student class, and principally, the interests of the students of the Colégio Pedro II."[33] The idea of a student class echoed the corporatist social order promoted by the Vargas regime, in which the rights of individuals flowed from their status as members of a group. This was intended to depoliticize the public by limiting political voice to officially recognized outlets. Thus, workers in a type of industry were represented by a single union before the Ministry of Labor, and the leadership of that union possessed the entire political voice of its members. *O Arauto* adopted a similar voice on behalf of all students, and the students of the colégio in particular.

The types of issues *O Arauto* raised illustrates the conservative and assimilationist language employed by students of the colégio. The main issue addressed in the paper was a demand for physical education facilities and programs in the school. Over the course of four issues, physical education was the subject of three separate articles and one editorial. Francisco Campos's 1931 secondary school reform mandated physical education, but reflecting the frequent lag between federal policy and practice no program had been instituted in the colégio. The students writing for O Arauto employed a full array of eugenic and racial discourse in their endeavor to have both physical education and athletic facilities provided for the school. Their call for physical education reflects the currency among students of the colégio of the eugenic arguments, even as physical education was first becoming a part of the federal education agenda.

In the first issue of O Arauto, students called for the hiring of a physical education instructor, arguing that students of the colégio had "weak physical development." Although there were physically fit exceptions, "the vast majority is comprised of weaklings with reduced thoracic capacity, bad posture, and some of them even growing bellies. And this is among people who are studying to tomorrow become one of the vital forces of the Fatherland. It is deeply alarming!" Thoracic capacity was one of the standard anthropometric measures by which eugenic vitality was assessed. It is remarkable that such technical terms from the science of eugenics had become commonplace among these students.[34]

Students argued that the lack of physical activity during the school day meant that the inadequate meals students had at home were not appropriately digested. The result was that their classmates "wind up weak and stunted . . . giving reason to those who say Brazil is a vast hospital." This was the hygienist and eugenic battle cry of the 1920s, appropriated by students as an argument for the school to take eugenic measures on their behalf. Their argument for physical education also adopted the common tendency of pointing to more developed nations: "We relegate physical education to an inferior plain, even though it is regarded as a vital problem to the more advanced nations of the world."[35]

The second issue of O Arauto built on the corporatist message by describing the "solidarity to a patriotic task . . . supported by our colleagues." The corporatist message was infused with an incipient generational identity. The introductory editorial declared that "the current generation, modern, dynamic, achieving, cannot and should not fall short of the confidence that is placed upon it and that results of the evolution of modernity."[36] The editorial echoed the optimism unleashed by the Revolution of 1930 that had taken place six months earlier. The student writers saw themselves as the dynamic agents of the nation's modernization, and represented themselves as the product of the revolution.

The issue again took up the question of physical education. To their previous arguments for physical education, the second issue added the endorsement for the idea expressed by the students of the colégio as a whole: "We are justified in our insistence on this matter by the interest that our last article . . . awoke in the hearts of our colleagues. A formidable number of students . . . gave us their whole and unconditional support for a campaign to reinstitute bodily education at the colégio." The students applauded Minister Campos for mandating the discipline, and they turned to the revolution as yet another reason for physical education: "Remember, Mr. Director, that you are the first director of the colégio since the revolution. Since the revolution is a project of regeneration and reconstruction, and since you are the person responsible for this project in the colégio, it is your duty to reconstruct and regenerate the colégio morally, materially, and physically."[37] Students of the colégio were not only versed in theories of eugenics, they related the themes of nationalism, eugenics, and education in ways that paralleled elite political discourse.

Physical education was the single most recurring theme of the newspaper. In the fifth issue, the editors reported that school director Delgado de Carvalho had agreed that "intellectual development depends on physical development," but that the school lacked athletic facilities. O Arauto continued its campaign, consulting Dr. Oliveira Santos, "our great friend, one of the leading figures in the world of sports, vice-president of Flamengo [soccer club]," about the potential for building athletic facilities on a lot adjoining the school. Santos replied that an adjoining lot would make a fine basketball court, which in turn would be suited to other physical educational activities as well.[38]

Director Delgado de Carvalho promised to seek money for a basketball court, and the newspaper optimistically predicted that "soon we will officially be able to practice sports, as is done in the educational institutions of the most advanced nations of the world."[39] A few years later a basketball court was built in the lot these students identified. The court was the main construction project conducted at the school during the Vargas era: physical education finally found a permanent place in the colégio. The director's report on the administration of the school from 1930 to 1940 gave as a motive for the establishment of physical education "the movement 1930," echoing the call issued by *O Arauto* nine years earlier.[40]

The newspaper also reported on the activities of the premilitary training program at the school. An article on a swearing of allegiance to the flag drew the commentary that "to the new reservists at the Externato Pedro II, *O Arauto* offers our most sincere congratulations," and it reprinted the text of the convocation speech that called on students to "love the Fatherland and the family, with the ends of making Brazil grandiose and strong."[41] Such nationalistic themes recurred, and the activities of the students in the premilitary program were a regular feature of the newspaper.

One of the few advertisements in *O Arauto* announced a conference on eugenics: "[In] the course in Brazilian Studies at the Nationalist Center, Mr. M. Pinto will give a lecture on the study of Eugenics, having examined the theories of Mendel on heredity."[42] This advertisement is curious in that it announced a lecture on Mendelian genetics, which, according to Nancy Stepan, "tended to be marginal until the late 1930s."[43] It is therefore remarkable that students of the Colégio Pedro II were counted among the few Brazilians who were not only conversant in the technical aspects of the dominant eugenic theories but could also access the scientific countertendencies of the movement. It is also noteworthy that the advertisement presumed that high school students, even at the exceptional colégio, would be interested in attending lectures on Mendel, heredity, or eugenics, and that the organizers of the lecture would seek out the presence of such students.

The impression student newspapers give is that students of the colégio had an intellectual, social, and cultural environment that was infused with eugenic racial and nationalist discourse largely similar to that which characterized the most erudite scientific, medical, and intellectual discourse on the "race" in Brazil. Regardless of their class of origin, students at the colégio were, by their very presence at the institution, invited into a role as builders of the nation. They were invited to lectures on the scientific underpinnings of eugenics, they published newspapers, and they sustained a dialogue about the need for the tools of eugenics in their school. At least some students, like the contributors to O Arauto and Pronome, embraced this role in all of its eugenic, disciplinary, and nationalistic forms.

Eugenic practices also worked their way into the colégio's administration in much the same way as in the city's public schools. In 1933, the director of the colégio's medical service, Dr. Severino Gasparini, began keeping records of students' health, their eating habits and nutrition, and their biometric and morpho-physiological development. These records were organized "on the same basis as in the army." Their multiple uses also corresponded with the work done by the Rio school system: "They are destined to both the medical examination of students, and to laboratory research."[44] Because the data set that could be collected by the colégio was insufficient for setting developmental norms, it would be compared with that collected by the YMCA, using the same methods.

Concern with questions of degeneracy and eugenic development permeated the Colégio Pedro II. Like other school systems, its medical service was guided by eugenic principles about hygiene, nutrition, and anthropometric development. To a much greater extent than in the city's public schools, students were fluent in the currents and countercurrents of eugenics. The physical education programs in the colégio were as plainly eugenic as those of the city's public schools, but their development arose more from student pressure than from federal directives. What is more, student advocacy of physical education was correctly phrased in the eugenic and nationalistic language that was used in elite circles.

The discourses of degeneracy and eugenics logically extended past student culture and school health—they were an important element of the school's curriculum; figured prominently in the textbooks colégio professors wrote; and entered into the contests for cátedras, when these arose. Two of the leading professors at the school, Raja Gabaglia and Jonathas Serrano, were also the authors of the principle geography and history textbooks. Jonathas Serrano's two main books, History of Civilization and Epitome of Brazilian History, took a nationalistic, Catholic, and Eurocentric perspective.

The fifth edition of History of Civilization, published in 1939, dealt with non-European civilizations only as phenomena of the premodern era. The modern era was a Eurocentric progression of national organization and technological development, culminating with a 1933 speech by Franklin Roosevelt about the need for world peace, as well as with the rise of fascism in Italy. Serrano described fascism sympathetically: "In a decade fascism has built Italy into a respectable power, with a first-rate army, navy, and airforce, and extraordinary enthusiasm for developing all of the resources of the country, as well as admiration for the man who has realized such a spectacular transformation." The book ends with a quotation by Mussolini: "The Fatherland is not an illusion: it is the greatest, the most human, the purest of realities."[45]

This conservative and nationalist tone carried over to the *Epitome of Brazilian History*, which excerpted much of the Brazilian history content from the five volumes of *History of Civilization*. This book was largely based on the Catholic/Portuguese historical experience. The section on slavery and African influence not only characterizes the Eurocentric perspective of the work but shows the degree of penetration that the stereotypes and sentimental images of Brazil's slaveocratic past had within Brazilian education during the very years that Freyre synthesized them into his classic works.

Throughout the book, afrodescendants were regarded largely as an exotic object, foreign to the reader, who was constructed by the text's voice as white. The section titled "The Black Contribution to Our Medium" cited the image of the *mãe preta* (roughly, "mammy") as "a moving fact of our domestic and social history." Alongside the *mãe preta* he added other influences: "Superstition, love for music and dance, a certain 'creole negligence,' heroic resignation in the face of misery, a fatalistic and lighthearted attitude in regard to work—these are some of the more or less favorable qualities we have inherited from the blacks."[46] Afrodescendants were treated as an element of the past, from which the white author and readers inherited certain characteristics of laziness and superstition that echoed Arthur Ramos's theory about the prelogical nature of Afro-Brazilian culture.

Serrano also presented a romanticized image of slavery. He acknowledged the harshness of slavery only to establish that the way Africans "huddled together without hygiene" resulted in their degeneracy. That done, he quickly moved to redeem the behavior of slave masters: "It is fair to say though that in Brazil the black was generally happier and less degraded than in other countries, including the North American colonies. Often the slave became dear to the masters and above all to the children." What was more, he argued, Catholic tradition and Portuguese law allowed religious instruction, baptism, and even marriage.[47]

Serrano glorified the Brazilian slave regime and relegated afrodescendants to anachronistic historical roles: "The black retempered the white race that came to America. The historic race being created undeniably profited greatly from African blood."[48] This passage contained the double meaning that black workers helped forge the nation and that black blood mixed into the nation's dominant European stock strengthened and adapted it to its new tropical civilization. Anthropologist Edgar Roquette Pinto worked closely with Serrano on some of his textbooks, an influence evident in the idea that miscegenation contributed to the health of the nation.

Abolition was naturally treated by Serrano as a white movement of charity. After giving a litany of legislation on the slave trade and a discussion of the gradual process of abolition, the chapter on slavery and Afro-Brazilian influences closes with a series of essay questions. As cast by Serrano, abolition was the result of a civic awakening on behalf of whites that only tangentially included or affected slaves. The questions are indicative of the passive role Serrano depicted for afrodescendants:

> I—Compare the indigenous element with the African and demonstrate the importance of each in our history.
> II—Demonstrate with examples that the abolitionist campaign was led by distinguished men of letters.
> III—Assess the consequences of abolition not only for the masters but also for the freed slaves themselves.[49]

For Serrano, and as a distinctive element of the leading high school history textbooks in Brazil, afrodescendants were marginalized into one-dimensional stereotypes, as a presence of the past and as a people who held a back seat in their own destiny. The discussion questions he proposes actively steered students away from slave resistance and compelled a reading of both slavery and abolition that centered on the free-white historical experience.

As a Catholic and a nationalist, Serrano wrote glowingly of the Vargas regime. He described the Revolution of 1930 as "the greatest and most important [movement] of our nation's history." As told to high school students, the Vargas administration was a combination of nationalist will and political genius: "President Getúlio Vargas knew how to increase constantly his personal prestige both within and outside Brazil, understanding how to unite energy and serenity, prudence and fearlessness, choosing dedicated and capable auxiliaries, revealing himself to be an administrator of exceptional moral character." He praised Vargas for advances in social policy and national organization, strengthening the military, and for being committed to visiting each region of the country so as to understand Brazil as a whole. In doing this Serrano echoed Alberto Tôrres.[50]

Reflecting the change in political currents, the closing passage of the book dealt with pan-Americanism. A speech by Vargas stressed the common objectives of the American nations, traced the idea of an "American system" back to José Bonifácio, and praised the diplomat Rio Branco for having realized it. Students learned that pan-Americanism was a Brazilian tradition. This closing theme to the book published in 1941 represents a dramatic break from the praise of Mussolini that appeared in the 1939 edition of *History of Civilization*. As the political currents of the Vargas era changed, the major textbooks followed suit.[51]

Racial ideology was only a backdrop in Serrano's books. It was evident when he discussed such issues as slavery and abolition, but conspicuously absent as a factor in the formation of the nation, its economic progress, and recent modernization. The Brazil that Serrano depicted in *Epitome* was not unlike the Africa he described in *Civilization*: the two pages about Africa dealt exclusively with European explorers Stanley and Livingstone, not once making reference to African individuals, cultures, or nations. What is more, the only two pages on Africa were paired with two pages on the exploration of the uninhabited north and south poles, underscoring the marginality of Africans to the history of civilization.[52] The existence of Africans in Africa was a mute backdrop to the adventures of Europeans. Similarly, afrodescendants were passive protagonists in slavery and abolition, and were invisible elements to the rest of Brazilian history and culture.

In the geography textbook *Readings in Geography*, by contrast, Raja Gabaglia enjoined the question of environmental and climactic degeneracy head-on. The chapter titled "Health and Climate" explored the prevalence of ideas of tropical degeneracy in European scholarship. Such notions of tropical disease, suggesting that climates of certain latitudes presented a constant threat to health and civilization, were presented by Raja Gabaglia as a myth that Europe paid for economically and culturally: "The easy justifications of superiority that each assumes at the expense of others, fear of travel, unreliable information, and fantasy, are responsible for the inveterate error that has cost and continues to cost Europe serious colonial problems and considerable economic losses because of the prejudices and shortcomings that emerge from such legends."[53]

In *Readings*, Raja Gabaglia provided students with critical skills to assess both ideas about climate and degeneracy, and to weigh the relevance of European scholarship to the Brazilian situation. He excerpted sections of leading works on climate and degeneracy to demonstrate the evolution of the debate. He began with Buckle's description of Brazil as a verdant paradise that was so lush as to be uninhabitable: "In the midst of this pomp, this splendor of nature, there is no room for man." But, as Raja Gabaglia explained, once arguments that Brazil was uninhabitable were proven ridiculous, the prejudice found new grounds.[54]

Brazil turned from uninhabitable to unhealthy; but the argument of unhealthiness was "false like the others." Citing Afrânio Peixoto's *Hygiene*, Raja Gabaglia put forward the case that the "sanitary notion of climate" was yet another myth, because such diseases as cholera and tuberculosis do not discriminate by climate. There was no such thing as tropical diseases, according to Peixoto, "there are only preventable diseases, against which hygiene has means of defense and attack."[55]

Gabaglia excerpted passages of Yale University geographer Ellsworth Huntington's *The Climate Factor* as examples of this vision of degeneracy in the tropics. According to Huntington, "heat is related in significant ways to character." His view was that "anyone who has spent time in a tropical country— missionaries, colonial administrators—knows that religion, education, and good government bring great benefits to a people, but nothing can surpass the effect of the environment. The willpower, industriousness, and self-confidence of people from temperate climates can only be repeated slowly in tropical countries—so slowly it takes centuries." By contrast, "in a fortifying climate, being honest, sober and master of one-self is easier. . . . People in such a climate are more likely to be inventive, industrious and reforming." But Huntington also states that people born in tropical countries were not inherently inferior. Instead, when one meets a Venezuelan of strong character, that person is much more impressive than someone of equal character from, say, Ohio, given the enormous difficulties he has overcome: "Thus our Southern Nations deserve greater respect for their achievements than do those of the North."[56] By the 1930s, Ellsworth Huntington had become a straw man for Brazilian scholars who used his climatological determinism to stress the failure of foreign ideas to explain the national reality.

RIO DE JANEIRO'S VOCATIONAL SECONDARY SCHOOLS

The Colégio Pedro II was a privileged space in Vargas-era Brazil. Students who defied the disciplinary, nationalist rules of the regime faced severe penalties. Conversely, the reward for correct behavior was membership in an elite that received the nation's most prestigious secondary education and almost guaranteed admission to higher education. Wilson Choeri, Aloysio Barbosa, Norma Fraga, and Cecilia Teixeira all went on to study at the University of Brazil. In general, students at the Colégio kept up the spirit of Pedro II as a "seminary of nationhood" by embracing the eugenic language that prevailed in official circles. Together, the students, faculty, and directors of the Colégio Pedro II maintained an institutional culture that in turn maintained the school's role as a model of the ideal, emerging Brazil. Students at the Colégio Pedro II were permitted and expected to be partners in defending social values and social hierarchies; students in Rio's few vocational secondary schools were given little latitude for social ascension.

The idea of a democratic society employed by Anísio Teixeira's team demanded that all citizens receive the education necessary to develop "consciousness and capacity for personal progress."[57] This meant vocational education should be complemented with classical disciplines, and that students attending Rio's vocational schools should also have the option of earning a classical secondary degree. But for adherents of the New School, building a democratic society through education did not simply mean eroding the difference between vocational and intellectual education, but reversing centuries of work culture and notions of hierarchy conditioned by the institution of slavery.

For the Colégio Pedro II's directors, building a democratic society meant

Table 7. Public Secondary Schools in Rio de Janeiro in 1940

School	Type of Course	Students	Format
Amaro Cavalcanti	Commercial	Mixed	Externato
Bento Ribeiro	Vocational	Female	Externato
João Alfredo	Vocational	Male	Internato
Orsina da Fonseca	Vocational	Female	Int. and Ext.
Paulo de Frontin	Vocational/Classical	Female	Externato
Rivadavia Corrêa	Vocational/Classical	Female	Externato
Santa Cruz	Vocational/Classical	Mixed	Externato
Souza Aguiar	Vocational	Mixed	Externato
Visc. de Cayrú	Vocational/Classical	Male	Externato
Visc. de Mauá	Vocational/Agricultural	Male	Int. and Ext.

Source: I N E P, *Oportunidades de educação na capital do país (Informações sobre as escolas e cursos para uso de pais, professores e estudantes)* (Rio de Janeiro: Imprensa Nacional, 1941), 58–64; Anísio Teixeira, *Educação Pública: Sua organização e administração* (Rio de Janeiro: Oficina Gráfica do Depto. de Educação do Distrito Federal, 1935), 149.

expanding access to the traditional gateways to status and privilege. By contrast, in the city's vocational schools, the development of classical curricula both to complement and to compete with the vocational program eroded the class dichotomy that prevailed in work and education. Conservatives saw this as a radical measure. They tolerated—even encouraged—expanding educational opportunity from the top down, as at the Colégio Pedro II, because the results in terms of student discipline and the development of class identity did not threaten traditional hierarchies. But they saw expanding opportunity from the bottom up as an anarchic inversion of hierarchy: a means of empowering dangerous classes. Their reaction to reforms implemented in the city's commercial school, Escola Amaro Cavalcanti, underscores the threat that U.S. ideas of social democracy posed to their vision of Brazilian social order.

In 1930, Rio possessed fewer than a dozen vocational schools. These taught basic trades such as carpentry, metalworking, textiles, hat making, and graphic production. An audit of these programs indicated that their facilities were entirely unsuitable—shop machinery was outdated and improperly distributed among the schools. One school "is in a state of little efficiency," while another was described as being in "a precarious state, absolutely inefficient . . . we recommend its extinction." None received a favorable evalua-

Table 8. Enrollments in Public Secondary Schools, Rio de Janeiro

School	1931	1934	1942
Amaro Cavalcanti	782	770	610
Bento Ribeiro	292	285	542
João Alfredo	292	323	275
Orsina da Fonseca	220	302	604
Paulo de Frontin	478	544	326
Rivadavia Corrêa	414	477	521
Santa Cruz	—	260	224
Souza Aguiar	180	237	263
Visc. de Cayrú	187	182	305
Visc. de Mauá	221	416	933
Total	3,066	3,796 (+24%)	4,603 (+21%)

Sources: I N E P, *Oportunidades de educação na capital do país (Informações sobre as escolas e cursos para uso de pais, professores e estudantes)* (Rio de Janeiro: Imprensa Nacional, 1941), 58–64; Anísio Teixeira, *Educação Pública: Sua organização e administração* (Rio de Janeiro: Oficina Gráfica do Depto. de Educação do Distrito Federal, 1935), 149.

tion.[58] As tables 7 and 8 show, by 1930 these schools had a combined total of little over three thousand students, and these students were educated poorly.

These schools—inefficient, small, and disorganized—could hardly be considered a secondary education system. Each had a different constituency. The commercial school, Amaro Cavalcanti, attracted a mixed student body with wealthier students from Copacabana and Botafogo along with poor students from the center and suburbs. Meanwhile, three internatos performed basically as orphanages, which for the director of secondary education, Faria Góes, hindered the reform program. He complained: "Attempting to enroll students from a slightly higher class is almost taken as an insult by families—'Put my child in vocational school? A school for orphans and the children of my maid?'"[59]

At the turn of the century, vocational schools were trade schools for boys, as well as finishing schools for girls of modest means who learned needlework, sewing, and other "feminine" skills. Decades of neglect left most of the schools incapable of providing more than basic social welfare, such as the "school soup."[60] As Faria Góes lamented: "The schools comprised of such students are often a spectacle of sadness because of the malnutrition, tuberculosis, weakness, and deformity of almost all of them. The mental level of these children is, naturally, a reflection of this psycho-social state."[61]

When the Department of Education expanded the mission of the vocational schools it instituted new criteria for admission. Candidates had to pass entrance exams modeled on the rigorous exams used for the secondary school of the Institute of Education, and had to have completed elementary education (although the internatos continued to provide some elementary education, preserving their social assistance role for a small number of destitute children). The requirement of an elementary school diploma alone meant that fewer than 10 percent of students beginning elementary school would qualify. But probably the greatest obstacle to attending one of the city's secondary schools was that the three thousand to five thousand spaces that were available during the 1930s made the very existence of the schools irrelevant to the one hundred thousand teens living in the city.

Secondary schools grew in size, but not dramatically. One new school was installed in 1934 in one of the buildings of the Santa Cruz stockyards. But this was the only new public secondary school established in Rio during the Vargas era. In some of the existing schools capacity was added, and in little over a decade 50 percent more students were enrolled full time in the city's vocational schools. The combined number of students enrolled in the ten vocational schools in 1942 was slightly less than the combined total of the Colégio Pedro II and the high school of the Institute of Education. These schools were not only national models—they offered most of the public secondary educational options available in the federal capital. By contrast, the city offered so little in the way of secondary education as to be almost irrelevant. Its vocational schools meant more as an exercise of educational philosophy than they did as centers of learning for the city's residents.

Although the Teixeira administration did not succeed in expanding the vocational education system, school expansion would have meant "above all, satisfying the democratic imperative of offering the greatest number of educational opportunities to the Brazilian, and on the other hand, giving the different classes and occupations a sense of equivalence and prestige." Students would have a choice between classical and vocational studies, and vocational students would have their cultural level elevated by classical courses as well. This idea clashed with the traditional division between vocational and classical learning, which paralleled the social distinction between manual and intellectual work. According to Teixeira, these two secondary education systems "differ in their social and cultural objectives so much that they are instruments for social stratification and class difference that are viscerally undemocratic."[62] This division could be eliminated by holding both vocational and classical courses in the same schools.

For Faria Góes, director of secondary education, the problem with public secondary education in the 1930s stretched back to the beginnings of colonization, when the indigenous population proved unassimilable to forced labor systems, the white settlers shunned work, and Africans were introduced as the colony's producers. Work culture was permanently affected by the introduction of African slaves: "Labor was for slaves. The infamous condition of the enslaved black conferred to manual labor an inextinguishable stigma." The nation's social and economic development was tied to the exploitation of Africans, and the unproductive work culture that slavery made them develop: "Labor was previously for slaves. Now it is for the poor, the lower classes, the less capable."[63]

Faria Góes explained that abolition failed to reverse this problem, netting instead only in greater social and economic disorganization. Echoing Alberto Tôrres, Faria Góes lamented that "with abolition we destroyed in a single blow a centuries-old labor system, the whole economic base of the society.... Slaves were dazzled by their freedom." National prosperity depended on the "valorization of Brazilian manual labor." But the Republic's educational institutions had failed at this aim: "The Republic that emerged when black slavery was replaced with the enslavement of illiterates could not prevent the preservation of the old division into two castes, a division paradoxically maintained by education."[64] Faria Góes acknowledged that abolition meant no real change in the experience of afrodescendants, and that the educational system, rather than help erode differences, worked to sustain them.

The reformed vocational school system would valorize manual labor, stimulate critical thinking among its students, and build citizenship. Graduates of the vocational schools would not be performing the work of slaves, nor would they be performing work as slaves. Instead, they would be skilled workers and educated citizens—a class that would break the centuries-old dichotomy between master and slave, intellectual and menial. Not all workers were to belong to this class, but rather an elite of workers. Faria Góes explained: "We did not intend to give industrial and commercial courses the qualities they needed to train the elite of men of science and thought of the nation, but we intended to train that elite of the labor system that develops the material wealth of the country."[65]

The main aim of the campaign to elevate vocational education was to endow schools with classical courses that supplemented the vocational training or provided the chance of pursuing a full classical education at the school. By 1934, a lack of resources and teachers, as well as limitations in physical facilities, prevented the classical programs from being offered in any but two of the schools. Paulo de Frontin and Rivadavia Corrêa, both girls' schools, had classical programs taught at night by teachers from the secondary school of the Institute of Education.

In these schools vocational courses were supplemented with classical courses and with programs in physical education and hygiene (which were, indeed, being gradually incorporated in all the schools). These largely eugenic programs were particularly directed at female students: "Women, whether married or single, whatever their profession, and much more than men, lack an understanding of Hygiene—especially nutritional Hygiene—that super important (but lamentably disregarded) element of the perfection or decadence of the race." Prominent among the female hygiene courses was the theme of puericulture: "Women cannot neglect puericulture, for to do so risks annihilating all of the efforts invested in the infancy and future of the Nation."[66]

Although all of the students at these two girls' schools (about a thousand in all) benefitted from the introduction of classical courses to their vocational programs, those girls wishing to pursue the classical degree accredited by the MES had to pay tuition. These schools did not have budgets of the size of the Institute of Education's, and the school system could not afford even these two programs. Teixeira lamented: "It was necessary to charge a special fee for those students who wanted to take the federal curriculum, in order to pay for its accreditation."[67]

In 1940, the matriculation fee for vocational programs was Cr$15 (US$0.90) while the fee for the classical program was Cr$263 (US$16), greater than the monthly industrial minimum wage. Even the vocational course cost more than several days' industrial wage, but a textile worker paid at this rate would have to spend well over a month's wages to enroll their child in the classical program of the city's public schools, a fee not including the cost of books and other supplies.[68] Only the children of already skilled or professional workers were likely to be able to afford the "public" secondary education. Erasing the divisions between manual and intellectual work was not so easy.

What resulted from the reform, at least at the outset, was a greater disparity in educational opportunities between boys and girls. Among city high schools, the boys were already at a disadvantage because regulations maintained that they could comprise at most 10 percent of the Institute of Education's student body. The male vocational schools lagged years behind in developing their classical programs because of a combined lack of space and resources. By 1940, only one of the male vocational schools and one of the coeducational schools had been adapted to offer classical courses. Moreover, combined enrollment in the four female vocational schools (2,096) was higher in 1942 than in the male schools (2,000). And even in the mixed schools, female enrollment was higher (489 to 340).[69]

Male students were at a disadvantage in pursuing public secondary education in Rio. It may have been coincidental that the only two vocational schools that had the space for new classes were female schools. But even in the coeducational schools, female students predominated, comprising 60 percent of the student body. A teenage boy in Rio who could not afford a private secondary school had few options for continuing his education. He could compete for a space at the institute but would be unlikely to succeed; if he were admitted, he would be ridiculed by the girls for whom the school was intended. He could enroll in one of the vocational programs, in which there were about 2,300 other boys enrolled. Or, he could compete for the Colégio Pedro II or for the Colégio Militar. The city school system was of little help.

Why were there more girls in the city's schools, and more and better opportunities for girls in the schools? The school system treated secondary education as a distant priority. This starved resources from secondary schools, with the notable exception of the institute, which, in turn, produced the teachers for the primary schools. This was a women's profession and the tendency toward professional women's development carried over to the other secondary school programs. Teachers for the vocational school's classical programs were generally teachers (or retired teachers) from the institute, who focused on training women.

Teachers and administrators saw a greater need for female classical education because most skilled industrial and technical jobs went to men. Industrial jobs available to women, such as textile manufacturing, were unskilled, low-paying jobs that did not require or reward an extended education. The options in commerce, administration, and government that were opening to women required skills developed through classical secondary education, and the Department of Education rose to meet this need. Men had more employment options and opportunities for apprenticeship.

While major curricular reforms, as well as expansion of the network of schools, were prevented by the financial and spatial limitations the system faced, some reforms of school culture were attempted. These reforms in school culture raised civic consciousness, developed notions of social and professional responsibility, and elevated the prestige of their training. For instance, the female Escola Bento Ribeiro "entertains several social and extra-curricular institutions, and the student policing is performed by the students themselves."[70] Students became responsible for their own self-discipline, a notion that was tolerated at the Institute of Education and the Colégio Pedro II; but in schools that catered to lower-class students, these exercises in autonomy, internal authority, and self-discipline were branded subversive or even outright anarchical.

STUDENT AUTONOMY AT THE ESCOLA AMARO CAVALCANTI

The school where the experiment in student autonomy was carried to its greatest extent, and where the project for student autonomy failed in the end, was the commercial school, Amaro Cavalcanti. At Amaro Cavalcanti, student councils were organized and charged with administration of many of the school's functions. These councils supervised student discipline, encouraged students who were falling behind, and developed supplemental courses and extracurricular activities. As historian Clarice Nunes describes, the councils "mobilized the students, making them electors and electables within the school, making them sentient of issues that enriched their lives."[71]

The student autonomy program at the school was developed by Anísio

Teixeira and Francisco Venâncio Filho, based on North American models of student self-government. Amaro Cavalcanti was a controlled medium for the experiment. Its director, Maria Junqueira Schmidt, was a leading educator and adherent to Dewey's (and Teixeira's) New School philosophy. Even critics of the self-government program acknowledged that she was "so justly sensible to questions of order and politeness."[72] Despite criticism by opponents, the purpose of the project was not anarchy: the school retained a full cohort of discipline monitors and both the student council and student newspaper had faculty advisors who oversaw their activities.

The experiment in self-government was conducted in a school that was more socially dynamic than other schools. Amaro Cavalcanti was a commercial school that charged tuition for its regular program, and higher tuition for its accountacy program. In 1940, the admissions exam cost Cr$15 (US$1), tuition cost Cr$50 (US$3), and for students intending to complete accounting studies, the diploma cost Cr$300 (US$18), more than the monthly minimum wage.[73] While some tuition waivers were issued, and some free books, uniforms, and materials were distributed, the school catered to a financially stable, if modest, clientele. This ranged from middle-class teens from Copacabana and Botafogo to poorer children from the city's center and northern suburbs.

Still, the experiment lasted little more than two controversy-filled years. When it collapsed in 1935, self-government had become another breech of Teixeira's reform program. An unsigned resignation letter by one of the school's discipline monitors illustrates the cloud under which self-government operated. The monitor resigned in protest over a student newspaper article critical of the school's administration. The monitor argued that "since the school cannot but reflect the society, and since our Brazil presently takes part in the crisis that afflicts the world," the experiment in self-government radicalized students and would incite anarchy.[74]

The monitor believed well-executed self-government worked if students had a tradition of social responsibility. In Europe, for instance, self-government was implemented safely because its schools were "still concerned with training elites, leaving mass education to calculated neglect." European nations would never allow self-government among the lower classes because it would result in "justifiable explosions." The monitor underscored that self-government was not adaptable to students from nonelite backgrounds, and cited a Harvard University president's remark that "there can be no doubt that authority must ultimately rest with the school's staff."

To the monitor, the self-government program at Amaro Cavalcanti did not meet these conditions. The students were of mixed, therefore incompatible, social backgrounds, and the administration had lost control. The advisor of the student newspaper failed to review the issue before it was printed and distributed, and the other monitor's disciplinary measures had been lax. The disciplinary mechanisms that made possible such autonomy had failed to police it. As a result, the monitor explained that "I refused further collaboration with disciplinary questions, disagreeing with the excessively bland way in which the little newspaper was punished."

One reason for the failure of self-government and the radicalization of students, the monitor argued, was the social influences outside of school, which indoctrinated them in the "tactics of disorder." Students supposedly brought radical influences from the home and their communities into the school. The monitor argued that self-government could work if students used notions of social and civic responsibility that they learned in school, rather than on the street: "It would be best not to practice anarchy to reach the new disciplinary regime. . . . Let us not abuse the regime of liberty by introducing it prematurely." To the monitor, these students were not mature enough to possess freedom.

Finally, the letter presented the impropriety of running such an experiment in a setting where students from different social classes interacted. In Amaro Cavalcanti:

> Class and social contrasts are plainly reflected in the mix of wealthy daddy's girls from Copacabana and Botafogo, who are sassy and ill-behaved if D. Schmidt forbids their wearing necklaces, earrings, rings and lipstick, or scolds them for their slack, . . . with the impoverished girls who the principal jumps through hoops to accommodate with uniforms and shoes. In this fruit salad atmosphere, the facts demonstrate the impracticability and the ridiculousness of self-government. "Autonomy" is a farce in schools and societies tied into the class struggle. In class struggle societies, autonomy can only be attempted in schools with narrower constituencies.

This letter of protest and resignation was an especially relevant critique of the experiment because the author was an administrator responsible for school discipline. Moreover, he was obviously well aware of educational currents and the debate over self-government in the United States and Europe, and recognized class struggle as a conceptual framework. In short, he was an insider who felt that the school was drifting toward anarchy. Student autonomy in that setting invited external tensions into the school, rather than fomenting disciplined internal authority based on the school. It was precisely the New School doctrine that the school be a microcosm of the society that, in the eyes of this disciplinary monitor, made self-government impracticable.

By 1935, Maria Junqueira Schmidt had left the school. The new director's notions of discipline collided with Amaro Cavalcanti's student culture, and student leader Antonio Houaiss expressed the school's discontent with the new director's style. The director expelled Houaiss. In response, the Amaro Cavalcanti students marched out of the school, demonstrating for their leader's reinstatement. The director refused and the students stayed on strike. Finally, Anísio Teixeira himself met with Houaiss. Clarice Nunes describes the encounter: "Anísio received him serenely and soberly. He heard his motives. Both were moved. The youth cried."[75]

Teixeira decided to reinstate the student and transfer the new director. The challenge to authority prevailed, but at the cost of the mechanism that permitted it. Nunes continues: "The cost of this gesture, which guaranteed a middle-class student, whose parents could not otherwise afford his education, continued matriculation . . . was the abandonment of self-government."[76] The experiment in self-government in the end became just one more point on which conservative and Catholic critics attacked the Teixeira administration.

Extending access to elite institutions, as took place at the Colégio Pedro II, was accepted by elites. On the other hand, increasing the status of an essentially lower-class institution was subversive. The Escola Amaro Cavalcanti collapsed class boundaries, inverted hierarchy, and placed the controls over social discipline in the hands of specifically the people to whom discipline was projected. For Teixeira, a democratic society demanded that such things be possible, and be handled by students with a sense of social responsibility. To the school's discipline monitor, this social responsibility did not yet exist, and therefore the experiment could never succeed. For outside critics, the experiment in self-government was no less than a deliberate step toward anarchy and communism.

THE DECLINE AND REBIRTH OF PUBLIC SECONDARY EDUCATION

Once Teixeira was purged from the school system, little attention was directed to public secondary education. The reforms that he commenced advanced only through institutional inertia—one male vocational school added the classical curriculum and enrollments overall grew by another 25 percent, as they had in the Teixeira years. But the city's secondary schools were basically ignored until 1941, when Director of Education Colonel Pio Borges eliminated the classical courses offered in the vocational schools. He maintained that he helped put the schools on a "realistic and stable footing" by focusing them on the primary purpose of industrial and commercial training.[77] Borges took the public school system out of the business of classical secondary education. To emphasize the point, the Institute of Education's secondary school was renamed the Colégio do Instituto de Educação, recasting it as a publicly maintained private school.

For the remainder of the Vargas era, the only public classical courses offered in Brazil's largest city were at the institute (now exclusively female), and at the Colégio Pedro II. The virtual elimination of public secondary education created an upswell of public pressure for the establishment of new secondary schools. A letter to mayor Henrique Dodsworth sent in May 1945 by Ricardo Teixeira, an army captain living in the suburbs, characterizes this public demand. As an army officer, he served as a spokesperson for the residents of Realengo, who petitioned the city to build a "municipal *ginásio* [high school with a classical curriculum] at Magalhães Bastos Station" on land they had already received as a donation from the army for that purpose.[78]

Captain Teixeira explained that such a school was needed because "currently, hundreds of children in the suburbs (Deodoro to Santa Cruz and Nova Iguassú) have their education paralyzed by the lack of transportation, for the great cost of fatiguing travel, by the excessive cost of private school, etc." As he asserted, the entire suburban region was devoid of public secondary schools. Teixeira added: "Your excellency will see the tremendous benefits this action will have upon hundreds of children that will be the men of tomorrow."

The letter was accompanied by the signatures of 108 residents of Realengo, who endorsed Teixeira as their spokesperson because, they stated, "he understands the difficulties we face in educating our children, even in elementary school."[79]

Characteristically, Teixeira's letter began an administrative inquiry, fielded to the head of the 13th Educational District, Secundino Ribeiro Júnior. In July 1945, two months after it was sent to the mayor, Ribeiro too endorsed the petition, confirming the conditions the petitioners described and exalting that "I cannot help but applaud those who, like these signators, seek an act of such great social scope." Ribeiro realized the propaganda potential of fulfilling the popular request, arguing that "since the current administration does everything in the interest of children, be it sanitary or pedagogical, I am certain their aspirations will be realized, and boldly, by this department."[80]

It took more than Ribeiro's enthusiasm to build a school. As the letter worked its way up the Department of Education, it met the opposition of Luiz Palmeira, director of the Department of Technical Education, who explained to the mayor that he had nothing against the city maintaining secondary programs, so long as they were not situated in vocational schools, because of the "negative results obtained by the Teixeira administration." He wrote: "Regarding the pretensions of the residents of Magalhães Bastos, I see no reason for special preference when other highly populated areas of the city also deserve attention."[81]

These preliminary reports on the petition took three months to assemble. From Palmeira's desk the petition worked its way up to Secretary of Education Jonas Correia's office, facing even more delays. Although the slowness of the bureaucratic apparatus was often enervating, in this particular case time was a powerful ally. Before the petition could be rejected outright, Getúlio Vargas was removed from power, and in little time the government had been replaced.

The new mayor, Philadelpho de Azevedo, chose Director Raja Gabaglia of Colégio Pedro II as the new secretary of education. Raja Gabaglia brought a new perspective to the school system's negligible secondary program. Four months after Palmeira declined the petition, Raja Gabaglia presented mayor Azevedo with an ex post facto response: "The hopes of the petitioners have been realized by the creation of two new city high schools."[82]

Raja Gabaglia's appointment as secretary of education of Rio began a new era in the city's public education. His experience at the Colégio Pedro II had taught him that "the ginásio, offering basic post-primary education, is essential to the adolescent who lacks the foundations of learning, with which he can devote himself to any professional activity."[83] He believed that classical secondary education, which he termed ginasial, was fundamental to all lines of work from intellectual to industrial to agricultural. Drawing on his experience at the Colégio Pedro II, he began his administration with a program for building ginásios throughout the city, creating a system for universal secondary education.

Under Raja Gabaglia's direction, the Colégio Pedro II provided a prestigious classical education to more students—and more poor students—than did the entire vocational school system to which Teixeira attached classical programs. The colégio succeeded where Teixeira's secondary schools failed. Gabaglia's conservative and nationalist strategies for opening the nation's most prestigious school to the masses enjoyed the sustained support of the government and its allies, even as political currents drifted rightward and into the ideological camp of the Catholic Church. By contrast, Teixeira's vocational school reform, supported by paid tuition, and his experiment in student autonomy placed the schools out of the reach of their poorer constituencies while drawing fire for promoting anarchy and communism.

Raja Gabaglia avoided Teixeira's course, choosing to build new, separate ginásios rather than reinstituting classical education in the vocational schools (which, in turn, preserved their technical and industrial orientation). Immediately after taking office, Raja Gabaglia proposed the construction of two ginásios, both in the suburbs. These ginásios met the needs expressed by Captain Teixeira. Raja Gabaglia and Mayor Azevedo obtained funding from the interim president, José Linhares, and began construction of the schools the same month that Raja Gabaglia took office.

Challenging the class divisions that had historically guided secondary education more effectively than had Teixeira, Raja Gabaglia situated the first two ginásios in the poorer sections of the city. He defended the decision in an article in the teachers' journal Revista de Educação Pública: "Statistics demonstrate that the vast majority of students who seek the model school, Pedro II, because of its low tuition, come from the rural and suburban zones. It is the administrator's responsibility to install the first new schools in these areas, and that is what we have done."[84] These first two schools would be part of a "chain of connected institutions" that would be built throughout the suburbs of the Leopoldina rail line, on the islands in Guanabara Bay, and in the north end of the city.

The two schools begun in 1945 symbolized for Raja Gabaglia the role played by secondary education in the development of the nation. The Ginásio Barão do Rio Branco in Madureira was named after the "definer of our borders," while Ginásio Benjamin Constant in Santa Cruz was named after the "founder of the Republic." Just as the schools were named after two of the figures responsible for defining the modern nation, so too would these schools define and serve as the foundations of the new Brazil, built through education.

The schools were situated where they could be fed by the greatest number of elementary schools in areas whose residents "never could have imagined having secondary education." What is more, in a significant break from the past (and correcting one of the fundamental limitations of Teixeira's secondary program), the schools would be entirely free: "Thanks to Mayor Philadelpho de Azevedo, the 1946 budget guarantees free education at city establishments; this measure of great democratic value and social reach, is introduced in our country for the first time."[85]

EPILOGUE: THE ENDURING
BRAZILIAN FASCINATION WITH RACE

In 500 years of history, Brazil has built in the tropics a country of immensely rich culture, colored by a completely special light in its celebrations, its food, and its music. Brazil is among the ten largest economies of the world, and its people—despite all the difficulties of income and education—learn fast and show an uncommon capacity to adapt to new things or to face disaster. That is a positive inheritance stressed by many contemporary thinkers. . . .

Grandpa came to make it in America and he lassoed grandma to satisfy his carnal appetites. So, from an anthropological standpoint, the Brazilian suffers from a bastard syndrome that is reflected in his self-image and in the culture he produces.—"Who Are We?" *Veja*, 20 December 2000[1]

Eugenics lost scientific legitimacy in the aftermath of the Second World War, but the institutions, practices, and assumptions it gave rise to—indeed, its spirit—lives on. The idea of a "Brazilian race" endures in many areas of public life. President Fernando Henrique Cardoso (1994–2002) repeatedly declared that he himself "has a foot in the kitchen," meaning he is in part descended from the "black help." In soccer, fans define their bond with their team through allusions to a "Red-Stripe Race" (Flamengo) or a "Super-Race" (Gremio Mineiro). The idea of a "Brazilian race" surfaced in more robust form in December 2000 as a cover story by José Edward for Brazil's glossy news weekly, *Veja*. In the story it was revealed that "researchers from Minas Gerais [have outlined] the first genetic profile of the Brazilian, and conclude that: (1) we really are the country of miscegenation; [and] (2) there are whites who are genetically black, and vice versa."[2]

According to Veja reporter Edward, Brazilian geneticists at the Federal University of Minas Gerais decoded the genomes of the Brazilian ethnicity and, in doing so, discovered that anthropologists and sociologists like Gilberto Freyre were right all along: Brazil is the "laboratory of races." This genetic study is not the eugenics of old, though. Veja reminded its readers of the dozens of eugenic measurements used by the Nazis to differentiate between supposed Aryans and inferior races (although it made no mention of similar practices used extensively by educators, the army, and the police in Brazil at the same time). That was "false science," but through the "true science" of contemporary genetics, Veja declared proudly, it is finally possible to identify the genetic markers of Jews and other ethnic groups. Using these methods, for example, DNA analyses of a grandson and a niece reveal the supposed Jewish ancestry of none other than Gilberto Freyre.

What does this study mean for understanding Brazilian society? The genetic test purportedly permits scientists "to determine how much European (more precisely, Eurasian) and African each Brazilian today possesses." The results, naturally, don't fail to surprise in the old familiar way: "60 percent of those who consider themselves 'whites' have the blood of Indians or blacks running in their veins." According to their study sample of 247 people from around the country, a Brazilian with all of the external characteristics of whiteness could possess the same genetic profile as a pure African. Similarly, a dark-skinned Brazilian could be as genetically white as a descendant of Europeans. The director of the study, Sergio Danilo Pena, defines this Brazilian paradox: "In Brazil the relationship between skin color and genetic makeup is very weak."[3]

Naturally, Veja applied the new technology to reveal the true genetic makeup of prominent national figures to its prurient readership. The conservative senate leader Antonio Carlos Magalhães turned out to be 99.999999 percent white. He represented the state of Bahia, whose population identified as 80 percent black or brown according to the 1990 census. Princess Paola, descended from Emperor Pedro II and as statistically European as Magalhães, reflected about her test: "That is what I expected, of course, although I would like to have a little bit of mixture." Sex symbols Paulo Zulu and Susana Alves

(Tiazinha), both of whom represent the *moreno* or brunette ideal and both of whom were the product of some racial mixture, turned up at opposite ends of the spectrum: respectively 99.5 percent African and 99.99 percent European. Vicente Paulo Silva, leader of the Central Única de Trabalhadores labor syndicate and, according to *Veja*, a "typical mulatto," is reported to have "probable Moorish" ancestry on his father's side and African origins on his mother's side. In a curious turn of phrase, *Veja* notes that the infusion of Eurasian genes on Silva's mother's side in recent generations has given him predominantly European genes, "which gives him the right to a 'diploma of whiteness.' "[4]

Although the labor leader Silva may have earned a genetic badge of whiteness, *Veja* also acknowledges that it has become fashionable for affluent, white Brazilians to stress possible race mixture in their backgrounds: "It is common among Brazilians, when they feel sufficiently secure, to joke about the miscegenated origins of their families. When it is convenient to present a progressive image or a *bon mot* in a prestigious setting, everyone has a 'grandmother captured by lasso' or a 'foot in the kitchen,' " as in the earlier quote by president and sociologist Fernando Henrique Cardoso. Cardoso declined *Veja*'s offer to verify his claim through the new genetic test.[5] The *Veja* article concluded by undermining critics of the "true science." Citing a critic of the study who argues that the genetic decoding "confers a simulacra of scientific support to the myth of racial democracy," author José Edward defended the article, declaring that "the study obviously has nothing to do with racial democracy. It uses genetics to scientifically prove and quantify what social scientists have long shown us."[6]

Both the study and the *Veja* article have everything to do with the idea of racial democracy. Both are founded on the assumptions that race is a "scientific" entity and that race matters. The study presumes that racial characteristics are genetically fixed, and *Veja* acknowledges that "one need not be a militant for black rights to recognize that . . . in Brazil, whiteness of skin continues to bring greater social and economic advantages."[7] In the year 2000, the elites debating questions of race in Brazil continued to conflate social values and scientific theory in much the same way as they had in the first half of the twentieth century.

This gem of pop genetics reflects how little has changed in the elite, scientific vision of race in Brazil. Scientists seek the genes of a Brazilian ethnicity just as raciologists debated the composition of the "Brazilian Man." The same researchers claim to identify traces of African ancestry among Brazilians with no outward phenotypical appearance through DNA samples rather than through Bastos D'Avila's Lapicque Index. Through race mixture, labor leader Silva can graduate into whiteness, fulfilling the potential of whitening through mixture that scientific racists and eugenicists dreamed of. The Brazilian cultural "inheritance" that *Veja* celebrates mirrors the legacies of African culture described in the history texts of the 1940s: love of food, music, and dance, as well as a heroic resignation to hardship. Finally, science remains the ultimate arbiter: confirming what anthropologists and sociologists have shown, promising "truth," and defining race to tiny fractions of a percent.

Two blanket assumptions bridge the eugenicists of 1930 with the geneticists of 2000: scientists of both periods have employed a white gaze, and because of it they have treated whiteness as the benchmark of Brazilian racial measurement. How white is a Brazilian? How nonwhite? Can a black person have whiteness inside? Can a white person really be black, deceiving us with their appearance? The gaze and the benchmark that have served as the tools of science have guided white social values as well. Once whiteness is securely established, blackness or race mixture become acceptable possibilities—even virtues to be celebrated. *Veja* itself points to this when it recognizes that the fashion of asserting ancestral miscegenation among elite white Brazilians depends on the level of comfort they feel in their environment.

Veja provides two crucial conceptual tools for understanding how elite Brazilian society navigates the complex question of race: the idea of being racially "comfortable" and the possibility of a "diploma of whiteness." Comfort applies to predominantly white elites, while the diploma can be bestowed on a racially mixed, typically lower-class individual—either "genetically" through miscegenation, or socioeconomically because they assume positions of leadership or wealth ("salon mestizos are treated as whites," *Veja* declares). The values cannot be inverted, though: the Brazilian elite does not graduate into blackness, and the nonwhite feel pressure more than they do comfort. President Cardoso can flirt with miscegenation, and senate leader Magalhães can prominently display his talismans of Afro-Brazilian religion in his Senate office because both men are secure on their perches of power, wealth, and whiteness.

In contemporary Brazil, white elite comfort is in part sustained by the structure of education. As in many Latin American nations, a strict division exists between private education for the wealthy, the middle-class, and even the aspiring middle class, and public education for the poor. Because the wealthy and the poor seldom commingle in the schools, the commingling between whites and nonwhites is also measurably diminished. The educational system builds a structural distance that makes white comfort possible, while on very rare occasions it awards a diploma of whiteness to a public school student. The division reinforced through education is compounded by a monthly minimum wage set at R$150 (the equivalent of US$80 in 2000)—the salary of many public schoolteachers—and with city social services choked by the ever-increasing demands posed by migrants from rural areas, where problems of land tenure remain mired in the legacy of the colonial plantation system.

Although the forms of social distance maintained through education have evolved considerably over the course of the twentieth century, three distinct phases are apparent. At the century's end, the distance has been sustained by a form of segregation between those who depend on the moribund public school systems and those who can afford private school. This breakdown of education into public and private spaces occurred during the 1960s and 1970s, when the military regime neglected primary and secondary education while lavishing resources on the more scientific—and less political—sectors of higher education. Concomitantly, teacher salaries were eroded by inflation. Although at mid-century, teachers' salaries were a mark of status and prestige, even equating the profession with the military officer corps, by the 1990s teacher earnings were at the bottom of the formal employment scale. Illustrative of the depth of the teacher salary crisis in Brazil, Paulo Maluf, who has been both governor of the state and mayor of the city of São Paulo, declared publicly that "there is no such thing as a badly paid teacher, there are only badly married teachers."[8]

At the outset of the century, a different form of segregation divided those children who had access to public education and those who did not, as Augusto Malta provocatively implied in his photo commentary on the 1921 inauguration of the Escola Bartolomé Mitre ("Children from the Morro do Pinto [favela] who don't go to school?" [see chapter 4]). Education reformers of the beginning of the century had to contend with a social system based on exclusion. In the nineteenth century, slaves were not allowed to attend school and almost all were illiterate. By the turn of the century, small networks of public schools existed in the state capitals and larger secondary cities, but these attended principally to the primary education of children from families of means. Some educational institutions attended to poorer children, providing a limited number of the urban poor with a vocational education. As was realized by the reformers of the 1920s and 1930s who tried to turn these institutions into secondary schools that might draw youths from different classes, the vocational schools built during the Empire and Republic were seen by the public as little more than orphanages for the destitute.

Between the extremes of rigid exclusion at the beginning of the century and the rigid socioeconomic segregation of the end of the century lies a distinctive moment in Brazilian public life. Beginning in the aftermath of the First World War, the school system in Rio de Janeiro—like others in Brazil—was transformed into an institution capable of drawing children of all social classes, ethnicities, and colors. This did not mean that reigning social hierarchies were inverted, or even diminished. To the contrary, the rare threats to the social hierarchy manifest in schools resulted in swift reprisals and furnished kindling for the Catholic conservative resurgence of the 1930s. The lewd dancing episode at the Institute of Education, Colégio Pedro II student jeering at military cadets, the collapse of self-government at the Escola Cavalcanti, and the extensive barrage of accusations of communism against a number of educators all reflected unacceptable exceptions to the norms of educational behavior.

The controversy over self-government at the Escola Amaro Cavalcanti, perhaps better than any other example, illustrates the complexity of maintaining social distance in a school that brought students of widely different classes together under a single roof. The school monitor who resigned in protest over the independence of the school newspaper believed that without self-government the school functioned in an orderly and disciplined manner. But self-government and social distance did not mix: "In this fruit salad atmosphere, the facts demonstrate the impracticability and the ridiculousness of self-government. 'Autonomy' is a farce in schools and societies tied into the class struggle. In class struggle societies, autonomy can only be attempted in schools with narrower constituencies."[9] For the historical moment in which educators experimented with the idea of the *escola única*—the universal public school—norms of order, discipline, and hierarchy had to prevail in the school.

But the public school system built between the world wars did not rely on order and discipline alone. The universal elementary school worked through the complex negotiation of values of race, class, and gender. These negotiations took place at all levels of the school system's operations, from curriculum to student selection, placement, and advancement; testing and tracking; teacher selection and training; health and hygiene programs; public events; and even in the building of schools and the arrangement of the school lunch program. The endeavor to build a universal public school system meant rewriting social values that had previously operated through institutional exclusion. The marginal status of poor and nonwhite Brazilians changed little under the new arrangement, but the ways educational institutions interacted with social hierarchies did change in significant ways.

The reformers who pushed for the universal public school and reshaped the format and content of education did so within a social context that had begun to look at culture and environment, rather than biology, as the roots of racial difference. The zeal of the interwar years for public education drew energy, resources, and leadership from the eugenics and health and hygiene movements, and educational reforms were championed by many of Brazil's pioneering social scientists. The elite cadre of intellectuals and social scientists that spearheaded education reform and expansion saw the public school as a vehicle for attaining a number of overlapping goals. The dominant objectives were the creation of a skilled and disciplined workforce, sanitizing the Brazilian popular classes, inculcating European habits and customs, and developing a coherent national identity.

Together, these objectives combined to forge an agenda for national development based on scientific and modern values. Yet old assumptions about race endured within this agenda. Reformers wrote their own assumptions about race, class, culture, gender, and health into the institutions they created. School policies recognized diverse forms of social difference. Some of these policies were aimed at reducing these differences and others were designed to maintain them, but in any case these policies reified perceptions of social difference, creating a metanarrative of race that reinforced inequality. A social order that had once been based on slavery and a monarchy was reinvented as an order based on science and merit without significantly changing the social hierarchy. Old inequalities were dressed in new clothes.

The ways a public school system contended with race and class illustrate the roles played by science and public power in reinforcing the institutional marginalization of the afrodescendant population. There are other ways to understand this process as well. Scholars have increasingly looked to other public institutions such as the police, the military, and the judicial system to dissect the operation of racial values within Brazilian society. This approach is crucial to understanding racial exclusion and inequality in a society such as Brazil, or in the postsegregation United States, where discrimination is pervasive but racism is not immediately apparent. These local institutions reveal the operation of inequality more effectively than can analyses of the broader public sphere.

The public schools of mid-century Brazil are privileged spaces for such analysis because they number among the few public places where people of different classes and colors regularly interacted, even if in structurally unequal terms. This study has considered the ways policymakers shaped that space, as well as the types of boundaries and bridges they built into the systems they created. This analysis of race within the public schools of Rio de Janeiro and within Brazilian educational policy opens a number of questions. It is based on a case study of Rio, although it examines evidence from other Brazilian states. Day-to-day educational practices outside of Rio, particularly in states with larger afrodescendant populations such as Bahia, merit more careful consideration. Some states, such as Ceará, Amazonas, and Pará, were sites of ambitious education reform and expansion as well, taking the initiative in developing rural educational systems.

Bahia is a striking case because it received the attention of many veterans of the Rio school system. During the Estado Novo years, public education there was headed by Isaias Alves, the psychologist who instituted intelligence testing in Rio and later flirted with Integralism and emerged as a fierce opponent of the New School reformers. After the collapse of the Estado Novo, Anísio Teixeira returned to public life as Bahia's director of public education, and he initiated yet another ambitious education reform in that state. The reform began with an extensive census of the Bahian interior to both determine the location of schools and ascertain the types of education most adequate to each region of the state.

When anthropologist Arthur Ramos set the groundwork for the UNESCO study of race relations in Brazil in 1948, Teixeira proposed that Bahia serve as the case study of the project, both because the state held the largest concentration of Brazilians of color and because he had the surveying staff already in place from his own programs. Ultimately, the bulk of the study was conducted in Rio de Janeiro and São Paulo, seen as the sites of Brazil's future and emerging society. The educational projects developed in Rio de Janeiro in the 1920s and 1930s served as the springboard for both national educational policies (the Law of Directives and Bases in Education, 1958, 1996) and for considerable research on race relations, not only that conducted by the Department of Education's Institute for Educational Research, but also the later work of Edgar Roquette Pinto and Arthur Ramos, who inspired the UNESCO study.

Teixeira's Bahian school reform culminated in the creation of "educational centers"—schools that provided space for an array of day and night, child and adult classes, and also served as an outpost of the public welfare system, offering health services and serving as a liaison with state authorities. These centers served as the basis for the extensive network of Integrated Public Education Centers (CIEPs) created throughout the city and state of Rio de Janeiro in the late 1980s and early 1990s during the government of Leonel Brizola. These prefabricated concrete schools—whose original design was created by Oscar Niemeyer, were of homogenous design and situated in highly visible locations, much like the schools built in the 1920s and 1930s. The schools were intended to serve as learning centers housing primary, secondary, vocational, and adult courses, as well as providing health and social services. Children in need could come to the schools early for breakfast and a shower, for lunch, and even stay for dinner.

Maria Yedda Linhares, who was the state secretary of education when the project was initiated, recalled high hopes of recreating the universal public school in the CIEP, but finished disappointed with the entire program. The schools failed to attract the middle class because they were seen as schools for the poor. Linhares recalls with particular bitterness the campaigns of calumny against the CIEPs waged by the networks of private schools that feared competition from public schools. Her criticism of private schools is much more extensive, though. Linhares saw the representatives of private schools who sat on the state school board as actively sabotaging public education in order to preserve their market by, for example, pressing to remove the classical curriculum from the state's public vocational and technical secondary schools.[10]

The CIEP project spearheaded by Darcy Ribeiro and Linhares failed to achieve the type of universal school that had been created in the interwar years. By the 1980s, the social distance in Brazilian education was based on the division between public and private schools. The collapse of the universal school calls for closer study, particularly in the racial dimension of what was essentially a "white flight" from public schools. Reversing this process proved to be a much more difficult endeavor than did the invention of the universal school, which took place in different circumstances. The failure of the CIEPs highlights the scale of the feat accomplished between the wars, as well as the significance of the ways the New School handled questions of race and class. The CIEPs did not overcome their image as a school for the poor. The New School's scientific embrace of race and class hierarchies, and its endorsement of the idea that most of the children in Rio suffered from a culture of poverty— from which only the state could redeem them—created a formula that fit the paradigms of the time.

When Arthur Neiva and Belissário Penna returned from their health expedition to the interior of Brazil in 1917 and called for the creation of a federal ministry of education and health, they galvanized a link between education and the question of race. The attentions that the scientific, intellectual, and political communities of the turn of the century lavished on questions of race and degeneracy dominated debates about progress, national identity, and modernization. The consensus among elites that emerged by the end of the First World War was that Brazil's existing population would have to suffice as the muscle of national progress. The challenge that this consensus presented was straightforward: how could the state cure Brazilians of their backwardness? Public health programs addressed one component of this formula; a system of labor relations addressed another. Public education touched on all aspects of the perfection of the race.

Educators working in Rio de Janeiro established a formula for bringing to fruition the school system that could perfect the race. This school system used whiteness as its baseline. The white and affluent were rewarded with innovative educational opportunities. Conversely, the school system provided a remedial experience for children who did not meet the white and affluent standards. The system worked efficiently and scientifically at sorting between these students based on their health and intelligence. The educational process was scientifically designed to provide health, discipline, and culture. Schools were staffed by increasingly white and higher-trained professionals. All of these processes were carefully studied, and reports on them were published and disseminated across Brazil, so that the solutions would radiate from the capital to all corners of the country. Guided by science and confident of their country's future, these educators offered Brazil a diploma of whiteness, giving new shape to enduring inequalities.

ABBREVIATIONS

FEDERAL INSTITUTIONS

DIP: Departamento de Imprensa e Propaganda (Department of Press and Propaganda)

DESPS: Delegacia Especial de Segurança Política e Social (Special Police for Political and Social Security)

EEFE: Escola de Educação Física do Exército (Army Physical Education School)

IBGE: Instituto Brasileiro de Geografía e Estatística (Brazilian Institute for Geography and Statistics)

INEP: Instituto Nacional de Estudos Pedagógicos (National Institute for Pedagogical Studies)

MES: Ministério de Educação e Saúde (Ministry of Education and Health)

SEES: Serviço de Estatística de Educação e Saúde (Health and Education Statistics Service)

SENAC: Serviço Nacional de Aprendizagem Comercial (National Service for Commercial Training)

SENAI: Serviço Nacional de Aprendizagem Industrial (National Service for Industrial Training)

SPHAN: Serviço do Patrimônio Histórico e Artístico Nacional (National Service for Historic and Artistic Patrimony)

CIEP: Centro Integrado de Educação Pública (Integrated Public Education Center)

DEN: Departamento de Educação Nacionalista (Department of Nationalist Education)

DGEC: Departamento Geral de Educação e Cultura (General Department of Education and Health)

DMP: Distrito Médico-Pedagógico (Medical-Pedagogical District)

IPE: Instituto de Pesquisas Educacionais (Institute for Educational Research)

SEMA: Serviço de Educação Musical e Artistica (Musical and Artistic Education Service)

SMF: Serviço de Matrícula e Frequência (Matriculation and Attendance Service)

SOHM: Serviço de Ortofrenia e Higiene Mental (Orthophrenology and Mental Hygiene Service)

SPAE: Serviço de Predios e Aparelhamentos (Buildings and Materials Service)

STE: Serviço de Testes e Escalas (Tests and Measures Service)

ASSOCIATIONS

ABE: Associação Brasileira de Educadores (Brazilian Association of Educators)

FIESP: Federação das Indústrias do Estado de São Paulo (Federation of Industries in the State of São Paulo)

IDORT: Instituto de Organização Racional do Trabalho (Institute for the Rational Organization of Work)

LBPPF: Liga Brasileira Pelo Progresso Feminino (Brazilian League for Feminine Progress)

ARCHIVES

AEL: Arquivo Edgar Leuenroth, Universidade Estadual de Campinas

AGC: Arquivo Geral da Cidade, Rio de Janeiro

AN: Arquivo Nacional do Brasil, Rio de Janeiro
CPII: Colégio Pedro II
CPDOC: Centro de Pesquisa e Documentação de História Contemporânea do Brasil, Fundação Getúlio Vargas
CUTC: Columbia University Teachers College
MIS: Museu da Imagem e do Som do Rio de Janeiro

NOTES

INTRODUCTION

Note: All translations are mine, unless otherwise noted.

1 Mauricio de Medeiros, "Uma recusa insultosa," *Diario Carioca*, 7 March 1944, 4. The *Diario Carioca* began publishing in 1929 with a circulation of five thousand and later "gained prestige" as an opposition newspaper during the Vargas era. Nelson Werneck Sodré, *A história da imprensa no Brasil* (Rio de Janeiro: Civilização Brasileira, 1966), 424.

2 *Caboclo* is defined as a person of mixed indigenous and European descent.

3 H. Sobral Pinto, "Uma injustiça a reparar," *Diario Carioca*, 12 March 1944, 9.

4 Letter from Sobral Pinto to Archbishop Jayme de Barros Câmara, 20 March 1944. Gustavo Capanema Collection, CPDOC, Relacionamento Estado-Igreja Católica 39.05.25 (0033).

5 Doraci de Souza, "Colégios estrangeiros," *O Globo*; reprinted in *Diario Carioca*, 11 March 1944, 4.

6 Letter from H. Sobral Pinto to D. Jayme de Barros Câmara, archbishop of Rio de Janeiro, 20 March 1944. Gustavo Capanema Collection, CPDOC, Relacionamento Estado-Igreja Católica 39.05.25 (0033).

7 A detailed discussion of the relationship between Gustavo Capanema and the Catholic Church can be found in Simon Schwartzman et al., *Tempos de Capanema* (São Paulo: EDUSP, 1984). For another source, see José Silveiro Baia Horta, *O hino, o sermão e a ordem do dia* (Rio de Janeiro: UFRJ, 1995). The centennial of Capanema's birth in 1900 witnessed the publication of two new books on his life and works: Angela de Castro Gomes, ed. *Capanema: O ministro e seu ministério* (Rio de Janeiro: Editoria FGV, 2000), and Murilo Badaro, *Gustavo Capanema: A revolução na cultura* (São Paulo: Nova Fronteira, 2000).

8 Undated note by Gustavo Capanema. Gustavo Capanema Collection, CPDOC, Relacionamente Estado-Igreja Católica 39.05.25 (0049). In the same note, Capanema ruled

over another controversy that is briefly worth noting. The issue centered on a father who complained that the Colégio Bennett in Rio discriminated by expelling his son because he refused to let him attend the religious education classes offered at the school. To this Capanema replied: "The commission verified that the Colégio Bennett did not demand that their students practice a specific religion; it required only that the student attend religious classes that are based on the reading and interpretation of the Bible."

9 This phrase was shorthand for the "eugenic perfection of the race," a process implicitly linked with health and education programs. This link was made explicit at even the highest circles of educational policy, such as was done by the Ministry of Education's Commission on Primary Education when it was listed among its four goals, alongside "social discipline, national defense, and improving productivity." National Commission on Public Education, "General Thoughts for the Organization of a 'Plan for the Popular Education Campaign,'" 8 November 1939. Gustavo Capanema Collection, CPDOC, 35.12.14g (0533).

10 According to Dain Borges, "Degeneration, though never far from colour in Brazil, was more than colour. It was a psychology of character, a science of identity, and a social psychology. As in Europe, it became an argument that national decline should be understood through the metaphor of progressive hereditary illness in a body, that the nation was a sick man. It survived the disrepute of racism and continued to shape the *Modernista* generation of Brazilian social criticism in the 1930s. The contemporary Brazilian social-welfare state and many contemporary themes of national identity derive from an ignored and discredited psychiatry of the nineteenth century." Borges, "'Puffy, Ugly, Slothful, and Inert': Degeneration in Brazilian Social Thought," *Journal of Latin American Studies* 25 (1993): 235–36.

11 Nísia Trinidade Lima and Gilberto Hochman, "Condenado pela raça, absolvido pela medicina: O Brasil descoberto pelo movimento sanitarista da Primeira República," in *Raça, ciência e sociedade*, ed. Marcos Chor Maio and Ricardo Ventura Santos (Rio de Janeiro: Editora FIOCRUZ, 1996), 24. The evolution of racial thought has been discussed extensively by both Brazilian and U.S. scholars. See Thomas E. Skidmore, *Black into White: Race and Nationality in Brazilian Thought*, 2nd ed. (Durham: Duke University Press, 1993); Nancy Leys Stepan, *"The Hour of Eugenics": Race, Gender, and Nation in Latin America* (Ithaca: Cornell University Press, 1991); Lilia Moritz Schwarcz, *O espetáculo das raças: Cientistas, instituições e questão racial no Brasil, 1870–1930* (São Paulo: Companhia das Letras, 1993); Gilberto Hochman, *A era do saneamento* (São Paulo: Editora Hucitec, 1998); and Mariza Corrêa, "As ilusões da liberdade: A escola Nina Rodrigues e a antropologia no Brasil" (Ph.D. diss., University of São Paulo, 1982).

12 Ann Stoler, *Race and the Education of Desire: Foucault's "History of Sexuality" and the Colonial Order of Things* (Durham: Duke University Press, 1995), 11.

13 This concept is employed in the way it was coined by Charles Wagley: "'Social race' (i.e. the way in which the members of a society classify each other by physical characteristics) is but one of a series of values which give individuals rank and determine their social relations." Wagley, *Race and Class in Rural Brazil* (Paris: UNESCO, 1952), 24.

14 For analyses of this transformation from nature to nurture, see Skidmore, *Black into White*; Stepan, *"The Hour of Eugenics"*; and Borges, " 'Puffy, Ugly, Slothful, and Inert.' "

15 Malcolm X, *The Autobiography of Malcolm X* (New York: Random House, 1975), 340.

16 David Roediger, *The Wages of Whiteness: Race and the Making of the American Working Class* (London: Verso, 1999), 6. On the construction of whiteness in the United States, see also Robin Kelley, *Race Rebels: Culture, Politics, and the Black Working Class* (New York: The Free Press, 1996); George Lipsitz, *The Possessive Investment in Whiteness: How White People Profit from Identity Politics* (Philadelphia: Temple University Press, 1998); and Noel Ignatiev, *How the Irish Became White* (New York: Routledge, 1996).

17 José Edward, "Quem somos nós?" *Veja*, 20 December 2000, 103.

18 Nelson do Valle Silva and Carlos Hasenbalg, "Race and Educational Opportunity in Brazil," in *Race in Contemporary Brazil: From Indifference to Inequality*, ed. Rebecca Reichmann (University Park: Pennsylvania State University Press, 1999), 65.

19 Gilberto Freyre, *The Masters and the Slaves: A Study in the Development of Brazilian Civilization*, 2nd ed. (New York: Knopf, 1956), xxvi–xxvii.

20 Ibid., xxxii.

21 Stepan, *"The Hour of Eugenics"*; Borges, " 'Puffy, Ugly, Slothful, and Inert.' "

22 Barbara Weinstein, *For Social Peace in Brazil: Industrialists and the Remaking of the Working Class in São Paulo, 1920–1964* (Chapel Hill: University of North Carolina Press, 1996), 336. On industrial rationalization as a social vision, see also Edgar de Decca, *O silêncio dos vencidos*, 2nd ed. (1981; São Paulo: Brasiliense, 1994), 150–55.

23 Weinstein, *For Social Peace in Brazil*, 27.

24 Such an approach has been taken by Kim Butler, *Freedoms Given, Freedoms Won: Afro-Brazilians in Post-Abolition São Paulo and Salvador* (New Brunswick: Rutgers University Press, 1998); Corrêa, "As ilusões da liberdade"; Silva and Hasenbalg, "Race and Educational Opportunity in Brazil"; Pierre Michel Fontaine, *Race, Class, and Power in Brazil* (Los Angeles: Center for Afro-American Studies, UCLA, 1985); Schwarcz, *O espetáculo das raças*; Skidmore, *Black into White*; Lima and Hochman, "Condenado pela raça, absolvido pela medicina." See also Jerry Dávila, "Expanding Perspectives on Race in Brazil," *Latin American Research Review* 35, no. 3 (2000): 188–98. For an excellent survey of literature on race in Brazil, see Rebecca Reichmann, ed., *Race in Contemporary Brazil: From Indifference to Inequality* (University Park: Pennsylvania State University Press, 1999), 1–36.

25 See George Reid Andrews, *Blacks and Whites in São Paulo, Brazil, 1888–1988* (Madison: University of Wisconsin Press, 1991); L. A. Costa Pinto, *O negro no Rio de Janeiro: Relações de raças numa sociedade em mudança* (São Paulo: Companhia Editora Nacional, 1953); Florestan Fernandes, *The Negro in Brazilian Society* (New York: Columbia University Press, 1969); Hendrik Kraay, ed., *Afro-Brazilian Culture in Bahia, 1790s to 1990s* (Armonk, N.Y.: M. E. Sharpe, 1998).

26 Marvin Harris, "Race Relations in Minas Velhas," in *Race and Class in Rural Brazil*, ed. Charles Wagley (Paris: UNESCO, 1952); Carl Degler, *Neither Black nor White: Slavery and Race Relations in Brazil and the United States* (New York: Macmillan, 1971).

27 Evelyn Brooks Higginbotham, "African-American Women's History and the Metalanguage of Race," *Signs* 17, no. 2 (winter 1992): 252.

28 These categories have been deconstructed by Melissa Nobles, who observes that "hoping to avoid asking Brazilians to respond to terms 'sometimes used with disdain,' IBGE decided to limit the choices to white, black, and yellow, with a horizontal line for 'mixed.' After the census was taken, however, all horizontal lines were tabulated and published under the category *pardo*. It is important to note that the meaning of *pardo* was—and is—ambiguous. In Portuguese-language dictionaries, it is defined as both 'gray' and 'brown,' and its connotations are equally ambiguous, because Brazilians infrequently use it in common parlance. Its most significant use is as a census term. Although controversy did not then surround *preto* (black), it has also been a peculiar term for IBGE to use. Brazilians usually use it in the third person, not the first person, as the census requires. Even more illuminating, it is commonly used to describe objects, not human beings." Nobles, *Shades of Citizenship: Race and the Census in Modern Politics* (Stanford: Stanford University Press, 2000), 99.

29 Bastos D'Avila, "Ensaio de raciologia Brasileira: Populações do Distrito Federal," *Revista de Educação Pública* 2, no. 1 (1944): 16.

30 This ambiguity is characterized by an observation by Charles Wagley: "Perhaps the most important difference between race relations in Brazil and in the United States is that color is but one of the criteria by which people are placed in the total social hierarchy. Before two Brazilians decide how they ought to behave toward each other, they must know more than the fact that one is dark-skinned and the other light-skinned. . . . Other criteria, such as income, education, family connections and even personal charm and special abilities or aptitudes come into play when placing a person in terms of the prestige hierarchy or even social class." Wagley, *An Introduction to Brazil* (New York: Columbia University Press, 1963), 142.

1. BUILDING THE "BRAZILIAN MAN"

1 Letter from Gustavo Capanema to Oliveira Vianna, 30 August 1937, in *As colunas da educação: A construção do Ministério de Educação e Saúde*, ed. Maurício Lissovsky and Paulo Sergio Moraes de Sá (Rio de Janeiro: IPHAN, 1996), 225 (doc. 149).

2 Letter from Gustavo Capanema to Getúlio Vargas, 14 June 1937, in *As Colunas da educação*, ed. Lissovsky and Sá, 224 (doc. 147).

3 Ibid.

4 Letter from Edgar Roquette Pinto to Gustavo Capanema, 30 August 1937, in *As Colunas da educação*, ed. Lissovsky and Sá, 226 (doc. 150).

5 Cited in Lauro Cavalcanti, *As preocupações do belo: Arquitetura moderna Brasileira dos anos 30/40* (Rio de Janeiro: Taurus Editora, 1995), 79.

6 Letter from Juvenil Rocha Vaz to Gustavo Capanema, 14 September 1937, in *As Colunas da educação*, ed. Lissovsky and Sá, 226 (doc. 151).

7   Gustavo Capanema memorandum, 14 December 1937, in *As Colunas da educação*, ed. Lissovsky and Sá, 230 (doc. 152).

8   Letter from Gustavo Capanema to Mario de Andrade, 1 February 1938, in *As Colunas da educação*, ed. Lissovsky and Sá, 232 (doc. 156).

9   Jaime Aroldo, "O Tipo Brasileiro," *A Nota*, 28 September 1938, 6.

10 M. Paulo Filho, "Homem Brasileiro," *O Correio da Manhã*, 23 September 1938, 4.

11 See Stepan, "*The Hour of Eugenics.*"

12 Between 1907 and 1945, more than seventy thousand people were sterilized in the United States. Those sterilized were mostly poor, frequently black, and deemed "feeble minded." The United States also conducted sterilization programs in Puerto Rico to combat "overpopulation." This was the most extensive eugenic sterilization program of any nation outside Nazi Germany. Although eugenics in the United States, Germany, and Great Britain was based mainly on Mendelian genetics, Brazil, along with much of Latin America, followed the Lamarckian school pioneered in France (Stepan, "*The Hour of Eugenics,*" 31, 134).

13 Quoted in Hochman, *A era do saneamento*, 64.

14 Stepan, "*The Hour of Eugenics,*" 48, 157.

15 Puericulture is a discipline that combines prenatal and postnatal infant and maternal care.

16 Nelson Rodrigues, "A realeza do Pelé," in *O melhor do romance, contos e crônicas* (São Paulo: Editora Schwarcz, 1993), 117.

17 For further reading on these models of scientific racism, see Stoler, *Race and the Education of Desire;* Stephen J. Gould, *The Mismeasure of Man* (1981; New York: Norton, 1996); and Skidmore, *Black into White.*

18 Lima and Hochman, "Condenado pela raça, absolvido pela medicina," 24.

19 Quoted in Skidmore, *Black into White,* 180.

20 *O urubú de nosso progresso* (Rio de Janeiro: Editora Francisco Fabiano Alves, 1935). Gustavo Capanema Collection, CPDOC, 35.12.14g (0549).

21 On the Juazeiro revolt, see Ralph Della Cava, *Miracle at Joazeiro* (New York: Columbia University Press, 1970).

22 Manoel Bergstrom Lourenço Filho, *O Juazeiro de Padre Cícero*, 3rd ed. (1928; São Paulo: Edições Melhoramentos, 1955), 17–18. Juazeiro received the Brazilian Academy of Letters prize and was published in at least three editions.

23 Ibid., 34.

24 Estado de Espírito Santo, Decreto No. 10.171: *Expede instrucções sobre o ensino normal e da outras providencias* (Victoria: Oficinas do "Diario da Manhã," 1930); Estado do Amazonas, *Programas do ensino primário, adotados pelo Conselho Superior de Instrução Pública em 28 de Janeiro de 1932* (Manaus: Imprensa Publica, 1932); Estado do Amazonas, *Regulamento geral da instrução pública, a que se refere ao Ato No. 1.267 de 19 de janeiro de 1932* (Manaus: Imprensa Publica, 1932); Estado de Parahyba, *Decreto No. 75 de 14 de março de 1931: Da novo regulamento a escola normal do estado—Acto do interventor federal* (João Pessoa:

Imprensa Oficial, 1931); Estado de Sergipe, Decreto No. 30 de 11 de março de 1931: "Dá novo regulamento à Escola Normal 'Rui Barbosa'" (Aracaju: Imprensa Oficial, 1931).

25 Maria Cristina de Albuquerque Araújo, "Antônio de Arruda Carneiro Leão," in Dicionário de educadores no Brasil, da colônia aos dias atuais, ed. Maria de Lourdes de Albuquerque Fávero and Jader de Medeiros Britto (Rio de Janeiro: Editora UFRJ, 1999), 67.

26 Ibid., 67–68.

27 Ibid., 66.

28 Cited in Gould, The Mismeasure of Man, 216.

29 Stepan, "The Hour of Eugenics," 60.

30 Bastos D'Avila remained in his position for at least eleven years, still holding his directorship at the end of the Vargas era. Arthur Ramos left in 1939 after completing the research for and publication of his monograph A criança problema.

31 The Lapicque Index, developed in France at the turn of the century, measured the relationship between the size of the radius bone in the arm and that of the ethmoid bone in the superior nasal category. The formula was the following: radial-pelvic index = (length of the radius × 100) / bi-crisiliac diameter. Bastos D'Avila, "Contribuição ao estudo do Indice de Lapicque," in Estudos Afro-Brasileiros (Trabalhos apresentados no 10 Congresso Afro-Brasileiro reunido no Recife em 1934), vol. 1 (Rio de Janeiro: Ariel Editora, 1935), 35.

32 Bastos D'Avila, "Secção de Antropometria," 16 October 1935. Lourenço Filho Collection, CPDOC, IPE (0010).

33 Letter from Bastos D'Avila to Lourenço Filho, 16 April 1936. Lourenço Filho Collection, CPDOC, IPE (0042).

34 Bastos D'Avila, "Ensaio de raciologia Brasileira," 16.

35 Ibid., 23.

36 Ibid., 24.

37 Bastos D'Avila and Pedro Pernambuco Filho, "Considerações em torno dos Indices de Kaup, Pelidisi e A.C.H.," Revista de Educação Pública 3, no. 1 (1945): 4.

38 Cited in Corrêa, As ilusões da liberdade, 232.

39 Ibid., 160.

40 Arthur Ramos, A família e a escola (Conselhos de higiene mental aos pais), Série D-Vulgarização (Rio de Janeiro: Oficina Gráfica do Departamento de Educação, 1934), 7.

41 Ibid., 8.

42 Ibid., 7.

43 Arthur Ramos, A criança problema: A higiene mental na escola primária (Rio de Janeiro: Companhia Editora Nacional, 1939), 10.

44 Ibid., 15.

45 Noêmi Alcântara Bonfim de Andrade, "A hygiene alimentar no serviço social das escolas," Cultura Política 2, no. 13 (1942): 24.

46 Pedro Pernambuco Filho, "Centro de Pesquisas Educacionais: Colaboração com o Ministério da Guerra," Revista de Educação Pública 2, no. 2 (1944): 211.

47 Inquérito sobre as causas de insegurança de trahalho, Mário Monteiro Machado, Secretario Geral de Viação, Trabalho e Obras Públicas, 1937. Pedro Ernesto Batista Collection, CPDOC, DO/Funcionalismo (0672).

48 On the Pedro Ernesto government and its social programs, see Carlos Eduardo Sarmento, *Pedro Ernesto: Um prefeito para o Rio* (Rio de Janeiro: Fundação Getúlio Vargas, 1995); Antonio Cesar Lemme, "Saúde, educação e cidadania na década de 30" (M.A. thesis, Centro Biomédico, UERJ, 1992); and Michael Conniff, *Urban Politics in Brazil: The Rise of Populism, 1925–1945* (Pittsburgh: University of Pittsburgh Press, 1981).

49 Jonas Correia, "Aspectos da educação primária no Distrito Federal," *Fon-Fon* (1941): 20.

50 C., interviewed by Anna Olga Lessa de Barros Barreto, "Contribuição para a história da escola pública primária do Distrito Federal, no período do Estado Novo (1937–1945)" (M.A. thesis, Pontifíficia Universidade Católica do Rio de Janeiro, 1986), 142.

51 Ibid., 136–42.

52 Relatorio apresentado pela diretora da escola Vicente Licínio (3–8) ao Exm. Snr. Superintendente da 3a circunscrição de ensino elementar, 1933. Anísio Teixira Collection, CPDOC, pi33.00.00 (3/293).

53 Ibid.

54 Nilo Romero, "Medicina e educação," *Revista de Educação Pública* 1, no. 3 (1943): 359.

55 Oscar Clark, "O papel da Secretaria de Educação na sociedade moderna," *Revista de Educação Pública* 3, no. 3 (1945): 323.

56 Romero, "Medicina e educação," 360.

57 Relatorio apresentado pela diretira da escola Vicente Licínio (3–8) ao Exm. Snr. Superintendente da 3a circuscrição de ensino elementar, 1933. Anísio Teixira Collection, CPDOC, pi33.00.00 (3/293).

58 Letter from Waldemar Pinto Victorio to Getúlio Vargas, 29 November 1943. Henrique Dodsworth Collection, AGC, Box 100–"Education, 1939–1944" (9060).

59 Ibid.

60 This image has been examined by Joel Wolfe, " 'Father of the Poor' or 'Mother of the Rich'? Getúlio Vargas, Industrial Workers, and Constructions of Class, Gender, and Populism in São Paulo, 1930–1954," *Radical History Review* 58 (1994): 80–111; and Robert M. Levine, *Father of the Poor? Vargas and His Era* (New York: Cambridge University Press, 1998).

61 Letter from Henrique Dodsworth to Getúlio Vargas, 24 April 1944; Letter from Waldemar Pinto Victorio to Getúlio Vargas, 29 November 1943. Henrique Dodsworth Collection, AGC, Box 100–"Education, 1939–1944" (9060).

62 Consulta do Diretor Geral da Fazenda, 18 January 1935. Pedro Ernesto Batista Collection, CPDOC, DO/Funcionalismo (0668).

63 Pio Borges, "A assistência médica à infância escolar," *Fon-Fon* (1941): 59.

64 Andrade, "A higiene alimentar no serviço social das escolas," 23–24.

65 A., interviewed by Barreto, "Contribuição para a história de escola pública," 105.

66 Romero, "Medicina e educação," 361.

67 Inezil Pena Marinho, "Evolução da educação física no Brasil," *Cultura Política* 4, no. 40 (1944): 76. See chapter 6 on the difficulties of instituting physical education at the Colégio Pedro II.

68 Peregrino Júnior, "Sentido político e biológico da educação física," *Cultura Política* 4, no. 36 (1944): 154–55.

69 Letter from the Bishops of São Paulo to Getúlio Vargas, 19 March 1940. Gustavo Capanema Collection, CPDOC, 34.07.14g (455).

70 Ibid.

71 Letter from Gustavo Capanema to the Bishops of São Paulo, 21 January 1940. Gustavo Capanema Collection, CPDOC, 34.07.14g (477).

2. EDUCATING BRAZIL

1 Mário Augusto Teixeira de Freitas, *A escolaridade primária e a política educacional*, chapter 5, "Revelações dos números no terreno social (1946)." Freitas Collection, AN, AP 48, Box 55, Folder 15.

2 See especially Nobles, *Shades of Citizenship*, chapters 2–4.

3 Boris Fausto, *A Revolução de 1930: História e historiografia*, 16th ed. (1970; São Paulo: Companhia das Letras, 1997).

4 Fausto adopts Francisco Weffort's definition of a compromise state: "A state in crisis that is formed and reformed in search of responses to the new conditions created by the crisis of the agricultural economy, the local (and global) crisis of liberal institutions, by the struggle of autonomous industrialization in a traditionally dependent society, by the social dependence of middle sectors and growing popular pressure." Fausto, *A Revolução de 1930*, 29. See also Francisco Weffort, *Classes populares e política* (São Paulo: Universidade de São Paulo, 1968).

5 de Decca, *O silencio dos vencidos*.

6 Weinstein, *For Social Peace in Brazil*, 50–66.

7 Edith Piza and Fúlvia Rosemberg, "Color in the Brazilian Census," in *Race in Contemporary Brazil: From Indifference to Equality*, ed. Rebecca Reichmann (University Park: Pennsylvania State University Press, 1999), 40. See also Fúlvia Rosemberg and Edith Piza, *Analfabetismo, raça e gênero nos censos Brasileiros* (São Paulo: Fundação Carlos Chagas, 1993).

8 Benedict Anderson, *Imagined Communities*, 2nd ed. (1983; London: Verso, 1991), 169.

9 Mário Augusto Teixeira de Freitas, "O exército e a educação nacional," *Jornal de Comercio*, 10 November 1935. Freitas Collection, AN, AP 48, Box 20, Folder 44.

10 Mário Augusto Teixeira de Freitas, "What the Numbers Say about Primary Education in Brazil," *Minas Gerais*, 24 June 1936. Freitas Collection, AN, AP 48, Box 9, Folder 28.

11 Alberto Tôrres, *O problema nacional Brasileiro* (Rio de Janeiro: Imprensa Nacional, 1914), 11.

12 Cited in Barbosa Lima Sobrinho, *A presença de Alberto Tôrres (Sua vida e pensamento)* (Rio de Janeiro: Editora Civilização Brasileira, 1968), 307. Similarly, Cândido Mota Filho, min-

ister of education in the 1950s, called Tôrres's work "an awakening of national consciousness." According to Lima Sobrinho, Tôrres was most widely read in the period between 1930 and 1935. Lima Sobrinho, 506, 508.

13 Alberto Tôrres, A organização nacional (Rio de Janeiro: Imprensa Nacional, 1914).

14 Tôrres, O problema nacional Brasileiro, 44, 11.

15 Skidmore, Black into White, 118–23.

16 Tôrres, O problema nacional Brasileiro, 146, 31.

17 Jeffrey Lesser, Welcoming the Undesirables: Brazil and the Jewish Question (Berkeley: University of California Press, 1994), 32; Lima Sobrinho, A presença de Alberto Tôrres, 511.

18 Lima Sobrinho, A presença de Alberto Tôrres, 506.

19 See especially Mary Kay Vaughan, Cultural Politics in Revolution: Teachers, Pesants, and Schools in Mexico, 1930–1940 (Tucson: University of Arizona Press, 1998); and Monica Esti Rein, Politics and Education in Argentina, 1946–1962 (Armonk, N.Y.: M. E. Sharpe, 1998).

20 For a detailed reading of the creation of the National Department of Public Health as a national public health agency and its projects in preventive health and sanitation, see Hochman, A era do saneamento.

21 Mário Augusto Teixeira de Freitas, "Custo do ensino público, primário geral, no decênio de 1932/1941." Freitas Collection, AN, AP 48, Box 55, Folder 116.

22 Saneamento is translated as both to sanitize and to cure.

23 "O Ministério da Educação e Saúde no quinquenio 1937–1942," Cultura Política 2, no. 21 (1942): 21.

24 Although the Colégio Pedro II ceased to be the curriculum-setting school, it continued to be administered by the federal government and to hold the prestige of being a model of national education (see chapter 6).

25 For an analysis of the role of SPHAN and historic patrimony in building the Estado Novo's idea of the nation, and the role of the state as cultural manager, see Daryle Williams, Culture Wars in Brazil: The First Vargas Regime, 1930–1945 (Durham: Duke University Press, 2001).

26 "O Ministério da Educação e Saúde no quinquenio 1937–1942," 21–39.

27 See Weinstein, For Social Peace in Brazil.

28 For a discussion of the nationalization of immigrant schools, see Schwartzman, Bomeny, and Costa, Tempos de Capanema.

29 Estado do Amazonas, Programas do ensino primário; Estado do Amazonas, Regulamento geral da instrução pública; Estado de Parahyba, Decreto No. 75 de 14 de março de 1931; Estado de Sergipe, Decreto No. 30 de 11 de março de 1931. For Ceará, see Lourenço Filho, Juazeiro de Padre Cícero; for Pará, Maranhão, and Amazonas, see also INEP, Organização do ensino primário e normal, vols. 1–3 (Rio de Janeiro: Ministério de Educação e Saúde, 1939, 1940).

30 "A situação do ensino primário," report by the Instituto Nacional de Estudos Pedagógicos [INEP] of the MES. Lourenço Filho Collection, CPDOC, 41.08.00.

31 Sueann Caulfield, In Defense of Honor: Sexual Morality, Modernity, and Nation in Early-

Twentieth-Century Brazil (Durham: Duke University Press, 1999), 189–90; Susan K. Besse, Restructuring Patriarchy (Chapel Hill: University of North Carolina Press, 1996). The expanding opportunities for (mostly white) women are addressed in chapters 3 and 6.

32 "Número e proporção dos habítantes de 5 anos e mais que sabem ler e escrever, presentes em 10-IX-1940 e em 10-IX-1950, por sexo e grupos de idade," in Conselho Nacional de Estatística, Contribuições para o estudo da demografia no Brasil (Rio de Janeiro: Serviço Gráfico da I BG E, 1961), 389–90; "Alfabetização em relação a côr nos estados," Gustavo Capanema Collection, CPDOC, 35.12.14g (569).

33 Hochman, A era do saneamento.

34 In 1944, Ceará spent Cr$101 (US$6) per student, half the national average of Cr$201 and less than a third of São Paulo's Cr$322 (US$19). "População geral e em idade escolar, em 1935," Secção de Documentação e Intercâmbio, INEP 1939. Gustavo Capanema Collection, CPDOC, 35.12.14g; "Estudo para o rateio do auxilio financeiro supletivo da União aos Estados e ao Distrito Federal," 1944, Freitas Collection, AN, AP 48, Box 8, Folder 27. This and other conversions to dollars are based on data from Ken Serbin, Igreja, Estado e a Ajuda Financeira Pública no Brasil, 1930–1964: Estudos de Três Casos Chaves (Rio de Janeiro: CPDOC/FGV, 1991), 43.

35 Everardo Beckeuser, "A educação primária como fator da unidade nacional," Cultura Política 2, no. 15 (1942): 67.

36 "Alfabetização em relação à côr, nos estados" Gustavo Capanema Collection, CPDOC 35.12.14g (569).

37 States counted in the south include São Paulo, Paraná, Santa Catarina, and Rio Grande do Sul. States counted in the northeast include Maranão, Piauí, Ceará, Rio Grande do Norte, Paraíba, Pernambuco, Sergipe, Bahia, and Alagoas. "Estudo para o rateio do auxilio financeiro supletivo da União aos Estados e ao Distrito Federal," 1944, Freitas Collection, AN, AP 48, Box 8, Folder 27.

38 Introduction by Mário Augusto Teixeira de Freitas, O ensino primário no Brasil no decênio, 1932–1941 (Rio de Janeiro: Serviço Gráfico do I BG E, 1945), xvii.

39 "Número e proporção dos habitantes de 5 anos e mais que sabem ler e escrever, por grupos de idade, com discriminação dos quadros urbanos," in Conselho Nacional de Estatística, Contribuições para o estudo da demografia no Brasil, 309.

40 Teixeira de Freitas, O ensino primário no Brasil em 1939, xx; "A escolaridade primária e a política educacional," Freitas Collection, AN, AP 48, Box 55, Folder 166.

41 Raimundo Pinheiro, "O papel da escola no aproveitamento da Amazonia," Cultura Política 1, no. 10 (1941): 80.

42 Mário Augusto Teixeira de Freitas, "O exército e a educação nacional," Jornal do Comercio, 10 November 1935. Freitas Collection, AN, AP 48, Box 20, Folder 44.

43 "População geral e em idade escolar, em 1935," Secção de Documentação e Intercâmbio, INEP, 1939. Gustavo Capanema Collection, CPDOC 36.12.14g.

44 "Número e proporção dos habítantes de 5 anos e mais que sabem ler e escrever, presentes em 10-IX-1940 e em 10-IX-1950, por sexo e grupos de idade," in Conselho Nacional de Estatística, Contribuições para o estudo da demografia no Brasil, 390.

45   "População geral e em idade escolar, em 1935," Secção de Documentação e Intercâmbio, INEP, 1939. Gustavo Capanema Collection, CPDOC, 36.12.14g; "Estudo para o rateio do auxilio financeiro supletivo da União aos Estados e ao Distrito Federal," 1944, Freitas Collection, AN, AP 48, Box 8, Folder 27; "Ensino primário geral, organização escolar e movimento nas unidades federativas em 1944," Freitas Collection, AN, AP 48, Box 19, Folder 36.

46   Thomas H. Holloway, *Policing Rio de Janeiro: Repression and Resistance in a Nineteenth-Century City* (Stanford: Stanford University Press, 1993), 25; Conselho Nacional de Estatística, *Contribuições para o estudo da demografia no Brasil*, 316; Alfred Agache, *Cidade do Rio de Janeiro: Extenção, remodelação e embellezamento* (Paris: Foyer Brésilien, 1930), 104.

47   See Teresa A. Meade, *"Civilizing" Rio: Reform and Resistance in a Brazilian City, 1889–1930* (Philadelphia: Penn State University Press, 1997).

48   Norma Evenson, *Two Brazilian Capitals: Architecture and Urbanism in Rio de Janeiro and Brasília* (New Haven: Yale University Press, 1973), 51.

49   Agache, *Cidade do Rio de Janeiro*, 90; Thomas W. Merrick and Douglas H. Graham, *Population and Development in Brazil, 1800 to the Present* (Baltimore: Johns Hopkins University Press, 1979), 60.

50   IBGE, *Censo Demográfico—População e Habilitação: Série Regional, parte XVI: Distrito Federal* (Rio de Janeiro: Serviço Gráfico do IBGE, 1950), 21.

51   Agache, *Cidade do Rio de Janeiro*, 100; Diretoria Geral de Estatística, *Recenceamento do Brazil, Realizado em 1 de setembro de 1920. . . . Vol. 4: População* (Rio de Janeiro: Typographia da Estatistica, 1930), 25.

52   SAARA is an acronym for the Sociedade de Amigos da Alfândega e Ruas Adjacentes. Jeffrey Lesser, *Negotiating National Identity: Immigrants, Minorities, and the Struggle for Ethnicity in Brazil* (Durham: Duke University Press, 1999), 78.

53   Agache, *Cidade do Rio de Janeiro*, 104.

54   José Alípio Goulart, *Favelas do Distrito Federal* (Rio de Janeiro: Serviço de Informação Agrícola, Ministério da Agricultura, 1957), 16.

55   IBGE, *O aproveitamento das apurações do Censo Demográfico de 1940 para a determinação das correntes de migração interior* (Rio de Janeiro: Serviço Gráfico do IBGE, 1948), 32–36.

56   Nereu de Sampaio, "Plano regulador das construções escolares," *Boletim de Educação Pública* 1, no. 1 (1932): 375.

57   Agache, *Cidade do Rio de Janeiro*, 189.

58   Nereu de Sampaio, "Plano regulador," 377.

59   Azevedo Lima, "O problema do prédio escolar no Distrito Federal," *Cultura Política* 1, no. 5 (1941): 77–78.

60   Costa Pinto, *O negro no Rio de Janeiro*, 130; José Alípio Goulart, *Favelas do Distrito Federal* (Rio de Janeiro: Serviço de Informação Agrícola, 1957).

61   Goulart, *Favelas do Distrito Federal*, 23; Agache, *Cidade do Rio de Janeiro*, 190.

62   H. Dias Cruz, *Os morros Cariocas no novo regime* (Rio de Janeiro: Grafica Olimpica, 1941), 41.

63   Costa Pinto, *O negro no Rio de Janeiro*, 106–8.

64 IBGE, *Censo Demográfico—População e Habitação*, 52.
65 Nereu de Sampaio, "Plano regulador," 376.
66 Costa Pinto, *O negro no Rio de Janeiro*, 135.
67 Fernandes argued that in postemancipation Brazil, "the Negroes and mulattos remained to the side or found themselves altogether left out of the general prosperity and cut off from political benefits, because they did not have the prerequisites for participating in the game or for abiding by its rules." Fernandes, *The Negro in Brazilian Society*, 56. On the UNESCO study, see Marcos Chor Maio and Ricardo Ventura Santos, eds., *Raça, ciência e sociedade* (Rio de Janeiro: Editora FIOCRUZ, 1996).
68 Costa Pinto, *O negro no Rio de Janeiro*, 133, 63, 41.
69 Ibid., 151–52, 162.
70 Nereu de Sampaio, "Plano regulador," 377.

3. WHAT HAPPENED TO RIO'S TEACHERS OF COLOR?

1 Dain Borges, *The Family in Bahia, 1870–1945* (Stanford: Stanford University Press, 1992), 364, n.36.
2 Diretoria Geral de Estatística, *Recenseamento do Brasil*, vol. 4, 27.
3 See David Hollinger, "Authority, Solidarity, and the Political Economy of Identity: The Case of the United States," *Diacritics* 29, no. 4 (1999): 119.
4 Directoria Geral de Estatística, *Recenceamento do Brasil*, vol. 4, xiii; IBGE, *Censo Demográfico—População e Habilitação*, 26–29.
5 On self-identification in the census, see Nobles, *Shades of Citizenship*, 99.
6 Maria Augusta dos Santos, "Cartas," *Getulino*, 5 August 1923, 1.
7 Aristides Barbosa and Francisco Lucrécio, in Márcio Barbosa, *Frente Negra Brasileira: Depoimentos* (São Paulo: Quilombhoje, 1998), 30–42.
8 Norma Fraga, interview by Jerry Dávila, 13 July 2000.
9 Maria Elizabete Xavier et al., *História da educação: A escola no Brasil* (São Paulo: Editora FTD, 1994), 62.
10 Maria Yedda Linhares, interview by Jerry Dávila, 20 July 2000. *Pistolão* has a double meaning. Its literal meaning comes from the latin *epistolam*, or letter, and means a letter of recommendation from a powerful individual. In conventional use, however, the meaning became intertwined with the concept of the powerful individual who provided the letter, thus acquiring the slang meaning "big gun." Aurélio Buarque de Holanda, *Novo Aurélio Século XXI: a dicionário da lingua portuguesa*. 3rd ed. (1975; Rio de Janeiro: Editora Nova Fronteira, 1999), 1340.
11 Aristides Barbosa, in Barbosa, *Frente Negra*, 29–30.
12 Teixeira de Freitas, *A escolaridade primária e a política educacional*, chapter 5, "Revelações dos Números no Terreno Social (1946)," Freitas Collection, AN, AP 48, Box 55, Folder 15.
13 Miguel Barros, "Discurso do representante da Frente Negra Pelotense," *Estudos Afro-*

Brasileiros (Trabalhos apresentados no 1° Congresso Afro-Brasileiro reunido no Recife em 1934), Vol. 1. (Rio de Janeiro: Ariel Editora, 1935), 271.

14 "Professor Norberto de Souza Pinto," Getulino, 15 June 1924.

15 Fernando de Azevedo, "A formação do professorado e a reforma," Boletim de Educação Pública 1, no. 4 (1930): 497, 495.

16 Decreto 3.810, organização do Instituto de Educação do Rio de Janeiro (Rio de Janeiro: Directoria Geral de Instrução Pública da Prefeitura do Distrito Federal, 1932), 21.

17 Lourenço Filho, "A Escola de Professores do Instituto de Educação," Arquivos do Instituto de Educação 1, no. 1 (1934): 15–16.

18 Francisco Campos, Regulamento do ensino normal do Estado de Minas Gerais (Decreto n. 9450 de 18 de fevereiro de 1930 (Belo Horizonte: Imprensa Oficial de Minas Gerais, 1930), 3.

19 Azevedo, "A formação do professorado e a reforma," 494.

20 Mário de Brito, "A admissão à escola secundária," Arquivos do Instituto de Educação 1, no. 1 (1934): 27.

21 See Dorothy Ross, The Rise of American Social Science (Cambridge: Cambridge University Press, 1991), and (ed.) Modernist Impulses in the Social Sciences (Baltimore: Johns Hopkins University Press, 1994); and Gould, The Mismeasure of Man.

22 Lawrence A. Cremin, David A. Shannon, and Mary Evelyn Townsend, A History of Teachers College, Columbia University (New York: Columbia University Press, 1954), 77.

23 Letter from James E. Russell to Wycliffe Rose, 18 December 1932, in Brahm David Fleisch, "The Teachers College Club: American Educational Discourse and the Origins of Bantu Education in South Africa, 1914–1951" (Ph.D. diss., Columbia University, 1995), 24.

24 Teachers College Report of the Dean for the Year Ending June 30, 1928, Columbia University Teachers College Archive, 40.

25 Students from Other Lands in Attendance at Teachers College to Date of Spring 1959, Columbia University Teachers College Archive, 2.

26 Letter from Lois Williams to Anísio Teixeira, 19 January 1934. Anísio Teixeira Collection, CPDOC, pi32.01.06.

27 Decreto 3.810, organização do Instituto de Educação do Rio de Janeiro, 21.

28 Eliane Marta Teixeira Lopes, "Júlio Afrânio Peixoto," in Dicionário de educadores no Brasil, ed. Fávero and Britto, 323.

29 Lourenço Filho, "A Escola de Professores do Instituto de Educação," 16–17.

30 Campos, Regulamento do ensino normal de Minas Gerais, 9.

31 Ibid.

32 Ibid., 9, 18.

33 Stepan, "The Hour of Eugenics," 64.

34 Teixeira, "O systema escolar do Rio de Janeiro, D.F.: Relatório de um anno de administração," Boletim de Educação Pública 1, no. 4 (1932), 353.

35 Diana Gonçalves Vidal, "O exercício disciplinado do olhar: Livros, leituras e práticas de

formação docente no Instituto de Educação do Distrito Federal" (Ph.D. diss., Universidade de São Paulo, 1995), 52.

36 Mário de Queiroz Rodrigues, "Educação física: Programa do curso normal do Instituto de Educação," *Revista de Educação Pública* 2, no. 2 (1944): 247.

37 Teixeira, "O systema escolar do Rio de Janeiro," 361.

38 Helena Silva de Oliveira, interviewed by Vidal, "Exercício disciplinado do olhar," 28.

39 Zilá Simas Enéas, *Era uma vez no Instituto de Educação*, 27.

40 Reed Tuddenham cited in Walt Haney, "Validity, Vaudeville, and Values: A Short History of Social Concerns Over Standardized Testing," *American Psychologist* 10, no. 36 (1981): 1022.

41 Brito, "A admissão a escola secundária," 31.

42 Ibid., 28.

43 Ibid., 29.

44 Enéas, *Era uma vez*, 28; Vidal, "Exercício disciplinado do olhar," 88.

45 Francisco Lucrécio, in Barbosa, *Frente Negra*, 55.

46 "A Côr e a Guarda Civil," *O Clarim d'Alvorada*, 14 July 1929, 1.

47 Francisco Lucrécio, in Barbosa, *Frente Negra*, 55.

48 "Instituto de Educação (Noticia mandada elaborar pelo Departamento de Educação para uma publicação sobre 'O Sistema Educacional do Rio de Janeiro, Distrito Federal')," *Arquivos do Instituto de Educação* 1, no. 1 (1934): 5, 10. Lourenço Filho, "A Escola de Professores," 19.

49 IBGE, *Censo Demográfico—População e Habitação*, 26–29.

50 Brito, "A admissão a escola secundária," 32.

51 "A escola primária do Instituto de Educação—relatório do ano 1933." Lourenço Filho Collection, CPDOC, Instituto de Educação (0482).

52 Letter from Mário de Brito to Anísio Teixeira, 12 December 1933. Anísio Teixeira Collection, CPDOC, 33.12.05 (0672).

53 "Conselho Nacional de Educação," Session from 27 October 1937. Lourenço Filho Collection, CPDOC, Conselho Nacional de Educação (0368).

54 Cited in Vidal, "Exercício disciplinado do olhar," 147–59. Teixeira even donated to the library the salary he drew from the Institute of Education for his chair in sociology.

55 "Conselho Nacional de Educação," Session from 27 October 1937. Lourenço Filho Collection, CPDOC, Conselho Nacional de Educação (0368).

56 Clarice Nunes, "Anísio Teixeira: A poesia da ação" (Ph.D. diss., Pontifícia Universidade Católica do Rio de Janeiro, 1991), 306.

57 "Conselho Nacional de Educação," Session from 27 October 1937. Lourenço Filho Collection, CPDOC, Conselho Nacional de Educação (0368).

58 Unsigned document, Anísio Teixeira Collection, CPDOC, pi 31/36.00.00 (0699).

59 Umbelina de Mattos, interviewed by Jerry Dávila, 23 July 1999. As the daughter of Baptista de Mattos, the highest-ranking black officer in the Brazilian army, Umbelina de Mattos's presence as a woman of color at the Institute of Education during the Estado Novo in part illustrates the rise of another strain of social power alongside social scientific technicalization: the will of the military. At the time, the Rio de Janeiro

Department of Education, the Institute of Education, and numerous top-ranking posts in the school system were occupied by military officers.

60 B., interviewed by Barreto, "Contribuição para a história da escola pública," 120.

61 Butler, *Freedoms Given, Freedoms Won*, 33. For more on the relationship between whiteness and modernity in Brazil, see also Michael Hanchard, "Black Cinderella? Race and the Public Sphere in Brazil," *Public Culture* 7, no. 1 (1994): 165–85; Lesser, *Negotiating National Identity*; and Reid Andrews, *Blacks and Whites in São Paulo, Brazil, 1888–1988*.

62 Victor Murray, cited in Fleisch, "The Teachers College Club," 56.

4. ELEMENTARY EDUCATION

1 "Relatório apresentado pela diretora da escola Vicente Licínio (3–8) ao Exm. Snr. superintendente da 3a circunscrição de ensino elementar, 1933." Anísio Teixeira Collection, FGV/CPDOC, pi33.00.00 (3/293). The principal's name was not included in the report. As discussed in chapter 2, urban renewal and the booming real estate market forced the poor out of downtown neighborhoods en masse. These working poor largely resettled in the northern and western zones of the city, which were linked to the city center by light rail. Bringing new schools to these populations was the principal and most successful goal of the Teixeira administration.

2 Ibid.

3 Ibid.

4 Azevedo Lima, "O problema do prédio escolar," 80.

5 For an analysis of the Pedro Ernesto Batista administration and political program, see Michael Conniff, *Urban Politics in Brazil*.

6 Peter Winn, "A Worker's Nightmare: Taylorism and the 1962 Yarur Strike in Chile," *Radical History Review* 58 (1994): 4–34. For a discussion of the widespread application of Taylorism within São Paulo industry, see Weinstein, *For Social Peace in Brazil*, 4–7.

7 Teixeira, "O systema escolar do Rio de Janeiro," 314.

8 Weinstein, *For Social Peace in Brazil*, 114.

9 *Decreto 3.810, organização do Instituto de Educação do Rio de Janeiro*, 21.

10 Teixeira, "O systema escolar do Rio de Janeiro," 311.

11 Ibid., 309.

12 Ibid., 317.

13 Ibid., 326.

14 Nereu de Sampaio, "Plano regulador," 384.

15 Ibid., 371.

16 Ibid., 395.

17 Ibid., 391.

18 Ibid., 376.

19 Map 6 only shows the school buildings that were owned by the city. Owing to a lack of data, it does not indicate the locations of the dozens of rented buildings or rooms that were used as temporary schools.

20 Azevedo Lima, "O problema do prédio escolar," 80.

21 Quoted in Beatriz Santos de Oliveira, "A modernidade oficial: A arquitetura das escolas públicas do Distrito Federal (1928–1940)" (Ph.D. diss., FAU/Universidade de São Paulo, 1981), 200.

22 For a detailed analysis of the architectural style of Teixeira's schools, see Oliveira, "A modernidade oficial."

23 Cited in Oliveira, "A modernidade oficial," 194.

24 Enéas Silva, cited in Oliveira, "A modernidade oficial," 194.

25 Teixeira, "O systema escolar do Rio de Janeiro," 324.

26 "Psicologia Educacional—Curso de Didática." Lourenço Filho Collection, CPDOC, PROG (0493).

27 José Adailson Medeiros, "Ulisses Pernambucano de Mello Sobrinho," in Dicionário de educadores Brasileiros, ed. Fávero and Britto, 472.

28 Regina Helena de Freitas Campos, "Helena Antipoff," in Dicionário de educadores Brasileiros, ed. Fávero and Britto, 241. See also Regina Helena de Freitas Campos, "Conflicting Interpretations of Intellectual Abilities among Brazilian Psychologists and Their Impact on Primary Schooling" (Ph.D. diss., Stanford University, 1989).

29 Manoel Bergstrom Lourenço Filho, Testes ABC para a verificação da maturidade necessária a aprendizagem da leitura e da escrita, 6th ed. 1933. (São Paulo: Edições Melhoramentos, 1957). While these tests were applied uncritically in Brazil, by 1930 Terman's test and other measures were openly questioned in the United States. Terman's test was criticized, for instance, by reknown journalist Walter Lippman in his essays "Mystery of the A Men" and "The Abuse of Tests." See Haney, "Validity, Vaudeville, and Values," 1023.

30 Isaias Alves, "Testes collectivos de intelligencia (Terman Group Test) e a sua applicação nas escolas públicas," Boletim de Educação Pública 1, no. 1 (1932): 397.

31 Alves, "Testes collectivos de intelligencia," 397.

32 Lourenço Filho, Testes ABC, 84.

33 Ibid., 86.

34 "Escola General Trompowsky," Anísio Teixeira Collection, CPDOC, pi35.00.00.

35 Ofélia Boisson Cardoso, "Curso de especialização em problemas de primeira série—Organizado pela Secretaria Geral de Educação e Cultura para o magistério primário no 20 semestre de 1943," Revista de Educação Pública 1, no. 4 (1943): 576.

36 Ibid., 587, 590.

37 "Secção de Antropometria," 16 October 1935. Lourenço Filho Collection, CPDOC, IPE (0010).

38 Bastos D'Avila to Lourenço Filho, 16 April 1936. Lourenço Filho Collection, CPDOC, IPE (0042).

39 See Nicola Pende, Scienzia Dell'Ortogenesi (Bergamo: Instituto Italiono D'Arti Grafiche, 1939).

40 Arthur Ramos to Lourenço Filho, 18 April 1936. Lourenço Filho Collection, CPDOC, IPE (0044).

41 "Condições de serviços odontológicos para alunos pobres," *Revista de Educação Pública* 1, no. 1 (1943): 40.

5. ESCOLA NOVO NO ESTADO NOVO: THE NEW SCHOOL IN THE NEW STATE

1 Paschoal Lemme, *Memórias*, vol. 2 (Rio de Janeiro: Cortez Editora/INEP, 1988), 241. Lemme's account of his months in jail with leading dissident intellectuals, as well as his participation in a prison university put together by 1935 detainees who provided lectures on their areas of expertise as well as general education courses for less-educated detainees, is a striking glimpse of life under repression during the Vargas era.

2 Ibid., 127.

3 Ibid., 130.

4 Zaia Brandão, "Paschoal Lemme," in *Dicionário de educadores do Brasil*, ed. Fávero and Britto, 426–34.

5 Heitor Villa-Lobos, *Canto orfeônico: Marchas, canções, e cantos marciais para educação consciente da "Unidade de Movimento,"* vol. 1 (Rio de Janeiro: E. S. Mangione, 1940).

6 Villa-Lobos, *Canto orfeônico*, 23.

7 Heitor Villa-Lobos, "Educação Musical," in *A presença de Villa Lobos*, vol. 13 (Rio de Janeiro: Museu Villa-Lobos, 1991), 8.

8 Ibid., 2.

9 Ibid., 12.

10 Villa-Lobos, *Canto orfeônico*, 1.

11 Ibid.

12 Villa-Lobos, "Educação Musical," 8.

13 Norma Fraga, interviewed by Jerry Dávila, 13 July 2000.

14 Ibid.

15 Maria Yedda Linhares, interviewed by Jerry Dávila, 17 July 2000. See also Eugen Webber, *Peasants into Frenchmen: The Modernization of Rural France, 1870–1914* (Stanford: Stanford University Press, 1976); and Jeffrey D. Needell, *A Tropical Belle Epoque: Elite Culture and Society in Turn-of-the-Century Rio de Janeiro* (Cambridge: Cambridge University Press, 1991).

16 "A agressividade do obscurantismo," Anísio Teixeira Collection, CPDOC, pi31/36.00.00 (0684).

17 Letter from Fernando de Azevedo to Anísio Teixeira, 12 March 1932. Anísio Teixeira Collection, CPDOC, 31.12.27.

18 On the politization between the Church and progressive educators over religious education, see Schwartzman et al., *Tempos de Capanema*; Horta, *O hino, o sermão, e a ordem do dia*; Conniff, *Urban Politics in Brazil*; Sarmento, *Pedro Ernesto*; and Marta Maria Chagas de Carvalho, "Molde nacional e forma cívica: Higiene, moral e trabalho no projeto da Associação Brasileira de Educação, 1924–1931" (Ph.D. diss., FEUSP/Universidade de São Paulo, 1996).

19 Letter from Alceu Amoroso Lima to Gustavo Capanema, 16 June 1935, Gustavo Capanema Collection, CPDOC, "Correspondence," GC/LIMA, Alceu Amoroso(0066).

20 Conniff, *Urban Politics in Brazil*, 146, 149.

21 Cited in Sarmento, *Pedro Ernesto*, 61.

22 "Conselho Nacional de Educação" Session of 27 October 1937. Lourenço Filho Collection, CPDOC, Conselho Nacional de Educação (0368).

23 "Relatório do ano 1936," Institute of Education. Lourenço Filho Collection, CPDOC, Instituto de Educação (0529).

24 Ibid.

25 Letter from Fernando de Azevedo to Anísio Teixeira, 26 August 1933. Anísio Teixeira Collection, CPDOC, 33.8.26 (0340).

26 Conniff, *Urban Politics in Brazil*, 149.

27 Letter from Anísio Teixeira to Assis Chateaubriand, 10 March 1932. Anísio Teixeira Archive, CPDOC, 32.02.17 (0450).

28 Undated memorandum, "Intellectual Production." Anísio Teixeira Collection, CPDOC, 31/35.00.00 (0681).

29 "A agressividade do obscurantismo." Anísio Teixeira Archive, CPDOC, pi31/36.00.00 (0684).

30 Letter from Mário Augusto Teixeira de Freitas to Fernando de Azevedo, 2 January 1936. Freitas Collection, AN, AP 48, Box 11, Folder 32.

31 Ibid.

32 Handwritten draft of the resignation letter from Anísio Teixeira to Pedro Ernesto. Anísio Teixeira Collection, CPDOC, 32.03.15 (0477).

33 The letter was signed by Afrânio Peixoto, former rector of the University of the Federal District, which had been organized by Teixeira; A. Carneiro Leão, former director of the Rio school system; Roberto Marinho de Azevedo, director of the Engineering School of the University of the Federal District; Gustavo Lessa, director of the Institute for Educational Research; Mario de Brito, director of the Institute of Education's secondary school; Paulo Ribeiro, chief of the Buildings and Education Material Division; and Celso Kelley, secretary of education for the state of Rio de Janeiro. Anísio Teixeira Collection, CPDOC, 35.12.01 (0919).

34 Draft of undated letter from Anísio Teixeira to U.S. Diplomat Barnette. Anísio Teixeira Collection, CPDOC, 36/45.00.00 (0952).

35 Conniff, *Urban Politics in Brazil*, 150–52.

36 Henrique Dodsworth dossier, Filinto Müller Collection, CPDOC, Biografias. In 1932, the state of São Paulo rebelled against the federal government, demanding a return to constitutional government. The renegade state was defeated, but in 1934 a national convention approved a new constitution for Brazil.

37 "Henrique Dodsworth: Traços biográficos," in *Revista de Educação Pública* 2, no. 3 (1944): 340. Henrique Dodsworth, *Relatório, 1932–1933, do Externato do Colégio Pedro II* (Rio de Janeiro: Imprensa Nacional, 1933).

38 Henrique Toledo Dodsworth, *Aspectos do ensino secundário: Relatório apresentado ao Exmo.*

Ministro da Justiça e Negocios Interiores, 1921 (Rio de Janeiro: Gazeta de Noticias, 1921), 11–12. Dodsworth went on to lament that "official inspection limits itself to punching the clock, bureaucratically counting teacher absences, and does not have the means to prevent the programs from being only partly taught, nor that laboratories represent only an experimental fiction."

39 Jonas Correia, "Reorganização do ensino primário do Distrito Federal: Exposição de motivos do Decreto No. 7718, de 5 de fevereiro de 1944," *Revista de Educação Pública* 2, no. 1 (1944): 103.

40 Ibid., 103–4.

41 Letter from Fernando de Azevedo to Anísio Teixeira, 26 August 1933. Anísio Teixeira Collection, CPDOC, 33.8.26 (0340).

42 "Expressão da moderna pedagogia social," *A Noite*, 26 February 1944, reprinted in *Revista de Educação Pública* 2, no. 1 (1944): 335.

43 "Educação Primária," *Jornal do Brasil*, 27 April 1944, reprinted in *Revista de Educação Pública* 2, no. 1 (1944): 338.

44 "Expressão da moderna pedagogia social," *A Noite*, 335.

45 Letter from Edgar de Pereira da Silva to Getúlio Vargas, 24 September 1941. Henrique Dodsworth Collection, AGC, Box 15—Education, 1939–1945 (11418).

46 "Colégio do Instituto de Educação," *Revista de Educação Pública* 1, no. 1 (1943): 134.

47 "Comemoração do aniversário do Departamento de Educação Nacionalista," *Revista de Educação Pública* 1, no. 1 (1943): 136–37.

48 Ibid., 137.

49 *Fon-Fon* (1941): 20. Henrique Dodsworth Collection, AGC, Box 15—Education, 1939–1945 (04106).

50 Clarice Nunes, "A escola redescobre a cidade: Reinterpretação da modernidade pedagógica no espaço urbano carioca, 1910–1935" (Niteroi: Universidade Federal Fluminense, 1993), 130.

51 "Projetadas escolas para a Zona Leopoldina," *Revista de Educação Pública* 3, no. 1 (1945): 117.

52 Romero, "Medicina e educação," 360.

53 *Fon-Fon* (1941): 20. Henrique Dodsworth Collection, AGC, Box 15—Education, 1939–1945 (01406).

54 Ibid.

55 Antônio Maria Teixeira and E. Corrêa de Azevedo, "Escolares desajustados (Considerações sôbre o relatório do 5o D.M.P., Relativo a 1942)," *Revista de Educação Pública* 1, no. 3 (1943): 325.

56 Ibid.

57 Joaquim Silveira Thomaz, "Desenvolvimento cefálico e sub-nutrição," *Revista de Educação Pública* 2, no. 4 (1944): 593.

58 Ibid., 595.

59 Alfredo Balthazar da Silveira, *História do Instituto de Educação* (Rio de Janeiro: Secretaria Geral de Educação e Cultura, 1954), 106–7.

60 A., interviewed by Barreto, "Contribuição para a história da escola pública," 111.

61 "Palavras de apresentação e de fé," Instituto 1, no. 1 (1941): 2.

62 "Hino do Instituto de Educação," Instituto 1, no. 1 (1941): 8.

63 "O Hino do Instituto," Instituto 1, no. 1 (1941): 9.

64 "O Dia da Bandeira," Instituto 1, no. 1 (1941): 14.

65 Williams, Culture Wars in Brazil, 10.

66 Getúlio Vargas, "Discurso de paraninfo com que o Presidente Getúlio Vargas se dirigiu aos professorandos de 1943, no Instituto de Educação, no ato de colocação de grau," Revista de Educação Pública 1, no. 4 (1943): 471.

67 Ibid., 473.

68 "Gravado o discurso de paraninfo do Presidente Getúlio Vargas," Revista de Educação Pública 2, no. 2 (1944): 330.

69 Jonas Correia, "Discurso pronunciado pelo Secretário de Educação e Cultura, Cel. Jonas Correia, no Instituto de Educação, paraninfando a segunda turma de professorandas de 1944," Revista de Educação Pública 3, no. 1 (1945): 695.

70 Ibid.

71 "Homenagem ao Professor Fernando de Azevedo no Instituto de Educação," Revista de Educação Pública 3, no. 4 (1945): 698.

72 "S.G.E.C. Instruções N. 2," Revista de Educação Pública 3, no. 3 (1945): 409.

73 Joel Wolfe, " 'Father of the Poor' or 'Mother of the Rich'?" 93.

74 Caulfield, In Defense of Honor, 14.

75 Request by the residents of Senador Camará for a school, 7 January 1944. Henrique Dodsworth Collection, AGC, Box 108—Education, 1939–1945 (07596).

76 Ibid.

77 Letter from the Companhia Confiança Industrial to Henrique Dodsworth, 24 November 1944. Henrique Dodsworth Collection, AGC, Box 108—Education, 1939–1945 (16948).

78 Letter from Felicidade Rodrigues to Getúlio Vargas, 27 June 1941. Henrique Dodsworth Collection, AGC, Box 15—Education, 1939–1945 (07183).

79 "Petition on the Allocation of Ground Floor to the Escola de Ciências, Artes e Profissões Orsina da Fonseca, 13 February 1941." Cardoso identified herself as an elementary school teacher assigned to the fiscalization of the 1st District. She occupied a role not unlike that of other women who entered teaching, and she had moved on to administrative posts within the school system. Henrique Dodsworth Collection, AGC, Box 15—Education, 1939–1945 (05172).

80 Letter from Fernando Perreira da Silva of the Comissão do Plano da Cidade to the Secretary of Education, 9 September 1941. Henrique Dodsworth Collection, AGC, Box 15—Education, 1939–1945 (05172).

6. BEHAVING WHITE: RIO'S SECONDARY SCHOOL

1 Wilson Choeri and Aloysio Barbosa, interviewed by Jerry Dávila, 1 August 1999.

2 Letter from Raja Gabaglia to Carlos Drummond de Andrade, 14 April 1942. Gustavo

Capanema Collection, CPDOC, Correspondence, GC/GABAGLIA, F (0466). Orlando de Barros, *Preconceito e educação no Governo Vargas (1930–1945)* (Rio de Janeiro: Colégio Pedro II, 1987), ii.

3   "Registro das Penas Disciplinares impostos aos alunos do Colégio Pedro II, 1934," entry by Raja Gabaglia, 16 November, 1940. Colégio Pedro II Archive, Marechal Floriano Branch.

4   Letter from Gaspar Dutra to Gustavo Capanema, 20 November 1940. Gustavo Capanema Collection, CPDOC, 35.10.18g (133).

5   "Registro das Penas Disciplinares," Raja Gabaglia, 12 December 1939. Colégio Pedro II Archive, Marechal Floriano Branch.

6   Letter from Raja Gabaglia to Gustavo Capanema, 14 December 1940. Gustavo Capanema Collection, CPDOC, 35.10.18g (136).

7   For a study of the Colégio Pedro II during the Republic, see Jeffrey Needell, *A Tropical Belle Epoque*.

8   Fernando Segismundo, *Excelências do Colégio Pedro II* (Rio de Janeiro: Colégio Pedro II, 1993), 91.

9   Ibid., 31.

10 Barreto, "Contribuição para a história da escola pública," 20.

11 Ibid., ii.

12 Segismundo, *Excelências do Colégio Pedro II*, 58.

13 Letter from Raja Gabaglia to Gustavo Capanema, 10 November 1941. Gustavo Capanema Collection, CPDOC, 41.10.11 (290).

14 Barreto, "Contribuição para a história da escola pública," 3.

15 Letter from Antonio Figuereira de Almeida to Gustavo Capanema, 28 October 1942. Gustavo Capanema Collection, CPDOC 35.10.18g (184).

16 Teixeira de Freitas, "Revelações dos números no terreno social (1946)," Freitas Collection, AN, AP 48, Box 55, Folder 15.

17 "Centro de Cultura e Civismo: Sindicato dos Educadores Brasileiros," in *Rio Ilustrado*, Special Edition, Homenagem às Classes Conservadoras, 1940.

18 "Turma de 1936—Colégio Pedro II—Internato." Colégio Pedro II Archive, São Cristovão Branch.

19 Ibid.

20 Clovis de Rêgo Monteiro, *Relatório do Diretor do Colégio Pedro II—Internato, ao Excelentíssimo Senhor Ministro da Educação e Saúde, Relativo aos anos de 1938 a 1943* (Rio de Janeiro: Colégio Pedro II, 1944).

21 "Turma de 1936—Colégio Pedro II—Internato." Colégio Pedro II Archive, São Cristovão Branch.

22 Barreto, "Contribuição para a história da escola pública," i–ii.

23 Maria Cecilia Teixeira, interviewed by Jerry Dávila, 13 July 2000.

24 Dodsworth, *Relatório, 1932–1933;* "Relatório Sucito de Ocurrencias e Atividades Verificadas no Externato do Colégio Pedro II (Periodo de Novembro de 1930 a Novembro de 1940)," Gustavo Capanema Collection, CPDOC, 35.10.18g (130).

25 "Matrícula do 50 Anno—1931." Colégio Pedro II Archive, Marechal Floriano Branch.

26 Ibid.

27 Dodsworth, *Relatório, 1932–1933.*

28 "Registro das penas disciplinares," Raja Gabaglia, 1 June 1942. Colégio Pedro II Archive, Marechal Floriano Branch.

29 "Registro das penas disciplinares," Raja Gabaglia, 14 July 1942. Colégio Pedro II Archive, Marechal Floriano Branch.

30 Norma Fraga, interviewed by Jerry Dávila, 13 July 2000.

31 "A Semana anti-alcoolica," *Pronome* 4, no. 21 (7 October 1932). Colégio Pedro II Archive, Marechal Floriano Branch.

32 "Effeitos do alcoolismo," *Pronome* 4, no. 21 (7 October 1932). Colégio Pedro II Archive, Marechal Floriano Branch.

33 Max Monteiro, "O Arauto," *O Arauto* 1, no. 1 (15 April 1931), 1. Colégio Pedro II Archive, Marechal Floriano Branch.

34 "Instrucção physica no Collegio Pedro II," *O Arauto* 1, no. 1 (15 April 1931), 2. Colégio Pedro II Archive, Marechal Floriano Branch.

35 Ibid.

36 Editorial, *O Arauto* 1, no. 2 (4 May 1931), 1. Colégio Pedro II Archive, Marechal Floriano Branch.

37 "Instrucção physica no Collegio Pedro II," *O Arauto* 1, no. 2 (4 May 1931), 5. Colégio Pedro II Archive, Marechal Floriano Branch.

38 "Instrucção physica," *O Arauto* 1, no. 5 (1 September 1931), 3. Colégio Pedro II Archive, Marechal Floriano Branch.

39 Ibid.

40 "Relatorio Sucinto de Ocurrecias e Atividades Verificadas no Externato do Colégio Pedro II (Periodo de Novembro de 1930 a Novembro de 1940)," Raja Gabaglia. Gustavo Capanema Collection, CPDOC, 35.10.18g (130).

41 "CPII" *O Arauto* 1, no. 2 (4 May 1931), 1. Colégio Pedro II Archive, Marechal Floriano Branch.

42 Ibid.

43 Stepan, "*The Hour of Eugenics*," 70.

44 Dodsworth, *Relatório, 1932–1933.*

45 Jonathas Serrano, *História da civilização (em cinco volumes, para o curso secundário)*, 5th ed. (Rio de Janeiro: F. Briguet & Cia., 1939), 209. The Campos reform of 1931 ended the separation of the disciplines of universal history and history of Brazil by creating a single discipline referred to as either universal history or history of civilization. This discipline was to give preference to Brazilian history within a world history context. The main text used for this discipline was Serrano's, which was divided into five volumes (one for each year of secondary education). The first volume, referred to above, was a general orientation that did not discuss Brazil. It made recourse to biographies of historical figures, followed by brief discussions of the historical contexts or events within which they participated. The intention was to incite student's interest in history. In later years, the books were divided into time periods that were

explored in greater thematic depth and with Brazilian history holding a privileged position. A decade later, the Capanema reform (1942) again divided Brazilian and world history, giving preference to Brazilian history.

46 Jonathas Serrano, *Epítome de história do Brasil*, 3rd ed. (1933; F. Briguet & Cia., 1941), 164.

47 Ibid., 160.

48 Ibid., 174.

49 Ibid., 175–76.

50 Ibid., 235–36.

51 Ibid., 242.

52 Serrano, *História da civilização*, 197.

53 Fernando Antonio Raja Gabaglia, *Leituras geográficas (Para o ensino secundário)* (Rio de Janeiro: F. Briguet & Cia., 1933), 116.

54 Ibid., 117.

55 Ibid., 119.

56 Ibid., 193.

57 Faria Góes, *Esboço para ensino secundário* (Rio de Janeiro: Oficina Gráfica do Departamento de Educação, 1935), 21.

58 Teixeira, "O systema escolar do Rio de Janeiro," 349.

59 Góes, *Esboço para ensino secundário*, 20.

60 Teixeira, "O systema escolar do Rio de Janeiro," 348.

61 Góes, *Esboço para ensino secundário*, 20.

62 Teixeira, "O systema escolar do Rio de Janeiro," 343, 344.

63 Góes, *Esboço para ensino secundário*, 10, 19.

64 Ibid., 15, 17.

65 Ibid., 29.

66 Ibid., 111.

67 Teixeira, "O systema escolar do Rio de Janeiro," 347.

68 INEP, *Oportunidades de educação no capital do país (Informações sobre as escolas e cursos para uso de pais, professores, e estudantes* (Rio de Janeiro: Imprensa Nacional, 1941), 60; Joel Wolfe, *Working Women, Working Men: São Paulo and the Rise of Brazil's Industrial Working Class, 1900–1955* (Durham: Duke University Press, 1993), 104. According to Wolfe, in 1940 the monthly minimum wage for São Paulo was Cr$220 (about US$13). Filinto Müller Collection, CPDOC, Relatórios chp.SIPS Pasta 1, "A indústria do livro, Considerações Gerais," 21 November 1938.

69 Yedda Chiabotto, "Ensino técnico-profissional no Distrito Federal: Movimento dos estabelecimentos e aproveitamento registrado no ano de 1942," *Revista Educação Pública* 1, no. 3 (1943): 363.

70 Teixeira, "O systema escolar do Rio de Janeiro," 348.

71 Nunes, "Anísio Teixeira," 294.

72 "Escola Técnica Amaro Cavalcanti," undated document, Anísio Teixeira Collection, CPDOC, pi32/36.00.00.

73 INEP, *Oportunidades de educação*, 60.

74 "Escola Técnica Amaro Cavalcanti," undated document, Anísio Teixeira Collection, CPDOC, pi32/36.00.00. Quotes in subsequent paragraphs also from this document.

75 Nunes, "Anísio Teixeira," 298.

76 Ibid.

77 Letter from Colonel Pio Borges to Henrique Dodsworth, 6 November 1941. Henrique Dodsworth Collection, AGC, Box 15—Education, 1939–1945 (11418).

78 Letter from Captain Ricardo Teixeira da Costa et al. to Henrique Dodsworth, 18 May 1945. Henrique Dodsworth Collection, AGC, Box 15—Education, 1939–1945.

79 Ibid.

80 Memorandum from Secundino Ribeiro Júnior to Henrique Dodsworth, 7 July 1945. Henrique Dodsworth Collection, AGC, Box 15—Education, 1939–1945 (07243).

81 Memorandum from Luiz Palmeira to Henrique Dodsworth, 3 August 1945. Henrique Dodsworth Collection, AGC, Box 15—Education, 1939–1945 (07243).

82 Letter from Raja Gabaglia to Philadelpho de Azevedo, 14 January 1946. Henrique Dodsworth Collection, AGC, Box 15—Education, 1939–1945 (5696).

83 Fernando Antonio Raja Gabaglia, "Ginásios Municipais," *Revista de Educação Pública* 3, no. 4 (1945): 489.

84 Ibid., 490.

85 Ibid., 491.

EPILOGUE: THE ENDURING BRAZILIAN FASCINATION WITH RACE

1 Edward, "Quem somos nós?" 103.

2 Ibid., 102.

3 Ibid., 106.

4 Ibid.

5 Ibid., 107.

6 Ibid., 108.

7 Ibid.

8 "Marta diz que Maluf é machista e sexista: Durante evento no centro da cidade, a candidata do PT aproveitou que a maioria dos presentes eram mulheres para lembrar frases do pepebista e para rebater críticas a programa de TV." *Folha de São Paulo*, 18 October 2000, 13.

9 "Escola Técnica Amaro Cavalcanti," undated document, Anísio Teixeira Collection, CPDOC, pi32/36.00.00.

10 Maria Yedda Linhares, interviewed by Jerry Dávila, 17 July 2000.

BIBLIOGRAPHY

INTERVIEWS

Aloysio Barbosa, Rio de Janeiro, 1 August 1999
Wilson Choeri, Rio de Janeiro, 1 August 1999
Norma Fraga, Rio de Janeiro, 13 July 2000
Maria Yedda Linhares, Rio de Janeiro, 17 July 2000
Umbelina de Mattos, Rio de Janeiro, 12 August 1999
Fernando Segismundo, Rio de Janeiro, 5 August 1999
Sara Hauser Steinberg, Rio de Janeiro, 5 August 1999
Maria Cecilia Teixeira, Rio de Janeiro, 13 July 2000

ARCHIVAL COLLECTIONS

Arquivo Edgar Leuernoth, Universidade Estadual de Campinas (AEL)

Arquivo Geral da Cidade, Rio de Janeiro (AGC)
  Henrique Dodsworth Collection

Arquivo Nacional do Brasil (AN)
  Jonathas Serrano Collection
  Liga Brasileira Pelo Progresso Feminino Collection
  Mário Augusto Teixeira de Freitas Collection

Centro de Memória de Educação, Prefeitura do Rio de Janeiro
  Escola Municipal Argentina
  Escola Municipal Darcy Vargas
  Escola Municipal Getúlio Vargas
  Escola Municipal Pedro Ernesto

Centro de Pesquisa e Documentação de História Contemporânea do Brasil, Fundação Getúlio Vargas (*CPDOC*)
Pedro Ernesto Batista Collection
(Manoel Bergstrom) Lourenço Filho Collection
Gustavo Capanema Collection
Filinto Müller Collection
Anísio Teixeira Collection

Colégio Pedro II Archive (*CPII*)

Columbia University Teachers College (*CUTC*) Archive

Fundação Darcy Vargas/Casa do Pequeno Jornaleiro Archive

Institute of Education Archive

Instituto de Estudos Brasileiros
Fernando de Azevedo Collection

Museu da Imagem e do Som do Rio de Janeiro (*MIS*) Augusto Malta Collection

Museu Villa-Lobos Archive

United States National Archives
Collection of the Office of the Coordinator for Inter-American Affairs (OCIAA)

NEWSPAPERS

A Chibata
A Liberdade
A Noite
A Nota
Diario Carioca
Elite
Getulino
Jornal do Brasil
Jornal do Comércio
Minas Gerais
O Alfinete
O Bandeirante
O Clarim d'Alvorada
O Globo
O Kosmos
O Menelick

JOURNALS AND MAGAZINES

Arquivos do Instituto de Educação
Boletim de Educação Pública
Cultura Política
Folha de São Paulo
Fon-Fon
Instituto
Jornal do Comércio
O Arauto
Pronome (orgão dos alumnos do Colegio Pedro II)
Revista de Educação Pública
Rio Ilustrado

PRIMARY SOURCES

Agache, Alfred. Cidade do Rio de Janeiro: Extensão, remodelação e embellezamento. Paris: Foyer
Bresilien, 1930.
Alves, Isaias. "Testes collectivos de intelligencia (Terman Group Test) e a sua applicação
nas escolas públicas." Boletim de Educação Pública 1, no. 1 (1932): 397–433.
Andrade, Noêmi Alcântara Bonfim. "A higiene alimenar no serviço social das escolas."
Cultura Política 2, no. 13 (1942): 23–29.
Andrade, Noêmi Alcântara Bonfim, and Miguel Elias Abu-Merhy. "Pesquisas sôbre o
indice de nutrição dos escolares do 30 distrito médico-pedagógico do Distrito Federal."
Cultura Política 2, no. 11 (1942): 65–80.
Azevedo, Fernando de. Brazilian Culture: An Introduction to the Study of Culture in Brazil. New
York: Macmillan, 1950.
———. "A formação do professorado e a reforma." Boletim de Educação Pública 1, no. 4 (1930):
495–97.
Azevedo Lima. "O problema do prédio escolar no Distrito Federal." Cultura Política 1, no. 5
(1941): 77–103.
Barros, Miguel. "Discurso do representante da Frente Negra Pelotense." Estudos Afro-
Brasileiros (Trabalhos apresentados no 1° Congresso Afro-Brasileiro reunido no Recife em 1934).
Vol. 1. Rio de Janeiro: Ariel Editora, 1935.
Beckeuser, Everardo. "A educação primária como fator da unidade nacional." Cultura
Política 2, no. 15 (1942): 64–71.
Bilac, Olavo, and Coelho Netto. Contos patrios. Rio de Janeiro: Livraria Francisco Alves, n.d.
Borges, Pio. "A assistência médica à infância escolar." Fon-Fon (1941): 59.
Brito, Mário de. "A admissão à escola secundária." Arquivos do Instituto de Educação 1, no. 1
(1934): 27–33.
Calmon, Pedro. Historia da civilização Brasileira para a escola primária. São Paulo: Companhia
Editora Nacional, 1934.

Campos, Francisco. *Regulamento do ensino normal do Estado de Minas Gerais (Decreto n. 9450 de 18 de fevereiro de 1930)*. Belo Horizonte: Imprensa Oficial de Minas Gerais, 1930.

Cardoso, Ofélia Boisson. "Curso de especialização em problemas de primeira série— organizado pela Secretaria Geral de Educação e Cultura para o magistério primário no 20 semestre de 1943." *Revista de Educação Pública* 2, no. 4 (1944): 576–90.

———. "Técnica de aplicação e julgamento dos Testes ABC." *Revista de Educação Pública* 2, no. 1 (1944): 33–42.

Chiabotto, Yedda. "Ensino técnico-profissional no Distrito Federal: Movimento dos estabelecimentos e aproveitamento registrado no ano de 1942." *Revista de Educação Pública* 1, no. 3 (1943): 363–66.

Clark, Oscar. "O papel da Secretaria de Educação na sociedade moderna." *Revista de Educação Pública* 3, no. 3 (1945): 321–41.

Confederação Católica de Educação. *O problema educativo na constituição*. Rio de Janeiro: Typographia Jornal do Comercio, 1934.

Conselho Nacional de Estatística. *Contribuições para o estudo da demografia no Brasil*. Rio de Janeiro: Serviço Gráfico do IBGE, 1961.

Correia, Jonas. "Aspectos da educação primária no Distrito Federal." *Fon-Fon* (1941): 20–24.

———. "Discurso pronunciado pelo Secretário de Educação e Cultura, Cel. Jonas Correia, no Instituto de Educação, paraninfando a segunda turma de professorandas de 1944." *Revista de Educação Pública* 3, no. 1 (1945): 1–3.

———. "Reorganização do ensino primário do Distrito Federal: Exposição de motivos do Decreto No. 7718, de 5 de fevereiro de 1944." *Revista de Educação Pública* 2, no. 1 (1944): 102–4.

Costa Pinto, L. A. *O negro no Rio de Janeiro: Relações de raças numa sociedade em mudança*. São Paulo: Companhia Editora Nacional, 1953.

D'Avila, Bastos. "Contribuição ao estudo do Indice de Lapicque." *Estudos Afro-Brasileiros (Trabalhos apresentados no 10 Congresso Afro-Brasileiro reunido no Recife em 1934)*. Vol. 1. Rio de Janeiro: Ariel Editora, 1935.

———. "Ensaio de raciologia Brasileira: Populações do Distrito Federal." *Revista de Educação Pública* 2, no. 1 (1944): 1–28.

D'Avila, Bastos, and Pedro Pernambucano Filho. "Considerações em torno dos Indices de Kaup, Pelidisi e A.C.H." *Revista de Educação Pública* 3, no. 1 (1945): 1–13.

Da Costa Sena, J. C. "Observações estatísticas sôbre o ensino público municipal." *Revista de Educação Pública* 2, no. 4 (1944): 697–704.

Departamento de Educação Nacionalista. *Boletim Mensal do Serviço de Educação Física* 3, no. 29 (1944).

Dewey, John. *John Dewey on Education: Selected Writings*. Chicago: University of Chicago Press, 1974.

DGEC. "Instituto de Educação (Noticia mandada elaborar pelo Departamento de Educação para uma publicação sobre 'o Systema Educacional do Rio de Janeiro, Distrito Federal." *Arquivos do Instituto de Educação* 1, no. 1 (1934): 1–10.

———. *Esboços de programas para ensino secundário.* Rio de Janeiro: Oficina Gráfica do Departamento de Educação do Distrito Federal, 1935.

———. "O Instituto de Educação no ano de 1936." *Arquivos do Instituto de Educação* 1, no. 3 (1937): 271–77.

Diaz Cruz, H. *Os morros Cariocas no novo regime.* Rio de Janeiro: Gráfica Olimpica, 1941.

Diretoria Geral de Estatística, Ministério da Agricultura, Indutria e Commercio. *Recenseamento do Brazil, realizado em 1 de setembro de 1920: Confirmação dos resultados do recenseamento demographico de 1920 e da estimativa feita pela Directoria Geral de Estatistica da população escolar de 6 a 12 annos existente no Distrito Federal em 31 de dezembro de 1926.* Rio de Janeiro: Typographia da Estatistica, 1927.

Dodsworth, Henrique Toledo. *Aspectos do ensino secundário: Relatório apresentado ao Exmo. Ministro da Justiça e Negocios Interiores.* Rio de Janeiro: Editora Gazeta de Noticias, 1921.

———. *Relatório, 1932–1933, do Externato do Colégio Pedro II.* Rio de Janeiro: Imprensa Nacional, 1933.

Estado de Espírito Santo. *Decreto No. 10.171: Expede instrucções sobre o ensino normal e da outras providencias.* Vitcoria: Oficinas do "Diario da Manhã," 1930.

Estado de Parahyba. *Decreto No. 75 de 14 de março de 1931: Da novo regulamento a escola normal do estado—Acto do interventor federal.* João Pessoa: Imprensa Oficial, 1931.

Estado de Sergipe. *Decreto No. 30 de 11 de março de 1931: "Dá novo regulamento à Escola Normal 'Rui Barbosa.'"* Aracaju: Imprensa Oficial, 1931.

Estado do Amazonas. *Programas do ensino primário, adotados pelo Conselho Superior de Instrução Pública em 28 de janeiro de 1932.* Manaus: Imprensa Publica, 1932.

———. *Regulamento geral da instrução pública, a que se refere o Ato No. 1.267 de 19 de janeiro de 1932.* Manaus: Imprensa Publica, 1932.

Freyre, Gilberto. *The Masters and the Slaves.* New York: Knopf, 1956.

Góes, Faria. *Esboço para ensino secundário.* Rio de Janeiro: Oficina Gráfica do Departamento de Educação, 1935.

Goulart, José Alípio. *Favelas do Distrito Federal.* Rio de Janeiro: Serviço de Informação Agrícola, 1957.

IBGE. *Censo Demográfico—População e Habitação: Quadros de totais para o conjunto da união e de distribuição pelas regiões fisiográficas e unidades federadas.* Rio de Janeiro: Serviço Gráfico do IBGE, 1950.

IBGE. *Censo Demográfico—População e Habitação: Série Regional, parte XVI: Distrito Federal.* Rio de Janeiro: Serviço Gráfico do IBGE, 1950.

IBGE. *Estatística do ensino: Separata do "Anuário Estatístico do Brasil—Ano IV—1938."* Rio de Janeiro: Serviço Gráfico do IBGE, 1940.

IBGE. *Estudos sôbre a composição da população do Brasil segundo a côr.* Rio de Janeiro: Serviço Gráfico do IBGE, 1950.

IBGE. *O aproveitamento das apurações do Censo Demográfico de 1940 para a determinação das correntes de migração interior.* Rio de Janeiro: Serviço Gráfico do IBGE, 1948.

INEP. *O ensino normal no Brasil: Relação dos estabelecimentos de ensino normal em funcionamento em dezembro de 1945.* Rio de Janeiro: Ministério de Educação e Saúde, 1946.

———. *Oportunidades de educação no capital do país (Informações sôbre as escolas e cursos para uso de pais, professores e estudantes)*. Rio de Janeiro: Imprensa Nacional, 1941.

———. *Organização do ensino primário e normal. Vol. 1: Estado de Amazonas*. Rio de Janeiro: Ministério da Educação e Saúde, 1939.

———. *Organização do ensino primário e normal. Vol. 2: Estado do Pará*. Rio de Janeiro: Ministério da Educação e Saúde, 1940.

———. *Organização do ensino primário e normal. Vol. 3: Estado de Maranhão*. Rio de Janeiro: Ministério da Educação e Saúde, 1940.

Lemme, Paschoal. *Memórias*. Vol. 2. Rio de Janeiro: INEP/Cortez Editora, 1988.

Leite, José Correia. *E disse o velho militante. . . .* São Paulo: CUTI, 1992.

Lourenço Filho, Manoel Bergstrom. "A Escola de Professores do Instituto de Educação." *Arquivos do Instituto de Educação* 1, no. 1 (1934): 1–26.

———. *O Juazeiro de Padre Cícero*. 3rd ed. 1928. São Paulo: Editora Melhoramentos, 1955.

———. *Testes ABC para verificação da maturidade necessária à aprendizagem da leitura e da escrita*. 6th ed. 1933. São Paulo: Edições Melhoramentos, 1957.

Magalhães, Basílio de. *História do Brasil para a quinta série do curso secundário*. Vol. 2. Rio de Janeiro: Livraria Francisco Alves, 1942.

———. *História do Brasil para a terceira série ginasial*. 3rd ed. 1942. Rio de Janeiro: Livraria Francisco Alves, 1945.

Marinho, Izenil Pena. "Evolução da educação física no Brasil." *Cultura Política* 4, no. 40 (1944): 69–77.

Marques, Olinda. "Como melhorar a frequência de nossas escolas." *Arquivos do Instituto de Educação* 1, no. 1 (1934): 91–97.

Mello, Cônego Olympio. "O Instituto de Educação no ultimo triênio: Dados constantes do Exmo. Sr. Prefeito Municipal, Cônego Olympio de Mello, à Câmara Municipal do Distrito Federal, em maio de 1936." *Arquivos do Instituto de Educação* 1, no. 2 (1936).

MES. *A Semana da Criança em 1943: 10 a 17 outubro—A infância abandonada*. Rio de Janeiro: Imprensa Nacional, 1943.

Monteiro, Clóvis de Rêgo. *Relatório Anual do Diretor do Colégio Pedro II—Internato ao Excelentíssimo Senhor Ministro da Educação e Saúde, Relativo ao ano de 1944*. Rio de Janeiro: Colégio Pedro II, 1945.

———. *Relatório Anual do Diretor do Colégio Pedro II—Internato, ao Excelentíssimo Senhor Ministro da Educação e Saúde, Relativo aos anos de 1938 a 1943*. Rio de Janeiro: Colégio Pedro II, 1944.

Mortara, Giorgio. *Interpretação e análise de algumas estatísticas do ensino primário no Brasil em relação com os resultados do Censo de 1940*. Rio de Janeiro: Serviço Gráfico do IBGE, 1942.

Nereu de Sampaio. "Plano regulador das construcções escolares (Annexo ao relatório do Diretor Geral de Instrução Pública)." *Boletim de Educação Pública* 1, no. 1 (1932).

Pende, Nicola. *Scienzia Dell'Ortogenesi*. Bergamo: Instituto Italiano D'Arti Grafiche, 1939.

Peregrino Júnior. "Sentido político e biológico da educação física." *Cultura Política* 4, no. 36 (1944): 154–72.

Pernambuco, Estado de. *Regulamento da escola normal, Estado de Pernambuco: Decreto No. 189, de 11 de maio de 1933*. Recife: Imprensa Oficial, 1933.

Pernambucano Filho, Pedro. "Centro de Pesquisas Educacionais: Colaboração com o Ministério da Guerra." *Revista de Educação Pública* 2, no. 2 (1944): 211–21.

———. "O valor do Serviço de Ortofrenia e Psciologia na aprendizagem escolar." *Revista de Educação Pública* 1, no. 3 (1943): 337–46.

Pinheiro, Raimundo. "O papel da escola no aproveitamento da Amazonia." *Cultura Política* 1, no. 10 (1941): 76–83.

Pombo, Rocha. *Historia do Brasil.* 3rd ed. São Paulo: Companhia Melhoramentos, 1925.

———. *Nossa pátria: Narração dos fatos da história do Brasil, através da sua evolução com muitas gravuras explicativas.* 79th ed. São Paulo: Companhia Melhoramentos, 1917.

Prefeitura do Distrito Federal. *Decreto 3.810, organização do Instituto de Educação do Rio de Janeiro.* Rio de Janeiro: Diretoria Geral de Instrução Pública da Prefeitura do Distrito Federal, 1932.

Raja Gabaglia, Fernando Antonio. "Apresentação de F. A. Raja Gabaglia, Sec. Geral de Educação e Cultura." *Arquivos do Instituto de Educação* 2, no. 4 (1945): 7–18.

———. "Ginásios Municipais." *Revista de Educação Pública* 3, no. 4 (1945): 489–91.

———. *Leituras Geográficas (Para o ensino secundário).* Rio de Janeiro: F. Briguet & Cia., 1933.

Ramos, Arthur. *A aculturação negra no Brasil.* São Paulo: Editora Nacional, 1942.

———. *A criança problema: A hygiene mental na escola primária.* Rio de Janeiro: Companhia Editora Nacional, 1939.

———. *A familia e a escola (Conselhos de higiene mental aos pais).* Série D—Vulgarização. Rio de Janeiro: Oficina Gráfica do Departamento de Educação do Distrito Federal, 1934.

———. *A higiene mental nas escolas: Esquema de organização.* Série B—Planos e Inquéritos. Rio de Janeiro: Oficina Gráfica do Departamento de Educação do Distrito Federal, 1934.

———. *The Negro in Brazil.* Washington, D.C.: The Associated Publishers, 1939.

———. *O folclore negro do Brasil: Demispicologia e psicanalise.* Rio de Janeiro: Editora Casa do Estudante do Brasil, 1935.

Ribeiro, Sylvio Salema Garção. "Documentação das grandes demonstrações civico-orpheônicas realizadas pela Secretaria Geral de Educação e Cultura." *Revista de Educação Pública* 1, no. 2 (1943): 184–85.

Rodrigues, Mário de Queiroz. "Educação física: Programa do curso normal do Instituto de Educação." *Revista de Educação Pública* 2, no. 2 (1944): 247–52.

Romero, Nilo. "Medicina e educação." *Revista de Educação Pública* 1, no. 3 (1943): 359–62.

Romero, Sylvio. *A história do Brasil: Ensinada pela biografia de seus heróes.* 9th ed. Rio de Janeiro: Livraria Francisco Alves, 1915.

Roquette Pinto, Edgar. "Apresentação." In *Estudos Afro-Brasileiros (Trabalhos apresentados no 1. Congresso Afro-Brasileiro reunido no Recife em 1934).* Rio de Janeiro: Ariel Editora, 1935.

Santos, Theobaldo Miranda. "A educação e a guerra." *Revista de Educação Pública* 1, no. 2 (1943): 317–22.

Serrano, Jonathas. *Epítome da história do Brasil.* 3rd ed. 1933. Rio de Janeiro: F. Briguet & Cia., 1941.

———. *História da civilização (em cinco volumes, para o curso secundário).* 5th ed. Rio de Janeiro: F. Briguet & Cia., 1939.

——. *História geral: História moderna e contemporânea.* Vol. 2. Rio de Janeiro: F. Briguet & Cia., 1944.

Secretaria Geral de Educação e Cultura. *Regulamento do ensino normal: Regime interno, resoluções.* Rio de Janeiro: Oficina Gráfica da SGES, 1947.

Silva, Joaquim. *História da civilização para o terceiro ano ginasial.* 5th ed. São Paulo: Companhia Editora Nacional, 1936.

Silveira, Alfredo Balthazar da. *História do Instituto de Educação.* Rio de Janeiro: Secretaria Geral de Educação e Cultura, 1954.

Stavrianos, L. S. "As ditaduras e o problema educacional." *Rio Ilustrado* (1936).

Teixeira, Anísio. *Educação não é Privilégio.* Rio de Janeiro: José Olympio Editora, 1957.

——. *Educação pública: Sua organização e administração.* Rio de Janeiro: Oficina Gráfica do Departamento de Educação do Distrito Federal, 1934.

——. "O systema escolar do Rio de Janeiro, D.F.: Relatorio de um anno de administração." *Boletim de Educação Pública* 1, no. 4 (1932): 307–70.

Teixeira, Antônio Maria, and E. Corrêa de Azevedo. "Escolares desajustados (Considerações sôbre o relatório do 50. D.M.P., relativo a 1942)." *Revista de Educação Pública* 1, no. 3 (1943): 323–32.

Teixeira de Freitas, Mário Augusto. *O ensino primário no Brasil em 1939.* Rio de Janeiro: Serviço Gráfico do IBGE, 1945.

——. *O ensino primário Brasileiro no decêncio, 1932–1941.* Rio de Janeiro: Serviço Gráfico do IBGE, 1946.

Thomaz, Joaquim Silveira. "Desenvolvimento cefálico e sub-nutrição." *Revista de Educação Pública* 2, no. 4 (1944): 593–609.

Tôrres, Alberto. *A organização nacional.* Rio de Janeiro: Imprensa Nacional, 1914.

——. *O problema nacional Brasileiro.* Rio de Janeiro: Imprensa Nacional, 1914.

Traverso, Antonio. "Fatores da formação dos póvos Sul Americanos." In *Concuso para cadeira catedrática.* Rio de Janeiro: Colégio Pedro II, 1941.

Vargas, Getúlio. "Discurso de paraninfo com que o Presidente Getúlio Vargas se dirigiu aos professorandos de 1943, no Instituto de Educação, no ato de colocação de gráu." *Revista de Educação Pública* 1, no. 4 (1943): 471–74.

Venancio Filho, Francisco. "A civilização Brasileira e a educação." *Anuário do Colégio Pedro II* 9 (1939): 1–103.

——. "Instituto de Educação no Distrito Federal." *Arquivos do Instituto de Educação* 2, no. 4 (1945): 19–32.

Villa-Lobos, Heitor. *Canto orfeônico: Marchas, canções, e cantos marciais para educação consciente da "Unidade de Movimento."* Vol. 1. Rio de Janeiro: E. S. Mangione, 1940.

——. "Educação musical." In *A presença de Villa-Lobos.* Vol. 13. Rio de Janeiro: Museu Villa-Lobos, 1991.

——. *Programa de música: Escolas elementar e secundária técnica e curso de especialização.* Rio de Janeiro: Oficina Gráfica do Departamento de Educação do Distrito Federal, 1934.

SECONDARY SOURCES

Abernathy, David B. *The Political Dilemma of Popular Education: An African Case.* Palo Alto: Stanford University Press, 1969.

Almeida, Lúcia Reis de. "O Instituto de Pesquisas Educacionais no antigo Distrito Federal e Estado de Guanabara." M.A. thesis, Faculdade de Educação/UFRJ, 1993.

Anderson, Benedict. *Imagined Communities: Reflections on the Origin and Spread of Nationalism.* 2nd ed. London: Verso, 1991.

Araújo, Joel Zito. *A negação do Brasil: O negro na telenovela brasileira.* São Paulo: SENAC, 2000.

Badaro, Murilo. *Gustavo Capanema: A revolução na cultura.* São Paulo: Nova Fronteira, 2000.

Barbosa, Marcio. *Frente Negra Brasileira: Depoimentos.* São Paulo: Quilombhoje, 1998.

Barreto, Anna Olga Lessa de Barros. "Contribuição para a história da escola pública primária do Distrito Federal, no período do Estado Novo (1937–1945)." M.A. thesis, Pontifícia Universidade Católica do Rio de Janeiro, 1986.

Barros, Orlando de. *Preconceito e educação no Governo Vargas.* Rio de Janeiro: Colégio Pedro II, 1987.

Besse, Susan K. *Restructuring Patriarchy: The Modernization of Gender Inequality in Brazil, 1914–1940.* Chapel Hill: University of North Carolina Press, 1996.

Bittencourt, Circe Maria Fernandes. "Pátria, civilização e trabalho: O ensino de história nas ecolas paulistas (1917–1939)." M.A. thesis, FFLCH/Universidade de São Paulo, 1988.

Bomeny, Helena. "Novos talentos, vícios antigos: Os renovadores e a política educacional." *Estudos Históricos* 6, no. 1 (1993): 24–39.

———. *Organização nacional da juventude: A política de mobilização da juventude no Estado Novo.* Rio de Janeiro: CPDOC/FGV, 1981.

Borges, Dain. *The Family in Bahia, 1870–1945.* Stanford: Stanford University Press, 1992.

———. " 'Puffy, Ugly, Slothful, and Inert': Degeneration in Brazilian Social Thought, 1870–1940." *Journal of Latin American Studies* 25 (1993): 235–56.

Butler, Kim. *Freedoms Given, Freedoms Won: Afro-Brazilians in Post-Abolition São Paulo and Salvador.* New Brunswick: Rutgers University Press, 1998.

Carvalho, Anelise Maria Miller de. "Reafirmação e delimitação do papel feminino nos livros didácticos dos anos 30/40." *Projeto História* 11 (1994): 171–78.

Carvalho, José Murilo de. *A formação das almas: O imaginário da Republica no Brasil.* São Paulo: Companhia das Letras, 1990.

———. *Os bestializados: O Rio de Janeiro e a República que não foi.* São Paulo: Companhia das Letras, 1991.

Carvalho, Marta Maria Chagas de. "Molde nacional e fôrma cívica: Higiene, moral e trabalho no projeto da Associação Brasileira de Educação, 1924–1931." Ph.D. diss., FEUSP/Universidade de São Paulo, 1986.

Caulfield, Sueann. *In Defense of Honor: Sexual Morality, Modernity, and Nation in Early-Twentieth-Century Brazil.* Durham: Duke University Press, 1999.

Cavalcanti, Lauro. *As preocupações do belo: Arquitetura moderna Brasileira dos anos 30/40.* Rio de Janeiro: Taurus Editora, 1995.

Conniff, Michael. *Urban Politics in Brazil: The Rise of Populism, 1925–1945.* Pittsburgh: University of Pittsburgh Press, 1981.

Corrêa, Mariza. "As ilusões da liberdade: A escola Nina Rodrigues e a antropologia no Brasil." Ph.D. diss., Universidade de São Paulo, 1982.

Cremin, Lawrence A., David A. Shannon, and Mary Evelyn Townsend. *A History of Teachers College, Columbia University.* New York: Columbia University Press, 1954.

Cunha, Célio da. *Educação e autoritarismo no Estado Novo.* 2nd ed. São Paulo: Cortez Editora, 1989.

Dávila, Jerry. "Expanding Perspectives on Race in Brazil." *Latin American Research Review* 35, no. 3 (2000): 188–98.

———. "Under the Long Shadow of Getúlio Vargas: A Research Chronicle." *Estudios Interdisciplinários de América Latina y el Caribe* 12, no. 1 (2001): 25–38.

de Decca, Edgar. *O silêncio dos vencidos.* 2nd ed. 1981. São Paulo: Brasiliense, 1994.

Degler, Carl. *Neither Black nor White: Slavery and Race Relations in Brazil and the United States.* New York: Macmillan, 1971.

de Jesus, Antonio Tavares. *Educação e hegemonia, no pensamento de Antonio Gramsci.* Campinas: Editora da UNICAMP, 1989.

Della Cava, Ralph. *Miracle at Joazeiro.* New York: Columbia University Press, 1970.

De Lorenzo, Helena Carvalho, and Wilma Peres da Costa, eds. *A década de 1920 e as origens do Brasil moderno.* São Paulo: Editora UNESP, 1997.

Diacon, Todd A. *Millenarian Vision, Capitalist Reality: Brazil's Contestado Rebellion.* Durham: Duke University Press, 1991.

Enéas, Zilá Simas. *Era uma vez no Instituto de Educação.* Rio de Janeiro: Zilá Simas Enéas, 1998.

Estatística, Conselho Nacional de. *Contribuições para o estudo da demografia no Brasil.* Rio de Janeiro: Serviço Gráfico do IBGE, 1961.

Evenson, Norma. *Two Brazilian Capitals: Architecture and Urbanism in Rio de Janeiro and Brasília.* New Haven: Yale University Press, 1973.

Fausto, Boris. *A Revolução de 1930: História e historiografia.* 16th ed. 1970. São Paulo: Companhia das Letras, 1997.

Fávero, Maria de Lourdes de Albuquerque, and Jader de Medeiros Britto, eds. *Dicionário de educadores no Brasil: Da colônia aos dias atuais.* Rio de Janeiro: Editora UFRJ, 1990.

Fernandes, Florestan. *The Negro in Brazilian Society.* New York: Columbia University Press, 1969.

Ferreira, Aurélio Buarque de Holanda. *Novo Aurélio Século XXI: O dicionário da lingua portuguesa.* 3rd ed. 1975. Rio de Janeiro: Editora Nova Fronteira, 1999.

Fleisch, Brahm David. "The Teachers College Club: American Educational Discourse and the Origins of Bantu Education in South Africa, 1914–1951." Ph.D. diss., Columbia University, 1995.

Fontaine, Pierre Michel. *Race, Class, and Power in Brazil.* Los Angeles: Center for Afro-American Studies, UCLA, 1985.

Foster, Philip. *Education and Social Change in Ghana.* Chicago: University of Chicago Press, 1965.

Foucault, Michel. *Discipline and Punish: The Birth of the Prison.* New York: Vintage Books, 1995.

Fox, Richard G., ed. *Nationalist Ideologies and the Production of National Cultures.* Vol. 2. Washington, D.C.: American Ethnological Society, 1990.

Garcia, Nelson Jahr. *Ideologia e propaganda política: A legitimação do estado autoritário perante as classes subalternas.* São Paulo: Edições Loyola, 1982.

Gay, Robert. *Popular Organization and Democracy in Rio de Janeiro: A Tale of Two Favelas.* Philadelphia: Temple University Press, 1994.

Ghiraldelli, Paulo. *Pedadagogia e luta de classes no Brasil, 1930–1937.* Ibitinga: Editora Humanidades, 1991.

Gomes, Angela de Castro, ed. *Capanema: O ministro e seu ministério.* Rio de Janeiro: Editora FGV, 2000.

Gould, Stephen Jay. *The Mismeasure of Man.* 2nd ed. 1981. New York: Norton, 1996.

Graham, Douglas H., and Sergio Buarque de Holanda Filho. *Migration, Regional and Urban Growth, and Development in Brazil: A Selective Analysis of the Historical Record, 1872–1970.* São Paulo: Instituto de Pesquisas Econômicas, U.S.P., 1971.

Green, James Naylor. *Beyond Carnival: Male Homosexuality in Twentieth Century Brazil.* Chicago: University of Chicago Press, 2000.

Guimarães, Manoel Luiz Lima Salgado. "Educação e modernidade: O projeto educacional de Anísio Teixeira." M.A. thesis, PUC-Rio, 1982.

Gumperz, J., ed. *Language and Social Identity.* Cambridge: Cambridge University Press, 1982.

Hanchard, Michael. "Black Cinderella? Race and the Public Sphere in Brazil." *Public Culture* 7 (1994): 165–85.

Haney, Walt. "Validity, Vaudeville, and Values: A Short History of Social Concerns Over Standardized Testing." *American Psychologist* 36, no. 10 (1981): 1021–34.

Harris, Marvin. *Amazon Town: A Study of Man in the Tropics.* New York: Macmillan, 1953.

Higginbotham, Evelyn Brooks. "African-American Women's History and the Metalanguage of Race." *Signs* 17, no. 2 (1992): 251–74.

Hochman, Gilberto. *A era do saneamento.* São Paulo: Editora Hucitec, 1996.

Hollinger, David. "Authority, Solidarity, and the Political Economy of Identity: The Case of the United States." *Diacritics* 29, no. 4 (1999): 116–27.

Holloway, Thomas H. *Policing Rio de Janeiro: Repression and Resistance in a Nineteenth-Century City.* Stanford: Stanford University Press, 1993.

Horta, José Silveiro Baía. *O hino, o sermão e a ordem do dia.* Rio de Janeiro: Editora UFRJ, 1994.

IBGE. *Contribuições para o estudo da demografia no Brasil.* Rio de Janeiro: IBGE, 1971.

——. *Estatísticas históricas do Brasil: Séries econômicas, demográficas e sociais de 1550 a 1988.* 2nd ed. Vol. 3. Rio de Janeiro: IBGE, 1990.

Ignatiev, Noel. *How the Irish Became White.* New York: Routledge, 1996.

Kelley, Robin. *Race Rebels: Culture, Politics, and the Black Working Class.* New York: The Free Press, 1996.

Kraay, Hendrik, ed. *Afro-Brazilian Culture in Bahia, 1790s to 1990s.* Armonk, N.Y.: M. E. Sharpe, 1998.

Leite, Dante Morreira. *O caráter nacional Brasileiro.* 1969.

Lemme, Antonio Cesar. "Saúde, educação e cidadania na década de 30." M.A. thesis, Centro Biomédico, UFRJ, 1992.

Lesser, Jeffrey. *Negotiating National Identity: Immigrants, Minorities, and the Struggle for Ethnicity in Brazil.* Durham: Duke University Press, 1999.

———. *Welcoming the Undesirables: Brazil and the Jewish Question.* Berkeley: University of California Press, 1994.

Levine, Robert M. *Father of the Poor? Vargas and His Era.* New York: Cambridge University Press, 1998.

———. *Pernambuco in the Brazilian Federation.* Stanford: Stanford University Press, 1978.

Lima, Magali Alonso de. *Formas arquiteturais esportivas no Estado Novo (1937–1945): Suas implicações na plástica de corpos e espíritos.* Rio de Janeiro: FUNARTE, 1979.

Lima, Nísia Trinidade, and Gilberto Hochman. "Condenado pela raça, absolvido pela medicina: O Brasil descoberto pelo movimento sanitarista da Primeira República." In *Raça, ciência e sociedade,* ed. Marcos Chor Maio and Ricardo Ventura Santos. Rio de Janeiro: Editora FIOCRUZ, 1996.

Lima Sobrinho, Barbosa. *A presença de Alberto Tôrres (Sua vida e pensamento).* Rio de Janeiro: Editora Civilização Brasileira, 1968.

Lippi e Oliveira, Lucia. *Estado Novo: Ideologia e poder.* Rio de Janeiro: Ediciones Zahar, 1982.

Lipsitz, George. *The Possessive Investment in Whiteness: How White People Profit from Identity Politics.* Philadelphia: Temple University Press, 1998.

Lissovsky, Maurício, and Paulo Sergio Moraes de Sá, eds. *As colunas da educação: A Construção do Ministério de Educação e Saúde.* Rio de Janeiro: IPHAN, 1996.

Lopes, Eliane Teixeira, Luciano Mendes Faria Filho, and Cynthia Greive Veiga, eds. *500 anos de educação no Brasil.* Belo Horizonte: Autêntica, 2000.

Machado, Mario Brockman. "Political Socialization in Authoritarian Systems: The Case of Brazil." Ph.D. diss., University of Chicago, 1975.

Maia, Maria. *Villa-Lobos: alma Brasileira.* Rio de Janeiro: Contraponto, 2000.

Maio, Marcos Chor, and Ricardo Ventura Santos, eds. *Raça, ciência e sociedade.* Rio de Janeiro: Editora FIOCRUZ, 1996.

Marson, Adalberto. *A ideologia nacionalista em Alberto Tôrres.* São Paulo: Editora Duas Cidades, 1979.

Marx, Anthony. *Making Race and Nation: A Comparison of the United States, South Africa, and Brazil.* New York: Cambridge University Press, 1998.

Meade, Teresa A. *"Civilizing" Rio: Reform and Resistance in a Brazilian City, 1889–1930.* Philadelphia: Pennsylvania State University Press, 1997.

Merrick, Thomas W. *The Demographic History of Brazil.* Albuquerque: The Latin American Institute, University of New Mexico, 1980.

Merrick, Thomas W., and Douglas H. Graham. *Population and Development in Brazil, 1800 to the Present.* Baltimore: Johns Hopkins University Press, 1979.

Needell, Jeffrey. *A Tropical Belle Epoque: Elite Culture and Society in Turn-of-the-Century Rio de Janeiro.* New York: Cambridge University Press, 1988.

Nemeth, Thomas. *Gramsci's Philosophy: A Critical Study*. Atlantic Highlands: Humanities Press, 1980.

Nobles, Melissa. *Shades of Citizenship: Race and the Census in Modern Politics*. Stanford: Stanford University Press, 2000.

Nunes, Clarice. "Anísio Teixeira: A poesia da ação." Ph.D. diss., Pontifícia Universidade Católica do Rio de Janeiro, 1991.

———. "A escola redescobre a cidade: Reinterpretação da modernidade pedagógica no espaço urbano carioca/1910–1935." Niteroi: Universidade Federal Fluminense, 1993.

Oliveira, Beatriz Santos de. "A modernidade oficial: A arquitetura das escolas públicas no Distrito Federal (1928–1940)." Ph.D. diss., FAU/Universidade de São Paulo, 1991.

Oliveira, Sueli Teresa de. "Escolarização profissional feminina, em São Paulo, nos anos 1910/20/30." *Projeto História* 11 (1994): 57–68.

Peard, Julyan. *Race, Place, and Medicine: The Idea of the Tropics in Nineteenth-Century Brazil*. Durham: Duke University Press, 1999.

Pereira, Lusia Ribeiro. "O fazer feminino do magistério (Tateando um objeto de pesquisa)." *Projeto História* 11 (1994): 115–29.

Piza, Edith. "Contaminação de prácticas no trabalho de magistério: Notas para fazer reflexão." *Projeto História* 11 (1994): 79–90.

Plank, David N. "The Expansion of Education: A Brazilian Case Study." *Comparative Education Review* 31, no. 3 (1987): 361–76.

Reichmann, Rebecca, ed. *Race in Contemporary Brazil: From Indifference to Inequality*. University Park: Pennsylvania State University Press, 1999.

Reid Andrews, George. *Blacks and Whites in São Paulo, Brazil, 1888–1988*. Madison: University of Wisconsin Press, 1991.

Rein, Monica Esti. *Politics and Education in Argentina, 1946–1962*. Armonk, N.Y.: M. E. Sharpe, 1998.

Reis, Maria Cándida Delgado. "Imagens flutuantes: Mulher e educação (São Paulo, 1910/1930)." *Projeto História* 11 (1994): 47–56.

Rodrigues, Nelson. "A realeza do Pelé." In *O melhor do romance, contos e crônicas*. São Paulo: Editora Schwarcz, 1993.

Roediger, David. *The Wages of Whiteness: Race and the Making of the American Working Class*. London: Verso, 1999.

Rosemberg, Fúlvia. "Educação e gênero no Brasil." *Projeto História* 11 (1994): 7–18.

Rosemberg, Fúlvia, and Edith Piza. *Analfabetismo, raça e gênero nos censos Brasileiros*. São Paulo: Fundação Carlos Chagas, 1993.

———. *Côr nos censos Brasileiros*. São Paulo: Núcleo de Estudo sobre Educação, Gênero, Raça e Idade, Pontifícia Universidade Católica de São Paulo, 1993.

Ross, Dorothy. *The Rise of American Social Science*. Cambridge: Cambridge University Press, 1991.

Ross, Dorothy, ed. *Modernist Impulses in the Human Sciences*. Baltimore: Johns Hopkins University Press, 1994.

Santos, Ricardo Ventura. "Edgar Roquette Pinto, os tipos antropológicos e a questão da degeneração racial no Brasil no início do século." In *XX Encontro Anual da* AN POCS *in Caxambú, MG.* Caxambú: AN POCS, 1996.

Sarmento, Carlos Eduardo. *Pedro Ernesto: Um prefeito para o Rio.* Rio de Janeiro: Fundação Getúlio Vargas, 1995.

Schwarcz, Lilia Moritz. *O espetáculo das raças: Cientistas, instituições e questão racial no Brasil, 1870–1930.* São Paulo: Companhia das Letras, 1993.

Schwartzman, Simon, Helena Maria Bousquet Bomeny, and Vanda Maria Ribeiro Costa. *Tempos de Capanema.* São Paulo: EDUSP, 1984.

Segismundo, Fernando, *Excelências do Colégio Pedro II.* Rio de Janeiro: Colégio Pedro II, 1993.

Serbin, Ken. *Igreja, estado e a ajuda financeira pública no Brasil, 1930–1964: Estudos de três casos chaves.* Rio de Janeiro: CPDOC/ FGV, 1991.

Silva, Marinette dos Santos. "A educação Brasileira no Estado Novo." M.A. thesis, Universidade Federal Fluminense, 1975.

Skidmore, Thomas E. *Black into White: Race and Nationality in Brazilian Thought.* 2nd ed. Durham: Duke University Press, 1993.

———. *Politics in Brazil, 1930–1964: An Experiment in Democracy.* Oxford: Oxford University Press, 1967.

Smolka, Ana Luiza Bustamante, and Maria Cristina Menezes, eds. *Anísio Teixeira, 1900– 2000: Provocações em educação.* Bragança Paulista: Editora Universidade de São Francisco, 2000.

Sodré, Nelson Werneck. *A história da imprensa no Brasil.* Rio de Janeiro: Civilização Brasileira, 1966.

Stepan, Alfred, ed. *Authoritarianism in Brazil.* New Haven: Yale University Press, 1974.

Stepan, Nancy Leys. *"The Hour of Eugenics": Race, Gender, and Nation in Latin America.* Ithaca: Cornell University Press, 1991.

Stoler, Ann. *Race and the Education of Desire: Foucault's "History of Sexuality" and the Colonial Order of Things.* Durham: Duke University Press, 1995.

Vaughn, Mary Kay. *Cultural Politics in Revolution: Teachers, Peasants, and Schools in Mexico, 1930– 1940.* Tucson: University of Arizona Press, 1998.

Vidal, Diana Gonçalves. "O exercicio disciplinado do olhar: Livros, leituras e practicas de formação docente no Instituto de Educação do Distrito Federal." Ph.D. diss., FEUSP/ Universidade de São Paulo, 1995.

Vidal, Diana Gonçalves, ed. *Na batalha da educação: Correspondência entre Anísio Teixeira e Fernando de Azevedo (1929–1971).* Bragança Paulista: Universidade de São Francisco, 2000.

Vilhena, Cynthia Pereira de Sousa. "Imprensa e educação Católicas na formação do público leitor feminino (1920/1950)." *Projeto História* 11 (1994): 147–60.

Villa-Lobos, Heitor. *A presença de Villa-Lobos.* Vol. 13. Rio de Janeiro: Museu Villa-Lobos, 1991.

Wagley, Charles. *An Introduction to Brazil.* New York: Columbia University Press, 1963.

———. *Race and Class in Rural Brazil.* Paris: UN ESCO, 1952.

Webber, Eugen. *Peasants into Frenchmen: The Modernization of Rural France, 1870–1914.* Stanford: Stanford University Press, 1976.

Weffort, Francisco. *Classes populares e política*. São Paulo: Universidade de São Paulo, 1968.

Weinstein, Barbara. *For Social Peace in Brazil: Industrialists and the Remaking of the Working Class in São Paulo, 1920–1964*. Chapel Hill: University of North Carolina Press, 1996.

Williams, Daryle. "Ad Perpetuam Rei Memoriam: The Vargas Regime and Brazil's National Historical Patrimony, 1930–1945." *Luso-Brazilian Review* (1994): 45–75.

———. *Culture Wars in Brazil: The First Vargas Regime, 1930–1945*. Durham: Duke University Press, 2001.

Winn, Peter. "A Worker's Nightmare: Taylorism and the 1962 Yarur Strike in Chile." *Radical History Review* 58 (1994): 4–34.

Wolfe, Joel. " 'Father of the Poor' or 'Mother of the Rich'? Getúlio Vargas, Industrial Workers, and Constructions of Class, Gender, and Populism in São Paulo, 1930–1954." *Radical History Review* 58 (1994): 80–111.

———. *Working Women, Working Men: São Paulo and the Rise of Brazil's Industrial Working Class, 1900–1955*. Durham: Duke University Press, 1993.

X, Malcolm. *The Autobiography of Malcolm X*. New York: Random House, 1975.

Xavier, Maria Elizabete, Maria Luisa Ribeiro, and Olinda Maria Noronha. *História da educação: A escola no Brasil*. São Paulo: Editora FTD, 1994.

INDEX

Afro-Brazilian Congress (1934), 100
Agache, Alfred, 55, 76, 78–82, 85, 88
Alagoas (state), 110
Alcoholism, 25, 33, 41–42, 208–209. See also
    Eugenics; Racial degeneracy
Alves, Isaias, 35, 123, 143–146, 166, 168,
    240
Amazonas (state), 10, 33, 65, 110, 120, 240
Anderson, Benedict, 59
Andrade, Carlos Drummond de, 64
Andrade, Mario de, 64
Antipoff, Helena, 143
Anti-semitism, 182, 194–196, 200, 208
Antonio, Celso, 22–24
Azevedo, Fernando de, 11, 25, 33, 62, 77,
    101–105, 123, 139, 172, 175, 183–184; at-
    tacked by Catholic nationalists, 166–170;
    reform by, 97, 102, 108–110, 129
Azevedo, Philadelpho, 183, 229–231

Bahia (state), 10, 33, 39, 69, 72, 168, 234,
    240
Barbosa, Aloisio, 192, 217
Batista, Pedro Ernesto, 42, 132, 156–157,
    170, 173
Beckeuser, Everardo, 69

Biotypology Association, 26
Boas, Franz, 9, 23, 28
Borges, Pio, 47, 176–178, 181–182, 228
Brazilian Association of Educators (ABE),
    60
Brazilian Institute for Geography and Statis-
    tics (IBGE), 52–55, 58–60, 66, 100
Brazilian race, 3, 27, 34, 37, 116, 222, 233
Brito, Mário de, 103, 111–112, 116, 264 n.33
Brizola, Leonel, 99, 241

Câmara, Jaime de Barros (archbishop of
    Rio), 3
Campos, Francisco, 77; authored Estado
    Novo Constitution, 107, 156, 173; federal
    education reform by, 63–64, 199, 268
    n.45; in Minas Gerais, 107–108, 143; as
    Minister of Education and Health, 63–64,
    209, 210; as Minister of Justice, 156; as
    Secretary of Education in Rio de Janeiro,
    155–156, 173, 176
Capanema, Gustavo, 6, 21–24, 41, 49–50,
    54, 64, 160, 163, 168; Catholic activism
    and, 3, 166–167; and the Colégio Pedro
    II, 193–196, 208; education reform by, 64;
    and the Estado Novo, 193–196

Cardoso, Fernando Henrique, 233, 235–236
Cardoso, Ofélia Boisson, 149–150
Carneiro Leão, Antonio, 33–34, 48, 101, 198, 264 n.33
Carvalho, Delgado de, 118, 198, 210
Catholic Church, 12; Catholic education, 1–2; and opposition to education reform, 17, 31, 49–50, 157–158, 165, 184, 195; political resurgence of, 159, 166–171, 238
Catholic Electoral League, 168
Catholic Nationalism, 107, 117–118, 202, 212, 214, 238; and religious education, 158–159, 165–172, 175
Ceará (state), 10, 30–32, 65, 68, 240
Chateaubriand, Assis, 171
Choeri, Wilson, 192, 217
Cícero, Father, 30–32
Claparéde, Edouard, 108, 143
Colégio Militar, 121, 177, 223
Colégio Pedro II, 17, 63–64, 99, 118, 176, 183, 191–231, 238; coeducation at, 205–206; Estado Novo at, 192–196; faculty of, 198, 212–217; Internato of, 202–204; physical education at, 209–210; race at, 207–217; student culture at, 197, 207–212
Columbia University, 9, 23
Columbia University Teachers College, 35, 103–104, 123, 132, 142–143, 168, 196
Communist Party of Brazil (PCB), 155, 157
Conniff, Michael, 170, 173
Constant, Benjamin, 197
Constitution of 1891, 67, 166
Constitution of 1934, 61, 105, 165, 201
Constitution of 1937, 107, 173
Correia, Jonas, 121, 175–179, 183, 229
Costa, Lúcio, 22
Costa Pinto, L.A, 55, 76, 81, 85–88
Criminology, 4, 25, 103, 106, 113, 142, 151. See also Pende, Nicola

D'Avila, Bastos, 36–39, 134, 151, 236
de Decca, Edgar, 57

Department of Press and Propaganda, 3, 195
DESPS. See Political Security Department
Dewey, John, 103, 107–108, 123, 134, 157, 198, 225
Dodsworth, Henrique Toledo, 46, 159, 173, 183–189; at Colégio Pedro II, 173–174, 198, 204; school reform by, 174–176, 182
Dória, Antonio de Sampaio, 106
Durkheim, Emil, 108
Dutra, Gaspar, 192

Education and Health Statistics Service (SEES), 59, 65, 171
Escola Amaro Cavalcanti, 218, 224–228, 238
Escola General Trompowsky, 146–151, 178
Escola Militar, 119, 180, 192–193, 195, 200
Escola Orsina da Fonseca, 189–190
Escola Profissional Souza Aguiar, 93–96
Escola Rivadavia Corrêa, 112, 222
Escola Vicente Licínio, 44–45, 126–129, 135
Espírito Santo (state), 10, 33
Estado Novo, 12, 46–47, 53, 62, 65, 79–80, 85, 99, 120, 138, 152, 154, 192–196, 198–201; Rio de Janeiro school system during the, 155–191
Eugenics, 9, 11, 24–27, 33–51, 64, 68, 100–107, 109, 112–116, 125–129, 132, 134, 141, 150–152, 156, 158, 173, 176–178, 184, 208–212, 222, 234, 236, 239. See also Alcoholism; Colégio Pedro II; D'Avila, Bastos; Intelligence testing; Racial degeneracy; Syphilis; Tuberculosis

Fausto, Boris, 57–59
Favelas. See Rio de Janeiro (city)
Federal District of Rio de Janeiro. See Rio de Janeiro (city)
Federation of Industries in the State of São Paulo (FIESP), 134
Fernandes, Florestan, 86–87, 122

Fontenelle, J.P., 146, 172

Fordism. *See* Rationalization

Fraga, Norma, 99, 163, 207, 217

Freitas, Mário Augusto Teixeira de, 52–55, 58–62, 71, 76, 171, 201. *See also* Brazilian Institute for Geography and Statistics (IBGE)

Frente Negra Brasileira, 97–100, 112–113

Freyre, Gilberto, 8–9, 33, 63, 100, 213, 234

Gabaglia, Fernando Antonio Raja, 118, 183; as director of the Colégio Pedro II, 192–201; as director of the Rio de Janeiro Department of Education, 229–231; as geographer, 212, 215–216. *See also* Colégio Pedro II

Genetic theory, 234–236; Lamarckian, 24–25, 48; Mendelian, 24–25, 152, 211

Góes, Joaquim Faria, 196, 219, 221–222

Health brigades, 33, 43–44, 127–128

Hochman, Gilberto, 28, 30, 67–68

Holanda, Sérgio Buarque de, 8

Huntington, Ellsworth, 216–217

IBGE. *See* Brazilian Institute for Geography and Statistics

Immigrant colonies, 63, 65

Immigrants and immigration, 75, 80–81, 88, 182, 189

INEP. *See* National Institute for Pedagogical Studies

Institute for the Rational Organization of Work (IDORT), 134

Institute of Education, 38, 68, 77, 90–93, 97–98, 101–125, 168–170, 198, 238; admissions process, 111–114, 220; during Estado Novo, 120–121, 180–184; elementary school of, 146; library of, 117–118; new building for, 101, 108–109; physical education at, 109–110; secondary school

of, 103, 109, 115–117, 176, 222–223, 228; teachers college of, 109–110, 114–117, 169

Integralist Action of Brazil (AIB), 155

Intelligence testing, 15, 35, 43, 111, 133–135, 141–150, 168, 177; ABC Test, 141–152; Binet I.Q. Scale, 142–143, 147, 150–152, 180; criticized, 157, 262 n.29; Terman Group Test, 35, 143–146, 152, 262 n.29

Kehl, Renato, 25

Kelly, Celso, 118, 264 n.33

Lamarck, Jean Baptiste. *See* Genetic theory

Leão, Antonio Carneiro. *See* Carneiro Leão, Antonio

Le Corbusier, Charles, 21

Legal medicine. *See* Criminology; Peixoto, Júlio Afrânio

Leme, Sebastião, 166

Lemme, Paschoal, 156–157, 172

Lima, Alceu Amoroso, 60, 167–168. *See also* Catholic nationalism

Linhares, José, 230

Linhares, Maria Yedda, 99, 165, 241–242

Literacy, 68–69, 71–74, 87, 89

Lobato, José Bento Monteiro. *See* Monteiro Lobato, José Bento

Lourenço Filho, Manoel, 6, 11, 33–34, 37, 41, 65, 77, 123, 134, 175; ABC Test by, 68, 104, 141–143; attacked by Catholic nationalists, 117–119, 168–170, 172; in Ceará, 30–32, 68; director of Institute of Education, 62, 68, 102, 104–105, 109–110, 114–115, 117–119, 180; director of INEP, 41, 62, 68, 157; at São Paulo normal school, 68. *See also* Institute of Education; Intelligence testing; National Institute for Pedagogical Studies

Machado, Pedro Monteiro, 41–42

Magalhães, Antonio Carlos, 234, 236

Malta, Augusto, 90–101, 131, 206, 237

Maranhão, 110

Marcondes Filho, Alexander, 187

Mattos, Umbelina de, 119–120, 260 n.59

Medeiros, Mauricio de, 1–2

Medical-Pedagogical Conference (1941), 178

Mello, Olimpio de, 168, 173

Mendel, Gregor. *See* Genetic theory

Mental Hygiene League, 25–26, 30

Migrants and Migration, 72, 75–76, 80–81, 88, 237

Minas Gerais (state), 10, 63–64, 72, 75, 82, 143; teacher training in, 102, 107–108

Ministry of Agriculture, 58, 60, 62, 171

Ministry of Education and Health (MES), 11, 16, 21–24, 32, 34, 41, 58, 62–65, 68–69, 193–195, 198; creation of, 28–29, 56, 107; National Commission on Primary Education of, 69; National Schoolbook Commission of, 198. *See also* Campos, Francisco; Capanema, Gustavo

Ministry of Justice, 156, 174, 187

Ministry of Labor, 56, 195, 208

Ministry of War, 193–194

Monteiro, Clóvis, 203–204

Monteiro Lobato, José Bento, 29–31, 54, 132

Müller, Filinto, 155, 173, 200. *See also* Political Security Department (DESPS)

Musical and Artistic Service (SEMA), 163. *See also* Villa-Lobos, Heitor

Mussolini, Benito, 213, 215

National Academy of Medicine, 28

National Defense League, 169

National Department of Public Health, 63, 67–68

National Institute for Pedagogical Studies (INEP), 30, 62–63, 65, 68, 102, 157, 172. *See also* Lourenço Filho, Manoel

National Institute of Statistics. *See* Brazilian Institute for Geography and Statistics (IBGE)

National Liberation Alliance (ANL), 119

National Museum of Anthropology, 9, 22, 38. *See also* Roquette Pinto, Edgar

National Physical Education School, 48, 64

National Service for Commercial Training (SENAC), 64

National Service for Historic and Artistic Patrimony (SPHAN), 64

National Service for Industrial Training (SENAI), 65

Neiva, Arthur, 4, 28, 242

New School educational philosophy, 105, 107, 117–119, 127, 148, 165–170, 183, 196, 217, 225, 227, 242

Niemeyer, Oscar, 22, 241

Nina Rodrigues, Raimundo, 28, 39

Normal School of Rio de Janeiro. *See* Institute of Education

Nunes, Clarice, 224, 227

Oswaldo Cruz Foundation, 64

Pará (state), 10, 65, 71, 110, 240

Paraíba (state), 10, 33, 65, 110

Paraná (state), 69, 72, 107

Passos, Francisco Pereira, 77, 79–80, 83, 88

Peixoto, Júlio Afrânio, 4, 25, 29, 33–34, 39, 77, 101, 106, 118, 129, 216, 264 n.33. *See also* Criminology

Pende, Nicola, 36, 151–152

Penna, Belissário, 4, 28, 61, 208, 242

Pereira, Miguel, 25, 28

Pernambucano, Ulisses, 143

Pernambuco (state), 10, 33–34, 107, 142

Physical education, 10, 26–27, 33, 48–50, 63–64, 109–110, 114–117, 176, 184, 209–210, 222

Pinto, Edgar Roquette. *See* Roquette Pinto, Edgar

Pinto, H. Sobral, 1–3

Pioneers of the New School, 105, 165–166, 183, 202. *See also* New School educational philosophy

Pires, Washington, 171
Political Security Department (DESPS), 118, 155–156, 200. *See also* Müller, Filinto
Prado Júnior, Antonio, 78
PRD-5 (radio station), 36, 120, 150, 183
Pro-Sanitation League, 26, 29–30
Psychological testing. *See* Intelligence testing
Puericulture, 26, 106–109, 222

Race as a scientific entity, 8–12, 235
Racial categories, 6–10, 17–19, 93–99, 144–146, 250 n.28. *See also* D'Avila, Bastos; Roquette Pinto, Edgar
Racial degeneracy, 3, 7, 11, 12, 15, 16, 17, 26–40, 54–55, 106, 125, 132, 150, 212–213, 216, 242, 248 n.10. *See also* Alcoholism; Colégio Pedro II; Eugenics; Intelligence testing; Syphilis; Tuberculosis
Racial democracy, 12, 14, 27, 101, 141, 235. *See also* Freyre, Gilberto
Racial identity, 6–10, 12–15, 250 n.30
Racial mixture, 8–9, 21–24, 31, 37–38, 235
Racial segregation, 84–87, 101, 177
Radio. *See* PRD-5
Ramos, Arthur, 6, 8, 34, 36, 39–40, 76, 86, 134, 213, 241
Rationalization, 11, 17, 33, 57, 125, 129, 133–134, 158, 171
Recife, Theobaldo, 181
Republican Party, 31
Revolution of 1930, 10–11, 32, 53, 55–58, 62, 107, 166, 210, 214
Rio de Janeiro (city): 72–89; autonomy of, 56, 132; educational spending in, 69, 74; favelas in, 76, 81, 84–88, 124, 131–132, 206; literacy in, 69, 72; race in, 72–73, 76, 81–89; suburbs of, 82–88, 126, 132, 137, 178, 206, 225; urban growth in, 73, 76–83
Rio de Janeiro (state), 72, 82, 157
Rio de Janeiro Department of Education, 4,

10, 11, 12, 17, 25, 33–47, 69–70, 87–89, 106, 121–122, 125–126, 135, 152; Buildings and Material Service of, 134–140, 187, 190; and choral song, 159–165; Curriculum Service of, 134; Department of Nationalist Education (DEN) of, 176–177, 184; as magnet for reformers, 74–76; Matriculation and Attendance Service (SMF) of, 135–136; Medical-Pedagogical Districts of, 178–180; public petitions to, 184–19; purged, 155; and religious education, 158, 165; Tracking and Advancement Service of, 135, 141, 178; vocational education of, 156, 175–176, 189, 196, 217–231, 242
Rio de Janeiro Institute for Educational Research (IPE), 35–42, 134, 241; Anthropometry Service of, 35–38, 134, 150–151, 180; Educational Radio and Cinema Service of, 35–36; Orthophrenology and Mental Hygiene Service of, 35–36, 39–40, 134, 149–151; Tests and Measures Service (STE) of, 35, 141–151, 178
Rio Grande do Norte, 10, 69, 72
Rio Grande do Sul, 75, 100
Rockefeller, John D., 103
Rockefeller, Nelson, 22, 161
Roosevelt, Franklin, 213
Roquette Pinto, Edgar, 9, 22–23, 25, 34, 36, 54, 61, 241; and definition of racial categories, 18. *See also* National Museum of Anthropology

Salgado, Plínio, 61
Sampaio, Nereu de, 86, 136–137
São Paulo (state): Constitutionalist revolt, 200, 264 n.36; education in, 10–11, 25, 33, 65, 73–75, 141–143, 167, 170, 178, 185; educational spending in, 69, 74; normal school of, 68, 104, 106–107, 142, 170; politics in, 56–57; racial discrimination in, 112–113; urban growth in, 73, 80, 82

São Paulo Eugenics Society, 25–26, 29–30, 108

Schmidt, Maria Junqueira, 225–227

Scientific Rationalization. See Rationalization

Secondary education, 17

Sergipe (state), 10, 33, 65, 110

Serrano, Jonathas, 6, 166, 198, 212–215

Silva, Enéas, 138

Slavery, 55, 61, 213–215, 217, 221

Soares, Átila, 168

Society of Friends of Alberto Tôrres, 60–62

Syphilis, 28, 177. See also Racial degeneracy

Systematic Rationalization. See Rationalization

Távora, Juárez, 61, 171

Taylorism, 107, 133. See also Rationalization

Teachers, 14, 18, 26, 44–45, 66, 70–71, 75, 80, 90–125, 140, 182–184, 237

Teacher Training, 16–17, 33, 64–65, 90–125, 163, 169, 189

Teixeira, Anísio, 17, 30, 33–36, 62, 77, 101, 177, 190–191, 240–241; attacked by Catholic nationalists, 155, 157–159, 165–173; as director of the Rio de Janeiro Department of Education, 116–117; reform of elementary education by, 79, 129–154, 158, 174–175; reform of secondary education by, 196–197, 217–228; reform of teacher training by, 102, 104–111; studies in U.S., 104, 110, 123; translation and publication by, 117, 134

Terman, Lewis, 35, 62, 103, 133, 262 n.29. See also Intelligence testing

Thomaz, Joaquim, 180

Tito, Arthur Rodrigues, 180–181

Tôrres, Alberto, 54, 60–62, 135, 175, 195, 215, 221

Toscano, Moacyr, 176

Tuberculosis, 25, 28, 64, 150, 208, 216, 219. See also Eugenics; Racial degeneracy

UNESCO, 76, 86, 241

United States: and educational ideas, 65, 102–103, 123, 133, 135, 143–144, 151–152, 156–159, 173, 196, 218, 225; and eugenics, 9; model for teacher training, 107, 111

University of Brazil, 63–64, 217

University of the Federal District, 118, 264 n.33

Vargas, Getúlio, 11, 12, 21, 23, 45–46, 52–57, 60, 62, 80, 113, 118–120, 155, 160, 163, 166, 173, 182–190, 193, 200, 215

Vaz, Juvenil Rocha, 22–23

Venancio Filho, Francisco, 183, 198, 225

Vianna, Francisco Oliveira, 22–23, 61

Villa-Lobos, Heitor, 159–165

Weinstein, Barbara, 11–12, 57–58, 134

Young Men's Christian Association (YMCA), 212

Jerry Dávila is Assistant Professor of History
at the University of North Carolina at Charlotte.

Library of Congress Cataloging-in-Publication Data
Dávila, Jerry.
Diploma of whiteness : race and social policy in Brazil,
1917–1945 / Jerry Dávila.
p. cm.   Includes bibliographical references and index.
ISBN 0-8223-3058-X (cloth : alk. paper)
ISBN 0-8223-3079-9 (pbk. : alk. paper)
1. Critical pedagogy—Brazil—History—20th century.
2. Discrimination in education—Brazil—History—20th
century. 3. Whites—Race identity—Brazil—History—20th
century. 4. Education—Social aspects—Brazil—History—
20th century. I. Title.
LC196.5.B6 D38 2003   371.829'00981—dc21   2002014073